Charles Bradlaugh

Political Essays

Charles Bradlaugh

Political Essays

ISBN/EAN: 9783337071820

Printed in Europe, USA, Canada, Australia, Japan

Cover: Foto ©Suzi / pixelio.de

More available books at **www.hansebooks.com**

THE
AUTOBIOGRAPHY
OF
MR. BRADLAUGH.

A Page of his Life.

[ENTERED AT STATIONERS' HALL.]

LONDON:
FREETHOUGHT PUBLISHING COMPANY,
28, STONECUTTER STREET. E.C.

PRICE THREEPENCE.

MR. BRADLAUGH'S AUTOBIOGRAPHY.

At the request of many friends, and by way of farewell address on leaving for America, I, for the first time in my life, pen a partial autobiographical sketch. I do not pretend that the narrative will be a complete picture of my life, I only vouch the accuracy of the facts so far as I state them. I have not the right in some cases to state political occurrences in which others now living are involved, nor have I the courage of Jean Jacques Rousseau, to photograph my inner life. I shall therefore state little the public may not already know. I was born on the 26th September, 1833, in a small house in Bacchus Walk, Hoxton. My father was a solicitor's clerk with a very poor salary, which he supplemented by law writing. He was an extremely industrious man, and a splendid penman. I never had the opportunity of judging his tastes or thoughts, outside his daily labours, except in one respect, in which I have followed in his footsteps. He was passionately fond of angling. Until 1848 my life needs little relation. My schooling, like that of most poor men's children, was small in quantity, and, except as to the three R's, indifferent in quality. I remember at seven years of age being at a national school in Abbey Street, Bethnal Green; between seven and nine I was at another small private school in the same neighbourhood, and my "education" was completed before I was eleven years of age at a boys' school in Coalharbour Street, Hackney Road. When about twelve years of age I was first employed as errand lad in the solicitor's office where my father remained his whole life through. After a little more than two years in this occupation, I became wharf clerk and cashier to a firm of coal merchants in Britannia Fields, City Road. While in their employment the excitement of the Chartist movement was at its height in England, and the authorities, frightened by the then huge continental revolution wave, were preparing for the prosecution of some of the leaders amongst the Chartists. Meetings used to be held almost continuously all day on Sunday, and every week-night in the open air on Bonner's Fields, near where the Consumption Hospital now stands. These meetings were in knots from fifty to five hundred, sometimes many more, and were occupied chiefly in discussions on theological, social, and political questions, any bystander taking part. The curiosity of a lad took me occasionally in the week evenings to the Bonner's Fields gatherings. On the Sunday I, as a member of the Church of England, was fully occupied as a Sunday-school teacher. This last-named fashion of passing Sunday was broken suddenly. The Bishop of London was announced to hold a confirmation in Bethnal Green. The incumbent of St. Peter's, Hackney Road, the district in which I resided, was one John Graham Packer, and he, desiring to make a good figure when the Bishop came, pressed me to prepare for confirmation, so as to answer any questions the Bishop might put. I studied a little the Thirty-nine Articles of the Church of England, and the four Gospels, and came to the conclusion that they differed. I ventured to write the Rev. Mr. Packer a respectful letter, asking him for aid and explanation. All he did was to denounce my letter to my parents as Atheistical, although at that time I should have shuddered at the very notion of becoming an Atheist, and he suspended me for three months from my office of Sunday-school teacher. This left me my Sundays free, for I did not like to go to church while suspended from my teacher's duty, and I, instead, went to Bonner's Fields, at first to listen, but soon to take part in some of the discussions which were then always pending there.

At the commencement I spoke on the orthodox Christian side, but after a debate with Mr. J. Savage, in the Warner Place Hall, in 1849, on the "Inspiration of the Bible," I found that my views were getting very much tinged with Freethought, and in the winter of that year, at the instigation of Mr. Packer, to whom I had submitted the "Diegesis" of Robert Taylor, I—having become a teetotaler, which in his view brought out my infidel tendencies still more vigorously—had three days given me by my employers, after consultation with my father, to "change my opinions or lose my situation." I am inclined to think now that the threat was never intended to have been enforced, but was used to terrify me into submission. At that time I hardly knew what, if any, opinions I had, but the result was that sooner than make a show of recanting, I left home and situation on the third day, and never returned to either.

I was always a very fluent speaker, and now lectured frequently at the Temperance Hall, Warner Place, Hackney Road, at the small Hall in Philpot Street, and in the open air in Bonner's Fields, where at last on Sunday afternoons scores of hundreds congregated to hear me. My views were then Deistical, but rapidly tending to the more extreme phase into which they ultimately settled. I now took part in all the gatherings held in London on behalf of the Poles and Hungarians, and actually fancied that I could write poetry on Kossuth and Mazzini.

It was at this time I made the acquaintance of my friend and co-worker, Mr. Austin Holyoake, at his printing office in Queen's Head Passage, and I remember him taking me to John Street Institution, where, at one of the pleasant Saturday evening gatherings, I met the late Mrs. Emma Martin. At Mr. Austin Holyoake's request, Mr. George Jacob Holyoake, to my great delight, presided at one of my lectures in Philpot Street, and I felt special interest in the number of the *Reasoner* which contained a brief reference to myself and that lecture.

I wrote my first pamphlet, "A Few Words on the Christian's Creed," about the middle of 1850, and was honoured by Dr. Campbell of the *British Banner* with a leading article vigorously assailing me for the lectures I had then delivered. After leaving home I was chiefly sheltered by Mrs. Sharples Carlile, with whose children, Hypatia, Theophila, and Julian, I shared such comforts as were at her disposal. Here I studied hard everything which came in my way, picking up a little Hebrew and an imperfect smattering of other tongues. I tried to earn my living as a coal merchant, but at sixteen, and without one farthing in my pocket, the business was not extensive enough to be profitable. I got very poor, and at that time was also very proud. A subscription offered me by a few Freethinkers shocked me, and awakened me to a sense of my poverty; so telling no one where I was going, I went away, and on the 17th of December, 1850, was, after some difficulty, enlisted in the Seventh Dragoon Guards. With this corps I remained until October, 1853, being ultimately appointed orderly-room clerk; the regiment, during the whole of the time I remained in it, being quartered in Ireland. While I was in the regiment I was a teetotaler, and used often to lecture to the men in the barrack-room at night, and I have more than once broken out of Portobello barracks to deliver teetotal speeches in the small French Street Hall, Dublin. Many times have I spoken there in my scarlet jacket, between James Haughton and the good old father, the Rev. Dr. Spratt, a Roman Catholic priest, then very active in the cause of temperance. While I was in the regiment my father died, and in the summer of 1853 an aunt's death left me a small sum, out of which I purchased my discharge, and returned to England, to aid in the maintenance of my mother and family.

I have now no time for the full story of my army life, which, however, I may tell some day. Before I left the regiment I had won the esteem of most of the privates, and of some of the officers. I quitted the regiment with a "very good character" from the Colonel, but I am bound to add, that the Captain of my troop would not have concurred in this character had he had any voice in the matter. The Lieutenant-Colonel, C. P. Ainslie, earned an eternal right to grateful mention at my hands by his gentlemanly and considerate treatment. I cannot say the same for my Captain, who did his best to send me to gaol, and whom I have not yet quite forgiven.

On returning to civilian life, I obtained employment in the daytime with a solicitor named Rogers, and in the evening as clerk to a Building Society; and soon after entering this employ I began again to write and speak, and it was then I, to in some degree avoid the efforts which were afterwards made to ruin me, took the name "Iconoclast," under which all my anti-theological work down to 1868 was done. I give Mr. Rogers' name now for he is dead, and malice cannot injure him. Many anonymous letters were sent to him to warn him of my irreligious opinions; he treated them all with contempt, only asking me not to let my propaganda become an injury to his business.

Soon after my discharge from the army I had a curious adventure. While I was away a number of poor men had subscribed their funds together and had erected a Working Man's Hall, in Goldsmiths' Row, Hackney Road. Not having any legal advice, it turned out that they had been entrapped into erecting their building on freehold ground without any lease or conveyance from the freeholder, who asserted his legal right to the building. The men consulted me, and finding that under the Statute of Frauds they had no remedy, I recommended them to offer a penalty rent of £20 a year. This being refused, I constituted myself into a law court, and without any riot or breach of the peace, I, with the assistance of a hundred stout men, took every brick of the building bodily away, and divided the materials, so far as was possible, amongst the proper owners. I think I can see now the disappointed rascal of a freeholder when he only had his bare soil left once more. He did not escape unpunished, for to encourage the others to contribute, he had invested some few pounds in the building. He had been too clever: he had relied on the letter of the law, and I beat him with a version of common-sense justice.

I lectured once or twice a week in the small Philpot Street Hall, very often then in the Hall of Science, City Road, and then in the old John Street Institution, until I won myself a name in the party and through the country. In 1855 I had my first notable adventure with the authorities in reference to the right of meeting in Hyde Park, and subsequently gave evidence before the Royal Commission ordered by the House of Commons, presided over by the Right Hon. Stuart Wortley. I was very proud that day at Westminster, when, at the conclusion of my testimony against the authorities, the Commissioner publicly thanked me, and the people who crowded the Court of Exchequer cheered me, for the manner in which I denied the right of Sir Richard Mayne, the then Chief Commissioner of Police, to issue the notices forbidding the people to meet in the Park. This was a first step in a course in which I have never flinched or wavered.

In 1856 I undertook, with others, the publication of a series of papers, entitled "Half-Hours with Freethinkers," the late John Watts being one of my co-workers. I also by myself commenced the publication of my "Commentary on the Pentateuch," which has since been entirely re-written, and now forms my "Bible: what it is."

During the autumn of 1857 I paid my first lecturing visit to Northampton.

Early in 1858, when Mr. Edward Truelove was suddenly arrested for publishing the pamphlet, "Is Tyrannicide Justifiable?" I became Honorary Secretary to the Defence, and was at the same time associated with the conduct of the defence of Simon Bernard, who was arrested at the instigation of the French Government for alleged complicity in the Orsini tragedy. It was at this period I gained the friendship of poor Bernard, which, without diminution, I retained until he died; and also the valued friendship of Thomas Allsop, which I still preserve. My associations were from thenceforward such as to encourage in me a strong and bitter feeling against the late Emperor Napoleon. Whilst he was in power I hated him, and never lost an opportunity of working against him until the *décheance* came. I am not sure now that I always judged him fairly; but nothing, I think, could have tempted me to either write or speak of him with friendliness or kindliness during his life. *Le sang de mes amis était sur son âme.* Now that the tomb covers his remains, my hatred has ceased; but no other feeling has arisen in its place. Should any of his family seek to resume the Imperial purple, I should remain true to my political declarations of sixteen years since, and should exert myself to the uttermost to prevent France falling under another Empire. I write this with much sadness, as 1870 to 1873 have dispelled some of my illusions held firmly during the fifteen years which preceded. I had believed in such men as Louis Blanc, Ledru Rollin, Victor Hugo, as possible statesmen for France. I was mistaken. They were writers, talkers, and poets; good men to ride on the stream, or to drown in honest protest, but lacking force to swim against, or turn back, the tide by the might of their will. I had believed too in a Republican France, which is yet only in the womb of time, to be born after many pangs and sore travailing.

In 1859 I saw Joseph Mazzini for the first time, and remained on terms of communication with the great Italian patriot until the year 1869, from time to time bringing him correspondence from Italy, where my business sometimes took me. After 1869 we found ourselves holding diverse opinions on the Franco-Prussian question—Mazzini went for Prussia, I for France—and I never saw him again.

In June, 1858, I held my first public formal theological debate with the Rev. Brewin Grant, B.A., at that time a Dissenting Minister at Sheffield. Mr. Grant was then a man of some ability, and if he could have forgotten his aptitudes as a circus jester, would have been a redoubtable antagonist. During this year I was elected President of the London Secular Society, in lieu of Mr. George Jacob Holyoake, who had theretofore led the English Freethought party, but who has of late years devoted himself more completely to general journalistic work.

In November, 1858, I commenced editorial duties with the *Investigator*, formerly conducted by the late Robert Cooper, which I continued until August, 1859. It had but a small circulation, and was financially a very great failure. For the encouragement of young propagandists, I may here insert a little anecdote of my early lecturing experience. I had lectured in Edinburgh in mid-winter; the audience was small, the profits microscopical. I, after paying my bill at the Temperance Hotel, where I then stayed, had only a few shillings more than my Parliamentary fare to Bolton, where I was next to lecture. I was out of bed at five on a freezing morning, and could have no breakfast, as the people were not up. I carried my luggage (a big tin box, corded round, which then held books and clothes, and a small black bag), for I could not spare any of my scanty cash for a conveyance or porter. The train from Edinburgh being delayed by a severe snow-storm, the corresponding Parliamentary had left Carlisle long before our arrival. In order to reach Bolton in time for my lecture, I had to book by a quick train, starting in about three-quarters of an hour, but could only book to Preston, as the increased fare took all my money, except 4½d. With this small sum I could get no refreshment in the station, but in a little shop in the street outside I got a mug of hot tea and a little hot meat pie. From Preston, I got with great difficulty on to Bolton, handing my black bag to the station-master there, as security for my fare from Preston, until the morning. I arrived in Bolton about quarter to eight; the lecture comenced at eight, and I, having barely time to run to my dgings, and wash and change, went onto the platform cold nd hungry. I shall never forget that lecture; it was in an ld Unitarian Chapel. We had no gas, the building seemed full of a foggy mist, and was imperfectly lit with candles. Everything appeared cold, cheerless, and gloomy. The most amusing feature was that an opponent, endowed with extra piety and forbearance, chose that evening to specially attack me for the money-making and easy life I was leading. Peace to that opponent's memory, I have never seen him since. It was while in Scotland on this journey I made the acquaintance, and ultimately won the friendship, of the late Alexander Campbell, of Glasgow—a generous, kindly-hearted old Socialist Missionary, who, at a time when others were hostile, spoke encouragingly to me, and who afterwards worked with me for a long period on this journal.

Occasionally, the lectures were interfered with by the authorities, but this happened oftener in the provinces than in London. In March, 1859, I was to have lectured in the Saint Martin's Hall on "Louis Napoleon," but the Government—on a remonstrance by Count Walewski, as to language used at a previous meeting, at which I had presided for Dr. Bernard—interfered; the hall was garrisoned by police, and the lecture prevented. Mr. Hullah, the then proprietor, being indemnified by the authorities, paid damages for his breach of contract, to avoid a suit which I at once commenced against him. Later in the same month I held a debate in Northampton with Mr. John Bowes, a rather heavy, but well-meaning, old gentleman, utterly unfitted for platform controversy. The press now began to deal with me tolerably freely, and I find "boy," "young man," and "juvenile appearance" very frequent in the comments. My want of education was an especial matter for hostile criticism, the more particularly so when the writer had neither heard nor seen me.

Discussions now grew on me so thick and fast that even some of the most important debates may perhaps escape notice in this imperfect chronicling. At Sheffield I debated with a Reverend Dr. Mensor, who styled himself a Jewish Rabbi. He was then in the process of gaining admission to the Church of England, and had been put forward to show my want of scholarship. We both scrawled Hebrew characters for four nights on a black board, to the delight and mystification of the audience, who gave me credit for erudition, because I chalked the square letter characters with tolerable rapidity and clearness. At Glasgow I debated with a Mr. Court, representing the Glasgow Protestant Association, a glib-tongued missionary, who has since gone to the bad; at Paisley with a Mr. Smart, a very gentlemanly antagonist; and at Halifax with the Rev. T. D. Matthias, a Welsh Baptist Minister, unquestionably very sincere. All these were formal debates, and were reported with tolerable fulness in the various local journals.

In the early part of 1860 I, aided by my friends at Sheffield, Halifax, and other parts of England, projected the *National Reformer* in small shares. Unfortunately, just after the issue of its prospectus, Joseph Barker returned from America, and was associated with me in the editorship. The arrangement was peculiar, Mr. Barker editing the first half of the paper and I the second. It was not precisely a happy union, and the unnatural alliance came to an end in a very brief period. In August, 1861, I officially parted company with Joseph Barker as editor. We had been practically divorced for months before : the first part of the paper usually contained abuse of those who wrote in the second half. He came to me originally at Sheffield, pretending to be an Atheist and a Republican, and soon after pretended to be a Christian, and spoke in favour of slavery. I am sometimes doubtful as to how far Mr. Barker deluded himself, as well as others, in his various changes of theological and political opinions. If he had had the slightest thoroughness in his character, he would have been a great man; as it is, he is only a great turn-coat.

In June, 1860, I debated again with the Reverend Brewin Grant, every Monday for four weeks, at Bradford, and during this debate had a narrow escape of my life. In one of my journeys to London, the Great Northern train ran through the station at King's Cross, and many persons were seriously injured. I got off with some trifling bruises and a severe shaking.

Garibaldi having at this time made his famous Marsala effort, I delivered a series of lectures in his aid, and am happy to be able to record that, though at that time very poor, I sent him one hundred guineas as my contribution by my tongue. This money was chiefly sent through W. H. Ashurst, Esq., now Solicitor to the General Post Office, and amongst the few letters I preserve, I have one of thanks from " G. Garibaldi," for what I was then doing for Italy.

In this year I debated for four nights with Dr. Brindley, an old antagonist of the Socialists, at Oldham; for two nights with the Rev. Dr. Baylee, the President of St. Aidan's College, at Birkenhead, where a Church of England curate manufactory was for some time carried on; and for two nights with the Rev. Dr. Rutherford, of Newcastle. Dr. Rutherford has since so identified himself with the cause of the Tyneside workers, that I read with regret any harsh words that escaped me in that debate. Although during late years I have managed to keep all my meetings free from violence or disorder, this was not always so. In October, 1860, I paid my first visit to Wigan, and certainly lectured there under considerable difficulty, and incurred personal danger, the resident clergy actually inciting the populace to physical violence, and part destruction of the building I lectured in. I, however, supported by one courageous woman and her husband, persevered, and, despite bricks and kicks, visited Wigan again and again, until I had, *bon gré mal gré*, improved the manners and customs of the people, so that I am now a welcome speaker there. I could not improve the morals of the clergy, as the public journals have recently shown, but that was their misfortune not my fault. In the winter of 1860, I held two formal debates in Wigan, all of which were fully reported in the local journals; one with Mr. Hutchings, a respectable Nonconformist layman, and the other with the Rev. Woodville Woodman, a Swedenborgian divine.

Early in 1861 I visited Guernsey in consequence of an attempt made by the Law Courts of the Island to enforce the blasphemy laws against a Mr. Stephen Bendall, who had distributed some of my pamphlets to the Guernseyites, and had been condemned to imprisonment in default of finding sureties not to repeat the offence. Not daring to prosecute me, although challenged in writing, the authorities permitted drink and leave of absence to be given to soldiers in the garrison, on condition they should try to prevent the lecture, and the house in which I lectured was broken into by a drunken and pious mob, shouting "Kill the Infidel." My antagonists were fortunately as cowardly as they were intolerant, and I succeeded in quelling the riot, delivering my lecture in spite of all opposition, although considerable damage was done to the building.

Shortly after this I visited Plymouth, where the Young Men's Christian Association arranged to prosecute me. They were, however, a little too hasty, and had me arrested at an open air meeting when I had scarcely commenced my speech, having only uttered the words—"Friends, I am about to address you on the Bible." Having locked me up all night, and refused bail, it was found by their legal adviser that a blunder had been committed, and a charge of "exciting a breach of the peace, and assaulting the constable in the execution of his duty," was manufactured. It was tolerably amusing to see the number of dinners, suppers, and breakfasts, all accompanied with pots or cups of Devonshire cream, sent in to the Devonport Lock-up, where I was confined, by various friends who wanted to show their sympathy. The invented charge, though well sworn to, broke down after two days' hearing, under the severe cross-examination to which I subjected the witnesses. I defended myself, two lawyers appeared against me, and seven magistrates sat on the bench, predetermined to convict me. Finding that the evidence of the whole of the witnesses whom I wished to call was to be objected to because unbelievers in hell were then incompetent as witnesses according to English law, I am pleased to say that several Nonconformists, disgusted with the bigotry and pious perjury of my prosecutors, came forward. The result was a triumphant victory, and a certificate of dismissal which I wrung from the reluctant bench of great unpaid. I was not yet satisfied; some of the magistrates had tried to browbeat me, and I announced in court that I would deliver the lecture I had been prevented from delivering to an audience assembled in the borough, and that I should sue at law the Superintendent of Police who had arrested me. The first portion of my defiance was the most difficult to give effect to; not a hall could be hired in Devonport, and nearly all the convenient open land being under military jurisdiction, it was impossible to procure the tenancy of a field for an open-air meeting. I, however, fulfilled my promise, and despite the police and military authorities combined, I delivered my lecture to an audience assembled in their very teeth. Devonport, Stonehouse, and Plymouth form one garrisoned and fortified town, divided by the River Tamar. All the water to the sea is under the separate jurisdiction of Saltash, some miles distant. I obtained a large boat on which a temporary platform was built, and this boat was quietly moored in the River Tamar on the Devonport side, about two fathoms from the shore. Placards were issued stating that, acting under legal advice, I should address the meeting and deliver the prevented lecture "near to the Devonport Park Gates." Overwhelming force was prepared by the Devonport authorities, and having already erred by too great haste, this time they determined to let me fairly commence my lecture before they arrested me. To their horror I quietly walked past the Park Gates where the crowd was waiting, and passing down a bye-lane to the river side, stepped into a little boat, was rowed to the large one, and then delivered my lecture, the audience who had followed me, standing on an open wharf, all within the jurisdiction of the Borough of Devonport, and I being about 9 feet outside the borough. The face of the Mayor ready to read the riot act, the superintendent with twenty-eight picked policemen to make sure of my arrest, and a military force in readiness to overawe any popular demonstration—all these were sights to remember. I am afraid the Devonport Young Men's Christian Association did not limit themselves to prayers and blessings on that famous Sunday.

As I had promised, the authorities refusing any apology for the wrongful arrest, I commenced an action against Superintendent Edwards, by whom I had been taken into custody. The borough magistrates indemnified their officer and found funds to resist me. I fought with very little help save from one tried, though anonymous friend, for Joseph Barker, my co-editor, but not co-worker, in our own paper, discouraged any pecuniary support. The cause was made a special jury one, and came on for trial at Exeter Assizes. Unfortunately I was persuaded to brief counsel, and Sir Robert Collier, my leader, commenced his speech with an expression of sorrow for my opinions. This damaged me very much, although I won the case easily after a long trial. The jury, composed of Devonshire landowners, only gave me a farthing damages, and Mr. Baron Channell refused to certify for costs. I was determined not to let the matter rest here, and myself carried it to the Court *in Banco*, where I argued it in person for two whole days, before Lord Chief Justice Erle and a full bench of Judges. Although I did not succeed in improving my own position, I raised public opinion in favour of free speech, and the enormous costs incurred by the borough authorities, and which they had to bear, have deterred them from ever again interfering either with my lectures, or those of any other speaker, and I now have crowded audiences in the finest hall whenever I visit the three towns. These proceedings cost me several hundred pounds, and burthened me with a debt which took long clearing off.

In 1862 I held a four nights' discussion with a Dissenting

clergyman, the Rev. W. Barker. My opponent was probably one of the most able and straightforward amongst my numerous antagonists. About this time a severe attack of acute rheumatism prostrated me, and having soon after to visit Italy, I, at first under medical advice, adopted the habit of drinking the light Continental wines, and although continuing an advocate of sobriety, I naturally ceased to take part in any teetotal gatherings.

In the struggle between the Northern and Southern States of America, my advocacy and sympathies went with what I am glad to say was the feeling of the great mass of the English people—in favour of the North; and my esteemed friend, and then contributor, W. E. Adams, furnished most valuable aid with his pen in the enlightenment of public opinion, at a time when many of our aristocracy were openly exulting in what they conceived to be the probable break-up of the United States Republic. During the Lancashire cotton famine I lectured several times in aid of the fund.

I began now also to assume a much more prominent position in the various English political movements, and especially to speak on the Irish Church and Irish Land questions. On the Irish question, I owe much to my late co-worker and contributor, poor Peter Fox André, a thoroughly honest and whole-souled man, whose pen was always on the side of struggling nationalities.

One of the disadvantages connected with a public career is, that every vile scoundrel who is too cowardly to face you openly can libel you anonymously. I have had, I think, my full share of this kind of annoyance. Most of the slanders I have treated with utter contempt, and if I had alone consulted my own feelings, should probably never have pursued any other course. Twice, however, I have had recourse to the judgment of the law—once in the case of a clergyman of the Church of England, who indulged in a foul libel affecting my wife and children. This fellow I compelled to retract every word he had uttered, and to pay £100, which, after deducting the costs, was divided amongst various charitable institutions. The reverend libeller wrote me an abject letter, begging me not to ruin his prospects in the Church by publishing his name; I consented, and he has since repaid my mercy by losing no opportunity of being offensive. He is a prominent contributor to the

Rock, and a fierce ultra-Protestant. He must have greater confidence in my honour than in his own, or fear of exposure would compel him to greater reticence. The other case arose during the election, and will be dealt with in its proper order.

It was my fortune to be associated with the Reform League from its earliest moments until its dissolution. It is hardly worth while to repeat here the almost stereotyped story of the successful struggle made by the League for Parliamentary Reform. E. Beales, Esq., was the President of the League, and I was one of its Vice-Presidents, and continued nearly the whole time of its existence a member of its executive. The whole of my services and journeys were given to the League without the slightest remuneration, and I repeatedly, and according to my means, contributed to its funds. When I resigned my position on the executive I received from Mr. George Howell, the Secretary, and from Mr. Beales, the President, the most touching and flattering letters as to what Mr. Beales was pleased to describe as the loyalty and utility of my services to the League. Mr. George Howell concluded a long letter as follows :— "Be pleased to accept my assurance of sincere regards for your manly courage, consistent and honourable conduct in our cause, and for your kindly consideration for myself as Secretary of this great movement on all occasions." These letters have additional value from the fact that Mr. Beales, whom I sincerely respect, differs widely from me in matters of faith, and Mr. Howell is, fortunately, far from having any friendly feeling towards me. It was while on the Executive of this League that I first became intimately acquainted with Mr. George Odger, and had reason to be pleased with the straightforward course he pursued, and the honest work he did as one of the Executive Committee. Mr. John Baxter Langley and Mr. R. A. Cooper were also amongst my most prominent co-workers.

My sympathy with Ireland, and open advocacy of justice for the Irish, nearly brought me into serious trouble. Some who were afterwards indicted as the chiefs of the so-called Fenian movement, came to me for advice. So much I see others have written, and the rest of this portion of my autobiography I may write some day. At present there are men not out of danger whom careless words might imperil, and as regards myself I shall not be guilty of the folly of printing language which a government might use against me. My pamphlet on the Irish Question, published in 1866, won a voluntary letter of warm approval from Mr. Gladstone, the only friendly writing I ever received from him in my life.

At Huddersfield, the Philosophical Hall having been duly hired for my lectures, pious influence was brought to bear on the lessee to induce him to break his contract. Fortunately, what in law amounted to possession had been given, and on the doors being locked against me, I broke them open, and delivered my lecture to a crowded and most orderly audience. I was arrested, and an attempt was made to prosecute me before the Huddersfield magistrates; but I defended myself with success, and defeated with ease the Conservative solicitor, N. Learoyd, who had been specially retained to ensure my committal to gaol.

In 1868 I entered into a contest with the Conservative Government which, having been continued by the Gladstone Government, finished in 1869 with a complete victory for myself. According to the then law every newspaper was required to give sureties to the extent of £800 against blasphemous or seditious libel. I had never offered to give these sureties, as they would have probably been liable to forfeiture about once a month. In March, 1868, the Disraeli Government insisted on my compliance with the law. I refused. The Government then required me to stop my paper. I printed on the next issue, "Printed in Defiance of Her Majesty's Government." I was then served with an Attorney-General's information, containing numerous counts, and seeking to recover enormous penalties. I determined to be my own barrister, and while availing myself in consultation of the best legal advice, I always argued my own case. The interlocutory hearings before the Judges in Chambers were numerous, for I took objection to nearly every step made by the Government, and I nearly always succeeded. I also brought the matter before Parliament, being specially backed in this by Mr. Milner Gibson, Mr. John Stuart Mill, and Mr. E. H. J. Craufurd. When the information was called on for trial in a crowded court before Mr. Baron Martin, the Government backed out, and declined to make a jury; so the prosecution fell to the ground. Strange to say, it was renewed by the Gladstone Government, who had the coolness to offer me, by the mouth of Attorney-General Collier, that they would not enforce any penalties if I would stop the paper, and admit that I was in the wrong. This I declined, and the prosecution now came on for trial before Baron Bramwell and a special jury. Against me were the Attorney-General, Sir R. Collier, the Solicitor-General, Sir J. D. Coleridge, and Mr. Crompton Hutton. I found that these legal worthies were blundering in their conduct of the trial, and at *nisi prius* I let them obtain a verdict, which, however, I reversed on purely technical grounds, after a long argument, which I sustained before Lord Chief Baron Kelly and a full court sitting in Banco. Having miserably failed to enforce the law against me, the Government repealed the statute, and I can boast that I got rid of the last shackle of the obnoxious English press laws. Mr. J. S. Mill wrote me: "You have gained a very honourable success in obtaining a repeal of the mischievous Act by your persevering resistance." The Government, although beaten, refused to reimburse me any portion of the large outlay incurred in fighting them.

It has always been my ambition to enter Parliament, and at the General Election for 1868 I, for the first time, entered the arena as a candidate. I was beaten; but this is scarcely wonderful. I had all the journals in England except three against me. Every idle or virulent tale which folly could distort or calumny invent was used against me. Despite all, I polled nearly 1,100 votes, and I obtained unasked, but not ungratefully listened to, the public acknowledgments from the Mayor of the borough, also from one of my competitors, Mr. Charles Gilpin, as to the loyal manner in which I had fought the contest through.

During the election struggle libels rained from all sides. One by the late Mr. Capper, M.P., seeking re-election at Sandwich, was the monstrous story, that in the open square at Northampton I had taken out my watch, and defied God to show his power by striking me dead in five minutes. Challenged for his authority, Mr. Capper pretended to have heard the story from Mr. C. Gilpin, M.P., who indignantly denied being any party to the falsehood. I insisted on an apology from Mr. Capper, which being refused, I sued him, but he died soon after the writ was served. The story was not an original invention by Mr. Capper; it had been reported of Abner Kneeland thirty years before, and is still a favourite one with pious missionaries at street corners. A still more outrageous slander was inserted in the *Razor*, a pseudo-comic weekly. I compelled this journal to give a full apology, but not until after two years' litigation, and a new trial had been ordered. When obliged to recant, the Christian proprietor became insolvent, to avoid payment of the costs. Unfortunately born poor, my life had been one continued struggle, and the burden of my indebtedness was sorely swollen in this and similar contests.

Probably the most severe, and to me certainly the most costly, struggle has been that on the oath question. Formerly it was a fatal objection against the competency of a witness who did not believe in a Deity and in a future state of rewards and punishments. Several attempts had been made to alter the law, but they had all failed; and indeed Sir J. Trevelyan's measures only provided for affirmation, and did not even seek to abolish the incompetency. In a case in which I was plaintiff in the Court of Common Pleas, my evidence was objected to, and I determined to fight the matter through every possible court, and to get the law changed if possible. I personally argued the case before Lord Chief Justice Bovill and a full Bench, in the Court of Common Pleas, and with the aid of the present Mr. Justice Denman and the late Lord Chancellor Hatherly, the law was twice altered in Parliament. Before victory was ultimately obtained I had to carry the case into the Court of Error, and I prepared and sent out at my own cost more than two hundred petitions to Parliament. Ultimately the Evidence Amendment Act, 1869, and the Evidence Further Amendment Act, 1870, gave Freethinkers the right to enter the witness box, and I won my suit. The Christian defendant finished by becoming bankrupt, and I lost a terribly large sum in debt and costs. The original debt and interest were over £300, and the costs of the various proceedings were very heavy.

In the winter of 1870 the Mirfield Town Hall, which had been properly taken and paid for for two nights' lectures, was refused by the proprietors, who barricaded the hall, and obtained a great force of police from the neighbourhood. In order that the law might be clearly settled on this matter, I brought an action to try the question, and although the late Mr. Justice Willes expressed himself strongly in my favour, it was held by Mr. Justice Mellor at *Nisi Prius* that nothing, except a deed under seal or an actual demise, would avail. A mere agreement for a user of a hall was a license revocable at will, even when for a valuable consideration. This convinced me that when hall proprietors break their contracts, I must myself enforce my rights as I did at Huddersfield, and have done in other places.

During the Franco-Prussian struggle I remained neutral until the 4th of September. I was against Bismarck and his blood-and-iron theory, but I was also utterly against the Empire and the Emperor; so I took no part with either. I was lecturing at Plymouth the day the *decheance* was proclaimed, and immediately after wrote my first article in favour of Republican France. I now set to work, and organised a series of meetings in London and the provinces, some of which were co-operated in by Dr. Congreve, Professor Beesly, and other prominent members of the Positivist party. These meetings exercised some little effect on the public opinion in this country, but unfortunately the collapse on the part of France was so complete, and the resources commanded by Bismarck and Moltke so vast, that, except as expressing sympathy, the results were barren. In October, 1870, I, without any previous communication from myself to them, received from the Republican Government at Tours a long and flattering letter, signed by Leon Gambetta, Adolphe Cremieux, Al Glais Bizoin, and Admiral Fourichon, declaring that they, as members of the "Gouvernement de la Defense Nationale, réunis en délégation à Tours," "tiennent à honneur de vous remercier chalereusement du noble concours que vous apportez à la cause de la France." On the 2nd of February, 1871, M. Tissot, the Chargé d'Affaires of France in England, wrote me: "Quant à moi, mon cher ami, je ne puis que constater ici, comme je l'ai deja fait, comme je le ferai en toute occasion, la dette que nous avons contractée envers vous. Vous nous avez donné votre temps, votre activité, votre eloquence, votre âme, la meilleure partie de vous même, en un mot; la France que vous avez été seule à defendre ne l'oubliera jamais." This is probably a too flattering estimate of my services to France, but coming from the official representative of the French Republic, I feel entitled to insert it. In September, 1871, Monsieur Emmanuel Arago, member of the Provisional Government of the 4th of September, wrote the following words upon the letter which had been sent me, as above mentioned, in October, 1870, by the Delegate Government of Tours: "En lisant cette lettre, j'eprouve tres vivement le regret de n'avoir pu, enfermé dans Paris, joindre ma signature à celles de mes collègues de la délégation de Tours. Mr. Bradlaugh est et sera toujours dans la République notre concitoyen."

During 1870, 1871, and 1872, I held several debates with the Rev. A. J. Harrison, formerly of Huddersfield. The first at Newcastle, in the splendid Town Hall of that place, was attended by about 5,000 persons. The second debate at Bristol, was notable from being presided over by Professor Newman. The third discussion was at Birmingham, and was an attempt at the Socratic method, and the last platform encounter was in the New Hall of Science, London. Of the Rev. Mr. Harrison it is enough I should say that, a few weeks since, when rumour put my life in danger, he was one of the first to write a kindly and unaffected letter of sympathy to Mrs. Bradlaugh.

When the great cry of thanksgiving was raised for the recovery of the Prince of Wales, I could not let it pass without protest. While he lay dangerously ill I had ceased to make any attack on himself or family, but I made no pretence of a grief I did not feel. When the thanksgiving day was fixed, and tickets for St. Paul's were sent by the Lord Chamberlain to working men representatives, I felt it right to hold a meeting of protest, which was attended by a crowded audience in the New Hall of Science.

The "right of meeting" has given me three important occasions of measuring swords with the Government during the last few years, and each time defeat has attended the Government. The first, the Hyde Park meeting, where I acted in accord with Mr. Beales, to whom as chief, let the honour go of this conflict. The second was on the 31st July, 1871, under the following circumstances. A meeting had been held by Mr. G. Odger and some of his friends in Hyde Park, on Sunday, the 30th of July, to protest against the grant to Prince Arthur; this meeting was adjourned until the following evening. Late on the Sunday afternoon, the adjourned meeting was forbidden by the Government. Early on Monday morning Mr. Odger applied to me to give the friends the benefit of my legal knowledge and personal influence. I consented, and the Government persevering, I took my share of the responsibility of the gathering, and signed with Mr. Odger a new notice convening the meeting. The Home Office not only served us also with a written prohibition, but threatened and prepared to use force. I immediately gave Mr. Bruce notice that the force would be illegal, and that it would be resisted. At the last moment, and in fact only some half hour before the meeting commenced, the Government abandoned its prohibition, and an enormous meeting of a most orderly character was held in absolute defiance of the authorities.

The more recent case was in December, 1872, when finding that Mr. Odger, Mr. Bailey, and others, had been prosecuted under some monstrous and ridiculous regulations invented by Mr. Ayrton, I, on my own responsibility, determined to throw down the gauntlet to the Government. I did this most successfully, and soon after the opening of Parliament the obnoxious regulations were annulled.

It is at present too early to speak of the Republican movement in England, which I have sought, and not entirely without success, to organise on a thoroughly legal basis. It is a fair matter for observation that my lectures on "The Impeachment of the House of Brunswick," have been delivered to crowded audiences assembled in some of the finest halls in England and Scotland, notably the Free Trade Hall, Manchester, the Town Hall, Birmingham, the Town Hall, Northampton, and the City Hall, Glasgow. It is, as far as I am aware, the first time any English citizen has, without tumult or disorder and in buildings belonging to various Municipalities, directly challenged the hereditary right of the reigning family.

In penning the foregoing sketch I had purposely to omit many facts connected with branches of Italian, Irish, and French politics. I have also entirely omitted my own struggles for existence. The political parts are left out because there are secrets which are not my own alone, and which may not bear full telling for many years to come. The second, because I hope that another year or two of hard work may enable me to free myself from the debt load which for some time has hung heavily round me.

THE REAL REPRESENTATION OF THE PEOPLE.

By C. BRADLAUGH.

SECOND EDITION.

LONDON:
FREETHOUGHT PUBLISHING COMPANY,
28, STONECUTTER STREET, E.C.

Price *Twopence.*

LONDON:
PRINTED BY CHARLES BRADLAUGH AND ANNIE BESANT,
28, STONECUTTER STREET, E.C.

THE REAL REPRESENTATION OF THE PEOPLE.

BY C. BRADLAUGH.

La multitude qui ne se réduit pas à l'unité est confusion. L'unité qui n'est pas multitude est tyrannic.—PASCAL.

La multitude, c'est la société; l'unité, c'est la verité—c'est l'ensemble des lois de justice et de raison qui doivent gouverner la société.—GUIZOT.

Government is a contrivance of human wisdom to provide for human wants. Men have a right that these wants should be provided for by this wisdom.—BUCKLE.

ANY one reading the parliamentary debates of 1793 to 1798, and again those immediately preceding the passing of the Reform Bill in 1832, will at once perceive how much of political power has been conceded by the governing classes to the governed on a pressure from without, and how little concession has been obtained by the people from their rulers from a sense of justice, when the demand has been unaccompanied by a powerful popular agitation. Enlargements of political privileges have been granted not cheerfully, but with fear and murmuring, and after a long and angry resistance. In the late debates on the reform question in the House of Commons, the working classes were, with some justice, upbraided for their apathy, yet when formerly active in their own interest they were not unfrequently the victims of state prosecutions for treasons and misdemeanours. I desire to see renewed political activity, believing that the present enormous and wasteful expenditure of the English Government calls for interference on the part of the people, who are the contributors of the great bulk of the revenue. Such an interference is only usefully practicable when a wide extension of political power has been obtained by the masses, and an alteration of the suffrage has rendered the House of Commons something nearer an assembly of the people's representatives. The unenfranchised are at the present time politically at the mercy of their more favoured brethren, and this subjection of one class to another is most disastrous in its effects on both. That men educated as are the English people should be controlled without the right to express an effective opinion as to the direction of such control, is a wrong demanding speedy remedy.

Believing it to be impossible that the masses can in the future rest satisfied for a period of any considerable duration without the enactment of some measure of parliamentary reform, and knowing that the attainment of a successful issue on the part of the people to any reform agitation must depend on the justice of the measure agitated for, and on the ability of the agitators to enforce their demands by sound argument, I deem it my duty to bring specially before the working classes, who are most interested in the renewal of a movement for reform, certain views which appear to me of vital importance to them, and which are promulgated by a writer who declares that "the problem of constitutional organism is, in what manner the individuals composing the entire community are to be classed, so that no opinions or interests shall be unheard, or extinguished in representation;" and who quotes with approval the statement of Guizot, that "the object of representative government is to examine publicly the great interests and diverse opinions which, while dividing society, seek to overcome each other, in the just confidence that out of their debates will grow the knowledge and adoption of those laws and measures which best conduce to the interests of the country. This object is only attained by the triumph of a true majority, the minority constantly being present and heard. If the majority is displaced by artifice, the result is falsehood. If the minority is excluded from the discussion, it is an oppression. In either case the principle of representative government is corrupted." The writer to whom I refer is Mr. Thomas Hare, of whom John Stuart Mill, in the supplement to his treatise on Parliamentary Reform, says that "he has raised the principle of the Representation of Minorities to an importance and dignity which no previous thinker had ascribed to it."

Holding, as I do, the opinion that every sane human being unconvicted of crime should have the means of exercising, through the electoral suffrage, an influence on the management of the public affairs of the state in which he or she is resident, I have been rejoiced to find in Mr. Hare's book an unfailing reply to one of the most vital objections made by those who contend against any considerable extension of the franchise to the masses. This objection was embodied by Mr. Burke in his expression of fear of a democratic majority, and is thus stated by Mr. Mill, who asks, " Why is nearly the whole educated class united in uncompromising hostility to a purely democratic suffrage? Not so much because it would make the most numerous class, that of manual labourers, the *strongest* power; *that* many of the educated classes would think only just. It is because it would make them the *sole* power, because in every constituency the votes of that class would swamp and politically annihilate all other members of the community taken together." That is, the minority who at present govern by the unjust exclusion of the masses from the exercise of the suffrage, claim to perpetuate this injustice, and to retain to themselves the usurped dominance, because they anticipate, at the hands of the people, the same kind of wrong which the masses suffer from them—namely, political annihilation. This political death (which occurring to any body of citizens is a most grievous injury to the state) has terror for the upper 10,000, notwithstanding which, they appear to deem it the rightful fate of the lower 10,000,000. John Stuart Mill says, " A person who is excluded from all participation in political business is not a citizen He has not the feelings of a citizen. To take an active interest in politics is, in modern times, the first thing which elevates the mind to large interests and contemplations; the first step out of the narrow bounds of individual and family selfishness, the first opening in the contracted round of daily occupations. The person who in a free country takes no interest in politics unless from having been taught that he ought not to do so, must be too ill informed, too stupid, or too selfish, to be interested in them; and we may rely on it that he cares as little for anything else which does not directly concern himself or his personal connections. Whoever is capable of feeling any common interest in his kind, or with his country, is interested in politics; and to be interested in them and not wish for a voice in them is an impossibility. The possession and the exercise of political, and among others of electoral rights, is one of the chief instruments both of moral and intellectual training for the popular mind; and all governments must be regarded as extremely imperfect until every one who is required to obey the laws, has a voice, or the prospect of a voice, in their enactment and administration" At present a fraction only of the community have a right to vote, the user of this right is far from complete, and a majority of the so-called representatives of the people are returned to the House of Commons by a minority of that fraction; so that, in fact, the minority of a minority rule the nation. This is clearly wrong, and the apology by the governing classes that theirs is the educated minority is deprived of much of its force on examination. Educated are the governors? Not so much in the wants of the poor as in the pauper toiler, not so fully in the needs of labour, as is the factory *employé;* in each phase of the labourer's existence various wrongs need remedy, and it is only in the living through these poor men's miseries that men can be educated to their full comprehension. There are many questions in the discussion of which the working classes are most fittingly educated to entitle them to a voice, and on which they have need as well as right to be heard by representatives from their own ranks. The pretence of education on the part of the politician is sometimes a tinsel, covering the most complete ignorance of the political requirements of the nation. An educated minority so misgoverned the uneducated majority of France that at last more than half a century of bitter wretchedness and starvation culminated in the decapitation of a king and a bloody convulsion of the nation. An educated minority in Austria at the present day rule by force against the will of the Hungarian, Venetian, and Gallician peasantry, and revolts and repressions result.

In our own country it has been the educated classes who

have impeded the education of their poorer brethren by the imposition of taxes on knowledge, and a variety of restrictions on the liberty of the press. To use the language of Mr. Buckle, "they could hardly have done worse if they had been the sworn advocates of popular ignorance." Especially have they hindered the diffusion of political information, and the pillory, prison, and transportation were the arguments used against the early instructors of the masses in their duties as citizens. The right to diffuse political knowledge amongst the crowd has been won by slow and painful processes, and in defiance of state trials, government-favouring judges, and county jails. No wonder that the masses have rested ignorant so long.

In England, even now, an educated minority waste in extravagant state expenditure million after million, coined by the hand labour of the political nonentities, who pay the taxes, and are deemed sufficiently educated to obey laws they have no share in making. Amongst the governing classes are some who from mean and selfish motives sustain a state of things which finds sinecures for younger sons; but there are many even in pure Belgravia who would willingly accord to the working man some share in the government, but who fear that if the right of suffrage be attained by the people, it will be used to destroy politically the whole of those in whom political power is at present vested. These urge that in every country, city, and borough the artizans and labourers outnumber the men of property and birth, and they declare their conviction that in a House of Commons returned by universal suffrage, there would be no justice done to the rights of property. If this argument were true to its fullest extent, it would only serve to show that those who have possessed the fullest opportunities for developing the national will, have not used their opportunities for the good of the nation. It can hardly be denied that the governing classes of the country have had to a great extent the power of controlling the education of the people, nor can it be contended that this power has been so advantageously used as it might have been if the real elevation of the masses had been sought.

So that in effect I reply, that even if the result of conceding to the working classes their political rights were as disastrous to the aristocracy as the most timid contemplate, yet even then there is no valid excuse for the withholding such political power from the people. Mr. Hare's proposal, which I desire to have discussed by my readers, meets this objection; and while he does not contend for such an extension of the suffrage as I should consider just, he proposes a scheme under which I conceive it possible to obtain the real representation of the people in the English House of Commons. Mr. Hare looks upon the Parliament House as a place where minorities, heresies, and protests of all sorts should be represented and entitled to a hearing; and in order to attain this he has in a most masterly manner framed a measure which should be fully examined by the people; for so long as the working classes are denied justice, and are not admitted to the suffrage in so ample a manner as to outnumber the upper class electors, it is to the working men that Mr. Hare's bill is peculiarly beneficial; and I trust that even if universal suffrage were obtained to-morrow the people would know that a permanent and progressive democracy can only subsist usefully by permitting its opponents to be heard in the national deliberative assembly. Guizot says that "an electoral system which in the formation of the deliberative assembly annuls in advance the influence and participation of the minorities, destroys the representative government, and would be as fatal to the majority as a law which in a deliberative assembly compelled the minority to remain silent."

At present elections are purely local, and the minority of electors in a particular borough are not only unrepresented, but are misrepresented. Of late several modes have been suggested for giving an effective voice to a minority; by limiting each elector to fewer votes than the number of members to be elected, or allowing him to concentrate all his votes on the same candidate. These various schemes are praiseworthy so far as they go, but they attain the object very imperfectly.

All plans for dividing a merely local representation in

unequal ratios, are limited by the small number of members which can be, and the still smaller which ought to be, assigned to any one constituency. There are considerable objections to the election even of so many as three by every constituent body. This, however, under present arrangements, is the smallest number which would admit of any representation of a minority, and in this case the minority must amount to at least a third of the whole. All smaller minorities would continue, as at present, to be disfranchised; and in a minority of a third, the whole number must unite in voting for the same candidate. There may, therefore, be a minority within the minority who have sacrificed their individual preference, and from whose vote nothing can with certainty be concluded but that they dislike less the candidate they voted for, than they do the rival candidate."* Mr. Hare would have principles represented rather than places, and he would not confine the voters to a local candidate, but would widen their sphere of choice, and permit the vote to be given to any one who was a candidate for election anywhere in the kingdom. That is, supposing there to be in all 658 members of parliament, and a total of 1,316,000 electors throughout the kingdom voting at a particular election, he would divide the latter by the former, thus leaving a quotient of 2000, and he would allow any candidate who obtained 2000 votes throughout the whole kingdom to be returned to parliament. This would much modify the constitution of the House, even without any extension of the suffrage. For example, there are the various Trades' Unions unrepresented in parliament, and although numerically strong, they are spread over a wide surface, and are so weak in suffrage power in any given town or borough, that there is probably no locality where the Trades' Unions would have the ghost of a chance to carry a candidate; but given all Great

---

* These semi-dissentients might even amount to a majority of the minority; for (as Mr. Hare remarks) if fifty persons agree to combine their strength, who, left to themselves, would have divided their votes among ten candidates, six of the fifty may impose their candidate on all the rest, though perhaps only relatively preferred by them.

Britain, and a hundred votes in one city, and twenty in that borough, and ten in this town, and five in that village, and so on, and the quotient may be attained, and the Trades' Union may pick their best man, and compel parliament to receive him. So with the Co-operative societies, the Odd-Fellows, and other large friendly societies. All these with their wide influences, might gather the necessary number of votes from different corners of the realm. This portion of Mr. Hare's scheme provides for the representation of every minority of not less than 2000 electors and the representation is more nearly equalised than is otherwise possible. Every candidate who is elected can boast that he is the representative of a constituency unanimous in their desire for his return, and no voter can complain that he is misrepresented by a man he has voted against. Some candidates of great popularity will probably get more than the quota of votes required, and if all these were counted for him, the House would be deficient of members, as none are to be returned who do not obtain the quota. To obviate this, Mr. Hare proposes that no more than the necessary quota of votes shall be counted to any candidate, and that whoever obtains that number shall be declared duly elected; all surplus votes being transferred to some one else. For this purpose the elector is to put on his voting paper more than one name, so that if the first named have elsewhere the necessary suffrages, then the vote passes to the second, or in case he shall already have sufficient, then to the third, or fourth, or fifth, or sixth, or seventh, and so on. Thus while the vote would in any case only be counted for one candidate, it would be sure to be counted for some candidate, and would not be thrown away as many votes are at present. John Stuart Mill regards it as certain that this scheme would, if carried out, prodigiously improve the *personnel* of the national representation. "At present, were they ever so desirous, a great majority of the most distinguished men in the country have little or no chance of being elected anywhere as members of the House of Commons. The admirers, and those who would be the supporters, of a person whose claims rest on acknowledged personal merit, are generally dispersed throughout the country, while there is no place in which his influence would not be far outweighed by that of some local grandee, or *notabilité de clocher*, who neither has, nor deserves to have, the smallest influence anywhere else. If a man of talents and virtue could count as votes for his return all electors in any part of the kingdom, who would like to be represented by him, every such person who is well known to the public would have a probable chance; and under this encouragement nearly all of them, whose position and circumstances were compatible with parliamentary duties, might be willing to offer themselves to the electors. Those voters who did not like either of the local candidates, or who believed that one whom they did not like was sure to prevail against them, would have all the available intellectual strength of the country from whom to select the recipient of their otherwise wasted vote. An assembly thus chosen would contain the élite of the nation."

The improvement anticipated would not be confined to representatives of minorities, better men would be chosen on either side. "A member who had already served in parliament with any distinction, would under this system be almost sure of his re-election. At present the first man in the House may be thrown out of parliament precisely when most wanted, and may be kept out for several years, from no fault of his own, but because a change has taken place in the local balance of parties, or because he has voted against the prejudices or local interests of some influential portion of his constituents." Instances of this have occurred, and will be familiar to the reader. "Under Mr. Hare's system, if he has not deserved to be thrown out, he will be nearly certain to obtain votes from other places, sufficient, with his local strength, to make up the quota of 2000 (or whatever the number may be) necessary for his return to Parliament. Consider next the check which would be given to bribery and intimidation in the return of members to Parliament. Who by bribery and intimidation, could get together 2000 electors from a hundred different parts of the country? Intimidation would have no means of acting over so large a surface; and bribery requires secrecy, and an organised machinery, which can only be brought into play within narrow local limits. Where would then be the advantage of bribing or coercing the 200 or 300 electors of a small borough? They could not of themselves make up the quota, and nobody could know what part of the country the remaining 1700 or 1800 suffrages might come from. In places so large as to afford the number of 2000 electors, bribery or intimidation would have the same chances as at present. But it is not in such places that, even now, these malpractices are successful. As regards bribery (Mr. Hare truly remarks), the chief cause of it is, that in a closely contested election where certain votes are indispensable, the side which cannot secure those particular votes is sure to be defeated. But under Mr. Hare's plan no vote would be indispensable. A vote from any other part of the country would serve the purpose as well: and a candidate might be in a minority at the particular place and yet be returned."

In each election the votes are necessarily given by voting papers, bearing the name and address of the speaker, which are preserved, each quota being kept distinct, and in case of a vacancy occurring by death, or otherwise, the returning officer in direction from the voter is to send a circular letter to each of the electors forming the constituency of the member who had filled the vacant seat with a list of the new candidates, and the candidate obtaining the largest number of suffrages out of such constituency will be returned as duly elected to the vacant seat.

In the event of a member accepting office under government, a circular letter is to be sent to the constituency represented by that member, informing them thereof, and unless in reply at least one fourth express their dissent, the representative who has so accepted office under government will not vacate his seat.

While Mr. Hare's plan does not propose to equalise the electoral districts in any of the modes heretofore suggested, it of course fulfils the whole object of those who desire this equalisation; and, unlike all other schemes, is self-adjusting, the quota being declared at each election as before stated.

REAL REPRESENTATION OF THE PEOPLE. 13

There are other points as to the ballot, the suffrage, disqualification of members, &c., upon which some differences of opinion may be expected. Mr. Hare objects to the ballot, and in another pamphlet this shall be fully discussed. The subject is of too much interest to dismiss here in a few lines only. Mr. Hare evidently hopes that undue influence will be so guarded against and checked by the heightened standard of electoral morals induced in the working out of the scheme of personal representation of which he is the author, that he provides for open voting by voting papers, signed by the elector, and these are to be delivered by the voter personally at the polling booth, save under special circumstances.

Mr. Hare's views on the suffrage are that the qualification should be accessible to every man when he acquires a home and settles to an occupation in life. He says with reference to woman, that given the same qualification as the man, there is no sound reason for excluding her from the parliamentary franchise. He would not disqualify judicial officers, clergymen, or officials from becoming representatives. Numerous readers will doubtless agree in thinking that too many probable causes of mischief abound in the adoption of this item. The Judge on the Bench who may have to try a political prisoner should be kept as free as possible from party bias. The system of government in England will most certainly have to undergo a thorough purification before civil service appointments can cease to be regarded as possible wages for ministerial support. He condemns the payment of members, but would limit each candidate's election expenses to £50. This sum would be a sort of guarantee against crowding the lists with sham candidates.

All the present machinery of elections would be thrown out of gear by the successful introduction of Mr. Hare's views. We should no longer have the inhabitants of each place divided into parties seeking to return their candidate against the desire of the political opponent. Instead of the elections being, as now, a contest for power in which some get their representative elected, and some vote and see all their labours fruitless, and their political effort entirely wasted, we should have the election an endeavour to select the ablest representative, each voter knowing that if he had anywhere in the country a quota of sympathising electors, he was sure of being represented in Parliament by the man of his choice. At present our electoral system divides the voters into adverse parties arrayed under formal names, and prevents the expression of the true and individual opinions of the members of either party. "It lowers the force of thought and conscience, reduces the most valuable electoral elements to inaction, and converts the better motives of those who act into an effort for success, and a mere calculation of the means of accomplishing it." Mr Hare's plan would enable the individual expression of opinion to become a reality, not a sham; it would develop a more self-reliant tone in those electors who at present are crushed out of vigour by the consciousness of their numerical helplessness. It would enable them to enter the House of Commons gathering their votes from east, west, north, and south, who under the present system could never get a majority in any one place, and who yet perhaps are better entitled to rank themselves as representative men in the country than are half the elected members of the Commons House of Parliament.

Those people who have not yet the suffrage right should submit Mr. Hare's views to careful investigation, in order to ascertain whether the bill he proposes would, if enacted, result, as I firmly believe it would, in increasing their opportunities of acquiring the franchise, by placing in Parliament various men having knowledge of and trusted by the people, to whom parliamentary action is at present impossible. Those who hold the reins of government entirely in their own grasp should seriously consider whether it would not be far wiser to carry such a measure now they have the ability, and while there is no hostile popular pressure, than to wait until a stormy reformation has swept them from power, and a manhood suffrage, conceded to the agitated masses to prevent a continuance of riot and revolt, has politically annihilated the classes who have hitherto usurped the entire government of the state. The governing minority might in a time of political repose, such as the present, gracefully enact Mr. Hare's measure on the ground that it was just and beneficial to the people; although, notwithstanding that it will be equally just in the next generation, its future benefits will be special to themselves. It would, however, be difficult for the minority of high birth and great estates to obtain the enactment for themselves from an irritated and overwhelming majority of a measure which, when themselves powerful, they had refused.

It is desirable that both sides should regard the question of the political enfranchisement of the people as of equal interest and common benefit. To adopt a phrase of Burke's, politics ought to be adjusted to human nature, and the proper business of the government ought to be to ascertain the general wish and requirements of the nation, legislating in accordance therewith. In one of his speeches the eloquent calumniator of the French Revolution said, "The people will have it so, and it is not for their representatives to say nay;" yet either of the members now sitting for Manchester may hear that the non-electors, inhabitants of that city, have assembled to the number of 40,000 in front of the Infirmary, declaring in favour of some measure, and he may, under present circumstances, altogether disregard their united voice, because politically they are dumb. Each individual of the 40,000 may be a tax-paying, law-observing machine, but he is destitute of any rights as a citizen: he has no vote, no voice in the government of his country. The Imperial Parliament is elected without his sanction, he contributes no choice, has no part in its selection; all his duty is to obey its edicts, his privilege to pay and pine.

That a great political struggle is impending, must be evident to every student of history. In every nation of the world, each period of assault by the governed on their governors for the obtainment of some share in the right to manage the business of the nation, has been preceded by a strong expression of heretical views. This is natural, for what is the latter but the manifestation of an education inconsistent with political slavery? While the masses are ignorant they believe everything and remain without the suffrage, but as they are gradually educated to confute the delusions of their ancient teachers, the superstitionists who frightened their children with bogey, so they are also educated enough to dispute the dictum of the great landed aristocracy who treat the nation as in its babyhood, and declare it incapable of self-government. At the present moment the nation, by its wide and fast increasing out-uttered heresy, manifests a rapid extension of education, and I therefore do not believe that it will wait for a very long time before its attention is turned to the achievement of some such result as the real representation of the people in Parliament.

No conclusion can be fitter for this brief pamphlet than the renewed recommendation to our readers to obtain for themselves Mr. Hare's volume, of which Mr. Mill says that —"it deserves a high rank among manuals of political thought," and that "the system it embodies will be recognised as alone just in principle, as one of the greatest of all practical improvements, and as the most efficient safeguard of further parliamentary reform."

GEORGE

PRINCE OF WALES;

WITH RECENT CONTRASTS AND COINCIDENCES.

BY

CHARLES BRADLAUGH.

LONDON:
FREETHOUGHT PUBLISHING COMPANY,
28, STONECUTTER STREET, E.C.

PRICE TWOPENCE.

THE LIFE OF GEORGE PRINCE OF WALES,

WITH RECENT CONTRASTS AND COINCIDENCES.

> "'God save the King!' It is a large economy
> In God to save the like; but if he will
> Be saving all the better: for not one am I
> Of those who think damnation better still."—BYRON.

GEORGE AUGUSTUS FREDERICK PRINCE OF WALES, was born on August 12th, 1762. He was the son of George III. by the Queen Sophia Charlotte. George III. was thrice married, once privately in 1759, at Curzon Street Chapel, May Fair, to Hannah Lightfoot, a Quakeress, and afterwards on September 18th, 1761, publicly to the Princess Sophia Charlotte of Mecklenberg Strelitz. As Hannah Lightfoot was living at the time of the second marriage, the offspring of that bigamous union would have been illegitimate if George III. had not been King of England. Fortunately it is one of the maxims of our glorious constitution, that the King can do no wrong; besides which, the marriage with Hannah Lightfoot has been positively denied, although it is said that the Earl of Abercorn and Lord Harcourt, amongst others, informed Queen Charlotte of the actuality of the first marriage. I accept the denial, even in the teeth of the fact, for a royal denial, as was shown in the case of the Fitzherbert marriage, of the Duke of York scandal, and of the Mordaunt divorce, is of greater value than any evidence; and in this case I accept the denial of the Lightfoot marriage the more readily, as if the story of that union were true it would cast grave doubts on the right of Her Most Gracious Majesty to reign over us. The only title English monarchs have to their crowns—and it must be admitted that this title is an all-sufficient one—is that of hereditary right. The monarchs of some countries have been selected by their peoples: our kings and queens are bred from special foreign stocks, and inherit the right to reign just as other persons inherit entailed estates, and any blot on the legitimacy would weaken the right. It is some comfort to know that George III. married Queen Charlotte twice, the second marriage being solemnised at Kew, in 1765; but whether Hannah Lightfoot was then dead or alive is a matter on which it is difficult to express an opinion. At any rate, if there had ever been any doubt as to the legitimacy of George Prince of Wales, the second solemnisation of the marriage with Sophia Charlotte may give all loyal subjects more ease of mind as to the title of the later born members of the Royal Family. Those who argue that Hannah Lightfoot died in 1765, make strange suggestions as to a severe attack of mental disease, which, commencing at this time, although partially repressed, ultimately reappeared, and many years after terminated in the absolute idiocy of George III.

There is a great contrast between the parents of Prince George and those of the present Prince of Wales. The late Prince Consort is known as Albert the Good, and the statues erected through the country testify more strikingly than his many less known grand deeds, to the great esteem in which his memory is held by all loyal Englishmen; but George III. was described by Lord Brougham in the following fashion:—" Of a narrow understanding, which no culture had enlarged; of an obstinate disposition, which no education perhaps could have humanised; of strong feelings in ordinary things, and a resolute attachment to all his own opinions and predilections, George III. possessed much of the firmness of purpose which, being exhibited by men of contracted mind without any discrimination, and as pertinaciously when they are in the wrong as when they are in the right, lends to their characters an appearance of inflexible consistency, which is often mistaken for greatness of mind, and not seldom received as a substitute for honesty. In all that related to his kingly office he was the slave of deeprooted selfishness; and no feeling of a kindly nature ever was allowed access to his bosom whenever his power was concerned." So one who had a fair opportunity of judging writes of the father, and the criticism may aid us to understand his son. It is said that on some rare occasions, George III. could be privately and munificently generous; the name of the father of our present Prince of Wales figured in many public lists of charitable subscriptions, but it has never been suggested that he in any way concealed the natural liberality of his disposition. George IV. was by letters patent created Prince of Wales and Earl of Chester; as first born, he was Duke of Cornwall and of Rothesay, Earl of Carrick and Baron of Renfrew. The present Prince of Wales was also created Earl of Dublin, a title afterwards deserved by his praiseworthy exertions at Punchestown Races for the amelioration of the condition of the Irish people. When George Prince of Wales was only nineteen, he became with his brother Frederick, who was not only Duke of York, but was elected Bishop of Osnaburgh when eleven months old, the subject of much hostile comment. One writer says, "at this period the Prince and his eldest brother were associated in dissipation of every species: their love of gaming was proverbial, and their excess of indulgence in voluptuousness was sufficient to drain the resources of the country."

How great the contrast between the conduct of these two royal princes and that of the present Prince of Wales and his brother the Duke of Edinburgh. Omitting the Continental papers, some of which have dared to print suggestions as to the habits of the first, and the Colonial papers, some of which have been wicked enough to charge the second with open and notorious licentiousness, and leaving as unworthy notice Sir Charles Mordaunt's reference to "the previous bad character" of the present heir-apparent, we defy the finger of slander to touch in any of our respectable journals the slightest remark of a depreciatory character against either of our well-beloved royal princes; except some provincial journal like the *Royal Leamington Chronicle*, or cheap paper like *Reynolds's*, all our free and independent press writers agreeing in testifying to the purity of the living scions of the House of Brunswick. George Prince of Wales called himself Florizel, and his *liaison* with Mary Robinson as Perdita was one of the most notorious amongst the escapades of his early life. Mrs. Baddeley states that it commenced when the Prince was little more than fourteen. "But," asks Thackeray, "shall we take the Leporello part, flourish a catalogue of the conquests of this royal Don Juan, and tell the names of the favourites to whom one after the other Prince George flung his pocket-handkerchief? What purpose would it answer to say how Perdita was pursued, won, deserted, and by whom succeeded?" As Thackeray refrained with George, so we refrain with Albert Edward, and from Broadwood downwards draw a discreet veil of reticence which only hides from those who cannot see:—

> "Who has a thing to bring
> For a gift to our lord the King,
> Our King all Kings above?
> A young girl brought him love;
> And he dowered her with shame,
> With a sort of infamous fame,
> And then with lonely years
> Of penance and bitter tears.
> Love is scarcely the thing
> To bring as a gift for our King."

The marriage of Prince George, in 1786, to Mrs. Fitzherbert, gained additional *éclat* from the fact that George is said to have written a letter to Charles James Fox, authorising him to deny in Parliament that the formal solemnity had ever taken place. Thackeray's answer ought to have been given to Mr. Rolle, in the House of Commons, in lieu of that spoken by C. J. Fox, who is alleged to have been present at the marriage, and yet asserted to the Legislature, if Hansard be reliable, that "it never did happen." The author of "Vanity Fair" says that George " did actually marry Mrs. Fitzherbert according to the rites of the Roman Catholic Church; that her marriage settlements have been seen in London, and that the names of the witnesses to her marriage are known." Yet, of what avail is an author's word against the denial of a Prince? When George attained his majority he had an allowance of £50,000 per annum, together with a grant of £60,000 for furnishing Carlton House. When Albert Edward attained his majority he had £40,000 a year voted him by Parliament, he had the income of the Duchy of Cornwall, exceeding net £60,000 per annum, and he had the enormous accumulations of his minority, amounting to something like a million sterling. Neither George

Prince nor Albert Edward Prince limited his expenditure to the amount of his income. The debts of George came before the Parliament; the pecuniary embarrassments of Albert Edward, although matter of common talk in some circles, are at present better concealed. The House of Commons in 1787, voted about £160,000 for the payment of the Prince of Wales's debts, solemn pledges of economy for the future being given by, and on behalf of, the royal insolvent. It is a question whether the present Parliament would vote, and whether the country would submit to a repetition of such a payment. In 1788, George III. was mad, and no greater proof can be advanced of the perfect and unimpeachable character of our monarchy than the fact that, with an insane head, the Government went on quite as well as when he was in possession of all his faculties. The mere fact that Jamaica had mutinied, that the American Colonies had broken our oppressive yoke, and that Ireland was held by force and fraud, must not be allowed to militate against our approval of George's reign. That war cost during it more than £1,200 000,000, renders the memory of George III. as dear to us, as the King was in life to the members of the London Corresponding Society. I know that one furious Radical, Earl Grey, speaks as if the monarchy were always better without the King than with him, for he declares that "the highly beneficial custom of holding Cabinet Councils without the presence of the Sovereign arose from George I. not knowing English." And Earl Grey had the audacity to publish this in the reign of her present Majesty, whose constant help and aid in the government of the nation is known to be so highly valuable. I once heard a public lecturer, describing the crowned head of this great empire, say—"What is the position which England's monarch occupies in the great vessel of the State? He is not the paddle-wheel nor the screw, neither the mast, the sails, the rigging, the bulwarks, nor the keel; he is the highly decorated figure-head, always costly, not always handsome, and never useful."

In consequence of the state of mind of George III., debates took place in the House of Commons as to the Regency. The friends of the Prince claimed it for him as a right; Pitt, on the contrary, maintained the terribly revolutionary doctrine, that in the event of incapacity on the part of the reigning monarch, the right to nominate the Regent rested with the Parliament. Everyone will see that this is a most dangerous doctrine, for it is equivalent to declaring that the nation has the legal right to select its own ruler on any vacancy occurring in the occupancy of the throne. Fortunately, the King temporarily recovered his reason. When sane, George III. bitterly disliked his eldest son, and showed that dislike in various fashions—the King and heir apparent were seldom or never seen together. To-day no such division can be shown between the reigning monarch and Crown Prince; and although it is true that on the recent royal visit to the City the Prince of Wales was unavoidably absent, it must not be forgotten that immediately his royal mother had left London for Windsor, Albert Edward delighted all loyal citizens by his attendance the same evening at one of the new theatres. George Prince of Wales was called the first gentleman in Europe; that is, he was so styled while he was alive, although posthumous critics have disputed his claim to the title; no such dispute is, however, likely to arise in any case with reference to the present Prince of Wales. His royal thoughtfulness for his guests, the sons of the Viceroy of Egypt, when a careless coachman had overturned them in the mud, will remain an ineffaceable testimony of his sensitive and well-trained nature. George is said to have been praised, and not unduly, for his highly cultivated mind, his elegant accomplishments, and his personal graces. Albert Edward has been honoured in the cartoon of the *Tomahawk* with a pictorial epitome of *his* elegant accomplishments.

In 1788, 1789, and 1790, in order to raise money, George Prince of Wales, Frederick Duke of York, and William Henry Duke of Clarence, issued joint and several bonds, bearing interest, and payable within six months after either of them should ascend the throne. These bonds were issued to an extent in all of nearly one million sterling nominal, but were of course placed at heavy discount. The holders, who were mostly foreigners, were prevented from being importunate creditors by deportation under the Alien Act from this country, and by accusations of treason in their own land. In 1794, the Prince of Wales owing then about £650,000, a bargain was made that George should marry his cousin Princess Caroline Louisa of Brunswick, and that the nation should not only pay all his debts, but also increase his annual allowance. George wanted his debts paid, but did not want to marry, and the copy of a letter is preserved, from him to his proposed spouse, in which he asks her to refuse to marry him, tells her that he loves another woman, and finally winds up: " You would find in me a husband who places all his affections upon another. If this secret which I name to you in confidence does not cause you to reject me; if ambition, or any other motive of which I am ignorant, cause you to condescend to the arrangements of my family, learn that, as soon as you shall have given an heir to the throne, I will abandon you, never to meet you more in public." It is wonderful how any woman could have married a man writing her such a letter. George said, "You cannot accuse me of having deceived you." Not only were the £650,000 debts paid, and the Prince's allowance increased from £60,000 to £100,000 per annum, but £71,000 additional was voted for plate, jewels, and marriage sundries, at Carlton House. Six months after the marriage the starving poor cried, " Give us bread," "No famine.' King George III. was pelted on his way to open Parliament, and, when he arrived at Westminster, was so frightened "that," says a Parliamentary writer, " his face was flushed and swollen, his eyes were momentarily turned from side to side, and his manner evinced the utmost perturbation." In great fear the Treason and Sedition Acts were hurried through Parliament.

It is alleged that George asked for a glass of brandy after his first interview with his bride elect, and that when he was married, on April 8th, 1795, he did not even remain sober on the wedding-day. No such disgraceful charge could be repeated against Albert Edward, whose constant sobriety, at home and abroad, might serve as an example for loyal temperance lecturers. That *La Cigale* should pretend against our prince, habits more like those of his princely predecessor, is an illustration of the licence of the foreign press, and that rumour should suggest an instance of public insobriety on the Boulevard des Italiens, shows how far mud may be thrown at royal ermine of the most spotless purity. Thackeray speaks of how George "reeled into chapel to be married; how he hiccupped out his vows of fidelity."

A daughter was born to Prince George on January 7th, 1796. She was named Charlotte Augusta, and immediately after her birth, Prince George, as he threatened, separated himself from his wife.

In 1803, the excesses of Prince George caused him further embarrassment, and £60,000 a-year extra were for three years and a half devoted to the liquidation of his liabilities. Who dare write at length the names of the women—some titled and fashionable—who helped to spend this money? In the Duke of Buckingham's letters, vague references at a later date to one titled dame might be explained in regard to the expenditure of this period:—

> "Who has a thing to bring
> For a gift to our lord the King?
> A harlot brought him her flesh,
> Her lusts, and the manifold mesh
> Of her wiles intervolved with caprice;
> And he gave her his realm to fleece,
> To corrupt, to ruin, and gave
> Himself for her toy and her slave.
> Harlotry's just the thing
> To bring as a gift for our king."

The Marchioness of Conyngham, one of the many temporary wives of this modern Solomon, amongst other gifts, had jewels value £80,000. Lady Jersey, another favourite, shared in the work of spoiling the Egyptians. Thackeray says, that the Prince of Wales' turf experiences were unlucky as well as discreditable. He was accused of cheating with his horse Escape, and although of course acquitted, left the Jockey Club in consequence. The Prince living separate from the Princess of Wales, all kinds of rumours were circulated, one allegation being that since the living apart, another and illegitimate child had been born to her, and a Royal Commission, including the Lord Chancellor and Lord Chief Justice of England, was issued to investigate these slanderous allegations; the official report made is supposed to have thoroughly cleared Princess Caroline's character, and to have demonstrated the most wicked conduct on the part of Queen Sophia Charlotte and Prince George, but King George III. " directed it should be destroyed, and every trace of the proceedings on the affair buried in oblivion." William Cobbett, however, obtained a copy of all the depositions, either from the Princess of Wales, or from Mr. Perceval, and printed them in a special number of his *Political Register*. In a letter printed some time after her acquittal, the Princess of Wales describes the evidence offered against her before the Royal Commissioners, as "the perjuries of my suborned traducers." In 1809, another royal scandal rang through Europe. His Royal Highness the Duke of York was Commander-in-Chief of his Majesty's forces, and it was proved before Parliament, by one of his many repudiated mistresses, a Mrs. Mary Ann Clark, that several sums of money had been paid to that lady by officers desirous of procuring promotion. One sum received by Mrs. Clark was shown, by corroborative testimony, to have been applied in part payment of a jeweller's bill, for which the Duke of York was liable. A note was produced which several witnesses, some of them of most unassailable character, declared to be in the Duke's handwriting, and the contents of which referred to the case. The Duke, however, declared the note to be a forgery, and the House of Commons, by a large majority, acquitted him of any participation in the scandalous corruption which undoubtedly took place.

The Duke of York declared, on "the honour of a Prince," that he knew nothing of the corruption proved at the bar of the House. One member of the House of Commons, Mr. Tierney, replied that "It was easy to conceive that His Royal Highness would have been prompt to declare his innocence upon a vital point; but why declare it upon 'the honour of a Prince?' for the thing had no meaning." Mr. Lyttleton, another member of the Parliamentary Committee, said, " If it were in the power of the House to send down to posterity the character of the Duke of York unsullied—if their proceedings did not extend beyond their journals, he should almost be inclined to concur in the vote of acquittal, even in opposition to his sense of duty. But though the House should acquit his Royal Highness, the proofs would still remain, and public opinion would be guided by them, and not by the decision of the House. It was in the power of the House to save its own character, but not that of the Commander-in-Chief." Mr. Wilberforce demanded the Duke of York's removal from office as " a reparation to the wounded morality of the country." Lord Temple urged that "His Royal Highness cannot be prudently continued a servant of the public." " Wherever he went the deep murmurs of public indignation would strike his ear." Lord Milton said, " His Royal Highness had given in a letter in which he declared on the honour of a Prince that he was innocent," " to his other guilt his Royal Highness had added that of falsehood." Fortunately for lovers of monarchy, a majority of 364 members against 123 brought in, in effect, a verdict of not guilty, and although the Duke of York resigned his high office, his character was freed from all stain. Now, his Royal Highness George William Frederick Charles Guelph Duke of Cambridge, son of the seventh son of George III., happens to be the present Commander-in-Chief. The nation pays to H.R.H. £12,000 per annum, as a slight mark of gratitude for having been born of Royal blood. It pays him also £4,432 for being Field Marshal Commander-in-Chief, and permits him also to receive another £5,000 a year for performing the task—so distasteful to his honourable nature—of holding four sinecure colonelcies. He has the full character of Brunswick bravery and—inheriting courage from his princely father, whose gallant conduct in leaving his command in Hanover, in 1803, covered his name with glory—has gathered enough of laurels in the Crimea to keep his reputation as a warrior green for ever. Of course, in the pure hands of H.R.H. the Duke of Cambridge, all suspicion of anything like improper influences in the administration of army patronage is out of the question, and any repetition of the Duke of York scandal simply impossible. Nevertheless, the *Belfast News Letter*, in a paragraph which went round the press about twelve months since, said—

"The whisper of a grave scandal has become so loud in circles where reliable information is generally to be found, that it is no longer possible to leave it unnoticed. It relates to a very high personage, whose position ought to place him high above the breath of suspicion, but whose private life is sullied by excesses which threaten to bring disgrace upon the order to which he belongs, and even to sully the ermine of Royalty itself. Had the causes of complaint or of reprobation been confined to private history alone, the probability is that the veil might not have been raised; but it is asserted that a flagrant abuse of patronage has long prevailed in the department over which the person in question holds imperial sway, and that the storm of dissatisfaction is attaining a strength which will probably lead the House of Commons, in the interests of the public, to direct an inquiry into the circumstances of the case. The subject is one of extreme delicacy, but, in a reforming age like the present, if suspicion justly attaches, it would seem but right that those who are responsible for the honour of the administration, whether it be military, naval, or civil, should interfere, ere it be too late, to prevent a great scandal, if not national reproach. It is rumoured that certain facts in connection with the matter have been laid before the chief adviser of the Crown."

His Royal Highness the Duke of Cambridge, ought to regret that neither Colonel Wardle, nor Lord Folkestone, nor Sir Francis Burdett is now in the House of Commons, to move for a parliamentary inquiry into the foundation of the above scandalous statement, for there can be no doubt that the Duke would be thoroughly cleared from all imputation, despite the allegation of the *Queen's Messenger*, that "his department is such an Augean stable of corruption, that it can never be cleansed unless the Serpentine is made to flow through it." Just as His Royal Highness the Duke of York was cleared by the vote of the House of Commons, and as His Royal Highness the Prince of Wales was freed from suspicion by the recent decision in the Mordaunt case, so would the Duke of Cambridge emerge unsullied from the ordeal of a parliamentary inquiry into the present distribution of army patronage. It is no light question; the money value of the preferment distributed in the department over which the Duke presides has already exceeded £2,000,000 sterling, and the central administration of the English army costs nearly three times as much as that of the French whose forces are at least five times as numerous. In 1810, a tragedy took place in connection with the Royal Family of an almost unparalleled character. His Royal Highness Ernest Augustus Guelph Duke of Cumberland, fifth son of George III.—whom Daniel O'Connell described as " the mighty great liar," and of whom another said that " sensibility and virtue were strangers to his breast"—was wounded in his own room on the night of the 31st May. The wounds are said to have been inflicted by the Duke's valet, Sellis, who was found dead in bed. Sir Everard Home, the physician, says that Sellis clearly killed himself; another account says that Sellis's " head was nearly severed from the body." An inquest was held on Sellis, but the jury not being permitted to see the body, refused to give any verdict, and a second jury was got together who returned a verdict of *felo de se* against Sellis. While it is not possible now to say one word which can clear this mystery, it must not be forgotten as an illustration of the general virtues popularly attributed to the Royal Family, that it was repeatedly alleged that Sellis did not commit suicide ; that no evidence was offered showing that he had any reasons for destroying himself, nor was it proved that he had shown any disposition towards such a course. On the contrary, it was urged that " the motive for getting rid of Sellis was the Duke's fear lest the man should reveal a secret inculpating his royal master in a crime of the most horrible description." While there is no reason for even supposing Sellis to have been murdered, it must be admitted that the Duke of Cumberland was extremely unfortunate in the matter of suicides. Twenty years later, Lord Graves committed suicide at a time when his existence interfered with the Duke's intimacy with Lady Graves, and Englishmen may rejoice that, bad as are some of the living Royal Princes, there is not one amongst them whose career can be regarded as coincident with that of the Duke of Cumberland.

In 1811, Prince George was appointed Regent, £100,000 extra being voted to him to enable him to bear the cost of the assumption of regal authority, and public opinion may be not unfairly judged by the following extract from a letter printed by the famous Junius, reproaching him for non-performance of his duties as ruler, and contrasting the Prince Regent with his father, the poor mad King :—

"It is true we had gained little by the private virtues of a sovereign, since they had neither benefited his people nor taught his children morality; but if not publicly useful, they were a barrier to reproach. He did not stain the throne with vice, nor drown the clamours of the people in the midnight revel. Content himself to walk soberly through his part, he left the busy action of the scene to others, but never shrunk his share in the performance. We did not call him from the stews to the Council-board; from the bed of adultery to the seat of honour. Sir, it is said you plume yourself upon that princely qualification called honour, but is it in the abandonment of every sacred tie or moral obligation? Is it in the open disregard of the world's reproof, and the stoical indifference to the calls of nature and humanity? Is it honour which prompts you to quit the arms of a wife for the endearments of a wanton; or with unblushing effrontery to introduce that wanton before the chaste eye of your Royal Mother? Is it a proof of princely honour to toy away the night in debauchery, the day in lascivious enjoyment, and bid the business of the world stand still? While your country groans in distress, and your people are sinking under their privations, is it a sense of princely honour which bids you revel in profusion, and mock their sorrows with your ostentatious prodigality? It is said you have so far outstripped the boundaries of enjoyment, that luxury and sensuality toil after you in vain; would you be redeemed from a state so calamitously despicable, go visit the abode of your wretched subjects, and take a lesson from patient indigence." "If this afford not an antidote to the listless apathy of your disposition, deign but to hearken to the grievances and wrongs which overwhelm your people, and the sense of apprehension must woo you back to reason."

No Junius lives to-day with fiery pen to scorch the princely vices of another George.

On May 3, 1816, Princess Charlotte of Wales was married to Prince Leopold, of Saxe Coburg. Prince Leopold had been previously married on January 2, 1815, to the Countess of Cohaky, who was alive at the time of the marriage with Princess Charlotte of Wales. That this was another instance of bigamy is an addition to our story so trifling that we pass it by without further comment. The Princess of Wales died in child-bed on the 6th November, 1817; Prince George never communicated the death to her mother, "the most brutal omission," says Mr. Wynn, in his letter to the Duke of Buckingham, " I ever remember, and one which would attach disgrace in private life."

On the 23rd January, 1820, the Duke of Kent died. On the evening of Friday, the 28th January, 1820, died officially King George III.

> "He died!—his death made no great stir on earth,
> His burial made some pomp; there was profusion
> Of velvet gilding, brass, and no great dearth
> Of aught but tears.
> The new world shook him off; the old yet groans
> Beneath what he and his prepared, if not
> Completed: he leaves heirs on many thrones
> To all his vices, without what begot
> Compassion for him—his tame virtues."

For some time the old King had been blind, deaf, and incurably mad, and yet his Grace of Buckingham and Sir William Knighton, tell us that the news of his death was received by George IV. "with a burst of grief which was very affecting." Living, the son had hated the father; for ten years that father had suffered chronic lunacy, but his good son finds affectionate grief for the dead as recompense for lack of filial love for the living.

In the succeeding month came the Thistlewood conspiracy, chiefly promoted, if not originally concocted, by an infamous scoundrel in the employ of the Castlereagh Government, who used the weaknesses of foolish and desperate men in order to terrify the timid by fear of treason and outrage from pursuing real political reform. Some coincidences quite as fearful, and even more thoroughly the result of police fabrication, might be found in Ireland and England in the present reign. Trials for sedition abounded. Henry Hunt, Sir Francis Burdett, Sir Charles Wolseley, Mr. Joseph Harrison, were all convicted and sentenced during the months of March and April. Colonel McMahon, who had been pimp and pander-general to the vicious appetite of George Prince of Wales, having died, and his private papers having passed into the hands of Mr. William Knighton, a physician, discreet reticence made Sir William Knighton the confidential adviser of the now worn-out and irritable debauchee. Next came the trial of the Queen, before the

House of Lords, for alleged adultery with Bartollomeo Bergami, of which Thackeray says, " As I read her trial in history I vote she is not guilty. I don't say it is an impartial verdict; but as one reads her story, the heart bleeds for the kindly, generous, outraged creature. If wrong there be, let it be at his door who wickedly thrust her from it." In August, 1820, one of Fremantle's letters to the Duke of Buckingham speaks of the treason, sedition, and blasphemy permeating the press, and a few weeks later Lord Cassilis writes, arguing against any reduction of the army, "a soldier less, and we shall have revolution and civil war." In July, 1821, King George IV. was crowned, his Queen, Caroline, whose name had been previously erased from the Liturgy, being refused admittance even to the Coronation ceremony. It was with George as Prince, not George as King that we desired here to deal. Some other time we may take the ten years of his reign from Coronation to death, and try to wade through the intrigues at the Cottage, the influence of Lady —, &c., of which the Buckingham letters say so much and tell so little. It is too much to try to sketch, in a few words, a concluding portrait of the rapidly-corrupting mass of foulness which seldom sat on the throne, or did kingly duty, but which Englishmen prayed for every Sunday, and honoured in their National Anthem,

" God save our gracious King."

"Here," says Thackeray, " was one who never resisted any temptation; never had a desire, but he coddled it and pampered it; if he ever had any nerve, frittered it away among cooks, and tailors, and barbers, and furniture-mongers, and opera dancers," "all fiddling, and flowers, and feasting, and flattery, and folly," "a monstrous image of pride, vanity, and weakness." From the accession of George III. in 1760, to the death of George IV., in 1830, the Royal Family of England received from the national treasury no less than £92,090,807.

Printed and Published by CHARLES BRADLAUGH and ANNIE BESANT, 28, Stonecutter Street, London, E.C.

A LETTER FROM A FREEMASON

TO GENERAL H.R.H. ALBERT EDWARD,

PRINCE OF WALES,

Duke of Saxony, Cornwall, and Rothesay; Earl of Dublin, Colonel 10th Hussars, Colonel-in-Chief of the Rifle Brigade, Captain-General and Colonel of the Hon. Artillery Company, K.G., G.C.S.I., K.T., G.C.B., K.P., etc., etc., etc.

TO BR∴ H.R.H. THE PRINCE OF WALES.

DEAR BR∴—I do not ask you to pardon this, to the profane, perhaps an apparently too familiar style of address, although I do pray pardon if I have unintentionally omitted many of your numerous titles in the formal superscription to this letter. I have never written before to a Prince, and may lack good manners in thus inditing; but to my brother Masons I have often written, and know they love best a plain, fraternal greeting, if the purpose of the epistle be honest.

You have voluntarily on your part, and unsought on my side, commenced by accepting me as a brother, and you have cemented this fraternity by specially swearing to protect me on appeal in my hour of danger; and though history teaches me that sworn promises are less well kept than steadfast, manly pledges, and that Princes' oaths are specially rotten reeds to lean upon; yet in the warmth of newly created brother, I am inclined to believe you brother—for we are brethren, you and I—not brothers perhaps as we should be of the same common humanity—for in this land I know that Princes are no fair mates for those who are pauper born; but we are brothers by your own choice, members of the same fraternity by your own joining; men self-associated in the same grand Masonic brotherhood, and it is for that reason I write you this letter. You, though now a Past Grand Master, are but recently a free and accepted Master

Mason, and probably yet know but little of the grand traditions of the mighty organisation whose temple doors have opened to your appeal. My knowledge of the mystic branch gained amongst the Republicans of all nations is of some years' older date. You are now, as a Freemason, excommunicate by the Pope—so am I. It is fair to hope that the curse of the Church of Rome may have a purifying and chastening effect on your future life, at least as efficacious as the blessing of the Church of England has had on your past career. You have entered into that illustrious fraternity which has numbered in its ranks Swedenborg, Voltaire, and Garibaldi. These are the three who personify grand Idealism and Poetic Madness; Wit and Genius, and true Humanity; manly Energy, sterling Honesty, and hearty Republicanism. My sponsor was Simon Bernard—yours, I hear, was the King of Sweden.

In writing, dear brother, I do not address you as a Prince of Wales, for some of our Princes of Wales have been drunken, riotous spendthrifts, covered in debt, and deep in dishonour; but you, dear brother, instead of being such an one, figure more reputably as the erudite member of a Royal Geographical Society, or as a steady fellow of the Worshipful Company of Fishmongers. Happily there is no fear that in your case a second Doctor Doran may have to pen the narrative of a delicate investigation. If Junius were alive to-day, his pen would not dare to repeat its fierce attack on another Prince of Wales. Junius charged George, Prince of Wales, with quitting the arms of his wife for the endearments of a wanton, with toying away the night in debauchery, and with mocking the sorrows of the people with an ostentatious prodigality. But your pure career, your sober and virtuous life, would win laudations even from Junius's ghost. You are an English gentleman, as well as Prince of Wales; a good and kind husband in spite of being Prince of Wales; with you woman's honour is safe from attack, and sure of protection. The draggled and vice-stained plumes on your predecessors' escutcheons have been well cleaned and straightened by modern journalism, and the Prince of Wales' feathers are no longer (like the Bourbon fleur de lis) the heraldic ornament of a race of princes *sans foi, sans mœurs*. Fit were you as profane to make the journeys to the Altar, for fame writes you as sober and chaste, as high-minded and generous, as kind-hearted and truthful. These are the qualities, oh Albert Edward, which hid your disability as Prince, when you knelt bare-kneed in our audience chamber. The brethren who opened your eyes to the light, overlooked your title as Prince of Wales in favour of your already famous manhood. Your career is a pleasant contrast to that of George Prince of Wales. Yet because you are as different from the princes whose bodies are dust, while their memories still remain to the historian as visible monuments of shame, I write to you, not as English Prince, but as brother Master Mason. Nor do I address you in your right as one of Saxony's princes, for amongst my memories of other men's readings, I have thoughts of some in Saxony's electoral roll, who were lustful, lecherous, and vile; who were vicious sots and extravagant wasters of their peoples' earnings, who have lured for their seraglios each fresh face that came within their reach : while you, though Duke of Saxony, have joined a brotherhood whose main intent is the promotion of the highest morality. I do not indeed regard your title of Duke at all in writing you, for when we find a Duke of Newcastle's property in the hands of Sherifis' Officers, his title a jest for bankruptcy messengers, and the Duke of Hamilton's name an European byeword, it is pleasant to be able to think that the Duke of Cornwall and Rothesay is not as these Dukes are ; that this Duke is not a runner after painted donzels, that he has not written cuckold on the forehead of a dozen husbands, that he is not deep in debt, has not, like these Dukes, scattered gold in filthy gutters, while deaf to the honest claims of justice. We know, brother, that you would never have voluntarily enrolled yourself in the world's grandest organisation, if you had been as these. It would have been perjury if you had done so—perjury which, though imperially honoured at the Tuileries, would be scouted with contempt by a Lancashire workman.

I do not write to you as Earl of Dublin, for Ireland's English-given earls have been as plagues to her vitals and curses to her peoples. For 700 years, like locusts, they have devoured the verdure of her fields, and harassed the tillers of her soil. From the Earl of Chepstow to the Earl of Dublin, is the mere journeying from iron gauntlet to greedy glove—take and hold ; and Irish peasantry, in deep despair, unable to struggle, have learned to hate the Earls with whom English rule has blessed them. Nor even is this letter sent to you as Knight of the Garter, for when I read "*Honi soit qui mal y pense*," I shrink from calculating the amount of evil that might fall upon some people in the world who occupy their thoughts with princes who are Gartered Knights. Nor do I pen this to you as Colonel either of Cavalry, Infantry, or Artillery, for I can but wonder at and admire the glorious military feats which, though your modesty has hidden them, have nevertheless entitled you to command your seniors, one at least with a Waterloo medal on his breast. Our history tells us of a warrior "Black Prince," who killed many foes; it can also in the future write of you as a gallant soldier before whom pheasant, plover, and pigeon could make no stand.

I write to you as a fellow Master Mason, as to one on an equality with myself, so long as you are true to your Masonic pledge, less than myself whenever you forget it. I address this epistle to you as fellow-member of a body which teaches that man is higher than king; that humanity is beyond church and creed; that true thought is nobler than blind faith, and that virile, earnest effort is better far than dead or submissive serfdom.

The Grand Lodge of England has just conferred upon you a dignity you have done nothing to earn; but you saw light in Sweden, and that initiation should have revealed to you that the highest honour will be won by manly effort, not squeezed from slavish, fawning sycophancy. Freemasonry is democracy, are you a Democrat? Freemasonry is Freethought, are you a Freethinker? Freemasonry is work for human deliverance, are you a worker? I know you may tell me in England of wine-bibbing, song-singing, meat-eating, and white kid glove-wearing fashionables who say "Shibboleth," make "royal salutes," and call this Freemasonry; but these are mere badge-wearers, who lift their legs awkwardly over the coffin in which truth lies buried, and who never either know the grand secret, or even work for its discovery. Come with me to-day, and I will show you, even in this country, lodges where the brethren work day and night to break through conventional fetters, where they toil hourly to break down imperial and princely shams, where as a prince they would scorn you, and where as a man they would give you a brother's grip, and die with you or for you in the fight for human redemption and deliverance. Go to Joseph Mazzini, and he will tell you of lodges where, for fifty years, Poles and Italians have kept the sparks of liberty alive whilst Russian and Austrian tyranny was striving to trample and crush them out. Go into France, and the imperial tottering Lie—which has stood too long in the shadow of the first Desolator's bloody reputation—will, if it can (now it is near its grave), forget its daily life-practice, and speak truth by way of change—tell you that the Masonic Lodges of France have been the only temples in which for twenty years it has been possible to preach the gospel of civil and religious liberty. Read Br.·. Adolph Cremieux's recent declaration: "La Maçonnerie n'est pas la religion, n'est pas la foi, elle ne cherche pas dans le Maçon, le croyant, mais l'homme." Get Odo Russell to ask Mastai Ferrati, or some old woman, to inquire of Monseigneur l'Eveque d'Orleans, and each will tell you that in the lodges are the greatest enemies of the falling churches, the bravest preachers of heretic thought, and the most earnest inculcators of Republican earnestness. Or instead of going, with some noble German glutton, to a paltry casino, read, if only once or twice, a page of Europe's history for forty years before '93, and then Germany's and Sweden's Master Masons, speaking from their graves, shall tell you how their teachings helped to pulverise crowns and coronets, and build up living citizens out of theretofore dead slaves.

You have joined yourself to the Freemasons at a right moment, for true Freemasonry is about to be more powerful than Royalty. In Spain, at this moment, they have a government without a king; nay, more, in that land disgraced by many an *auto da fé*, there is hope of the growth of a people not in the hands of priests. The Revolution which trampled on the Crown, has raised the brain, and heresy has been spoken boldly in the legislative chamber. Freemasonry has in Iberia a grand mission, an arduous task. The Revolution has exiled the weak and wicked Queen. Freemasonry, to prevent the return of such royalty, has to strive for the development of a strong and useful people. In Italy, where the Honorary G.·. M.·. is our brother, Joseph Garibaldi, to-day they dream of a Government without a monarch. Turin, Florence, Naples, Rome, forgetting petty dissensions and local differences, no longer misled by royally-tinselled vice, are striving and hoping for the time when an Italian Republic, with a Roman Senate, may once more claim the right to be in the vanguard of civilising peoples. Read, Brother, how at the recent Masonic Banquet at Florence, Frederic Campanella was greeted with *vivas* for the union "di tutti i Galantuomini" for the salvation of Italy. In England, even at this hour, we are—if the organs of blood and culture speak truly—very near forgetting the use of a Queen. The least learned in politics amongst our peoples now know that kings and queens here are only the costly gilded figureheads of the ship of State, its helm being in the hands of the nominees of our territorial aristocracy. Some begin to wonder whether the State might not be better served by sign less gaudy, and more in accordance with the material of which the bulk of the vessel is built. Others grumble downright that a sort of base Dutch metal should be imported in large quantities, as if we had no good British oak out of which to carve a king without disfiguring German silver or Dutch leaf. In France, men are working, with prospect of near success, to overthrow the fear-stricken, *soi-disant* nephew of the great Emperor; and in Europe, the Republic of United Germany is not so far away but that the grandchildren of living Prussian and Austrian subjects may read with wonderment of the value that foolish Englishmen set upon petty German princes. *Liberté, Egalité, Fraternité,* form the Masonic trinity in unity. Do you believe in this trinity? Which will you be, prince or man? You give me the right to ask, for, cradled a prince, you have to-day (in the time which ought to be your manhood) sought admission to the ranks of men. In Freemasonry there are no princes; the only nobles in its true peerage muster-rolls must be noble men—men noble in thought, noble in effort, noble in endurance—men whose peerage is not of a parchment patent, but foot-trodden on the world's weary-to-climb life's ladder. In our Masonry there are no kings save in the kingship of manhood, "*Tous les hommes sont rois.*" Kings with pens for sceptres, king poets who make burning verse, and grand music to give life to the half-dead nation. Kings of prose, who pen history as impeachment of the few cruelly strong in the past, and who pen it that the many may learn neither to be cowardly nor weak in the grand struggle of the future.

You are a prince, but dare you be a man: for the sake of
the Danish flower, whose bloom should gladden your life;
for the sake of the toiling millions who are loyal from habit,
and who will revolt reluctantly, but for peace will pay taxes
readily; for the sake of the halo that history will show round
your head in its pages? If you dare, let us see it. Go to
Ireland—not to Punchestown races, at a cost to the people
of more than two thousand pounds—but secretly amongst
its poor, and learn their deep griefs. Walk in London, not
in parade at its horse shows, where snobs bow and stumble,
but in plain dress and unattended; in its Spitalfields, Bethnal
Green, Isle of Dogs, and Seven Dials; go where the unemployed commence to cry in vain for bread, where hunger
begins to leave its dead in the open streets, and try to find
out why so many starve. Don corduroy and fustian, and
ramble through the ploughed fields of Norfolk, Suffolk,
Northamptonshire, Wiltshire, and other counties, where
thirteen shillings per week are high wages, out of which the
earner has to feed and clothe man, wife, and family, and
pay rent.

Brother, before you die you will hear cries for a Republic
in England, cries that will require the brains of a grand
man to answer, cries which are gathering now, cries from the
overtaxed, who pay, without thought and without inquiry,
many more pounds in unearned pensions, for yourself and
brother princes, than they will by-and-bye pay shillings,
unless indeed you all work miracles, and make yourselves
worth your money to the nation. Yet even this you might
do; you might—you and your fellow princes in Europe—
if you would disband your standing armies, get rid of the
tinselled drones and gaudy court caterpillars, the State
Church leeches, and hereditary cormorant tax-eaters, and
then there would be a renewed lease of power for you, and
higher happiness for the people. But whatever you determine to do, do quickly, or it will be too late. The *Vive la
République* now heard from some lips in Paris, Lyons, Marseilles, Bordeaux, will soon be the voice of France, and
there is an electric force in the echo of that cry—a force
which evokes the lightning-like flash of popular indignation
with such directness against princes who mock peoples,
against kings who rule for themselves, and against peers who
govern for their own class, that as in a moment the oak

which has stood for centuries, is stripped of its brown bark, and left bleached and blasted to wither, so is royalty stripped of its tinselled gilding and left naked and defenceless to the cold scorn of a justly indignant nation. As a Freemason you are bound to promote peace, but peace makes the strength of peoples, and discovers the weakness of princes. As a Freemason you are bound to succour the oppressed of the world, but then it will be against your fellow-princes. As a Freemason you are bound to aid in educating the ignorant, but if you do this you teach them that the sole authority kings can wield they derive from the people; that a nation may elect a chief magistrate to administer its laws, but cannot give away their liberties to a master who shall have the right to bequeath his authority over their children to his child. As a Freemason you are bound to encourage the development of Freethought, but Freethought is at war with the Church, and between Church and Crown there has ever been most unholy alliance against peoples. You were a prince by birth, it was your misfortune. Your have enrolled yourself a Freemason by choice, it shall either be your virtue or your crime—your virtue if you are true to its manly dutifulness; your crime if you dream that your blood royalty is of richer quality than the poorest drop in the veins of

A FREE AND ACCEPTED MASON.

PRICE ONE PENNY.

Printed by ANNIE BESANT and CHARLES BRADLAUGH, 28, Stonecutter Street London, E.C.

FIVE DEAD MEN

Whom I Knew when Living:

ROBERT OWEN, JOSEPH MAZZINI, CHARLES SUMNER, J. S. MILL, & LEDRU ROLLIN.

BY

CHARLES BRADLAUGH.

LONDON:
FREETHOUGHT PUBLISHING COMPANY,
28, Stonecutter Street, E.C.

PRICE FOURPENCE.

LONDON
PRINTED BY ANNIE BESANT AND CHARLES BRADLAUGH,
28, STONECUTTER STREET, E.

FIVE DEAD MEN WHOM I KNEW
WHEN LIVING.

In selecting as the subject for a lecture "Five Dead Men Whom I Knew when They were Living"—Robert Owen, Joseph Mazzini, John Stuart Mill, Charles Sumner, and Alexandre Auguste Ledru Rollin—I do not mean more than that the accidents of my chequered life, having thrown me into contact with these men, I take their lives for the lessons such lives give, without either pretending to maintain their several views, or to imply that all, or either of, the five are, or is, in any fashion identified with my own advanced opinions, except where such identity shall be expressly stated. Naturally, the compass of a lecture is prohibitive of any biographic detail, or of any completeness of statement of the respective teachings of the men I briefly deal with.

I.—ROBERT OWEN.

ROBERT OWEN, the great advocate of English Socialism, was born at Newtown, a Montgomeryshire village, on the 14th May, 1771. His early life-struggles—his rapid, but sober and business-like, conquest of that wealth which the world worships so much, but to which he seems to have attached little value, except as it gave him facilities for spreading his views—are familiar enough. It is at New Lanark, in 1797, and thenceforth for twenty years, that one would wish to show Robert Owen, for if he had never done aught outside New Lanark, he did enough there alone to win grateful recollection. Surrounding the factory workers in his employment with humanising conditions, ameliorating their position, he made the wage-winners something more than mere human machines. Recognising that it was easier to bend and mould the tendencies of the child than to break the long-acquired habit of the grown man or woman, Robert Owen set an example to all Britain by introducing infant schools in his New Lanark village. It was Robert Owen who practically demonstrated that the child's mind is a sheet of paper, varying in colour, quality, and size, but which cannot be left blank; it must be ornamented or disfigured, fact or falsehood must be written on it. It was Robert Owen who gave an example which might be followed with advantage by teetotal advocates. He made New Lanark a sober village, not so much by denouncing drink, as by providing home inducements and evening amusements which outrivaled the beer-shop or whisky store. Many an unfortunate man, returning to his overcrowded unwholesome dwelling, wearied with his toil, finds that it is foul with the breath of so many huddled together, and he consequently escapes to the glare of the gin palace or the gathering at the beerhouse to fly from the misery he finds at home. It is true that he thus aggravates the ill, but we cannot make men sober unless we purify their lives, unless the domestic hearth has its charms and enticements for them; what we want is, that the workers shall have a dwelling to go to from their work which has in it the real tokens of comfort, purity, and health of life. No four-leaved shamrock, nor magician's wand, could have even been supposed to effect so great a transformation as the persistent Humanitarianism of this earnest Robert Owen effected at New Lanark. His doctrines on the formation of character have found practical and authoritative expression more recently in the law-established reformatory schools. Instead of trampling juvenile criminals still lower into the earth, society now adopts the view which Robert Owen was the first to popularise—although not the first to enunciate —that man is better or worse according to the conditions surrounding the parent previous to the birth of the child, and those which surround the infant itself during its childhood, and accompany the boy or girl during youth. Young criminals are now sought to be made less criminal by being placed for lengthy periods under conditions which shall modify and improve their characters.

In 1817 Robert Owen—who had up to this time been regarded by fashionable society as an amiable but eccentric philanthropist, whose whims were to be pardoned on account of his wealth—startled all England by his famous declaration at the London Tavern. Impeaching the religions of the world, he aroused against him all the clergy, and frightened away most of his titled admirers. It has been the custom of late years for street-corner tub-thumpers—utterly incapable of imitating Owen's unselfish devotion to human improvement—to malign Robert Owen's name, and to cast all kinds of opprobrious epithets against his life. Undoubtedly Robert Owen furnished some cause to his foes, when he declared in his London Tavern speech that all the religions of the world were founded in error. And yet every religious man will contend that all the religions of the world save one, and that one his own, are false. It is said, too, that the doctrine that man is the creature of circumstances involves a theory of fatalism demoralising to the human character. Those who take ground against Mr. Owen overlook the fact that it is better to teach the truth, whatever that truth may be, so that the knowledge may furnish the motive for the selection of improving conditions. Nor is man a merely passive figure to be acted on ; he re-acts and modifies his surroundings, improving or aggravating them and their effects. As each drop of water is to the ocean, so is each human unit to the world—part of the great whole, from which it cannot escape, and from which it cannot be eliminated. Freewill theorists delude themselves with empty words when they claim for the phenomena of volition that they are outside all law. The formula that man's character is formed for him, and not by him, does not express all the truth, but it expresses much more than is taught by those whose dogma it is that man may will, uninfluenced by events. Robert Owen has been too fiercely assailed for his views on marriage, those who are his assailants, forgetting how much the laws affecting woman's position and property, and regarding divorce, have been modified during the last fifty years. The marriage question is one hedged round with huge difficulties. In Roman Catholic countries extreme harshness forbids all divorce. In some States of the American Republic great facilities are given for determining a contract, which holds by force of law only, against the desire of each. Human passion enters too much with some into the consideration of this question, and is too utterly excluded by others. It is chiefly as the inaugurator of the English Socialist Propaganda that Robert Owen will be remembered. No Socialist myself, I yet cannot but concede that the movement had an enormous value, if only as a protest against that terrible and inhuman competitive struggle, in which the strong were rewarded for their strength, and no mercy was shown to the weakest. I am probably too much of an individualist to judge a system fairly which seems to me to neutralise individual effort; but it is only necessary to look to the enormously beneficial results of co-operative effort in the North of England, in order to affirm that the Socialist Missionaries, with good old Robert Owen at their head, have left proud monuments of the effect of their teachings. If any early reconcilement is possible, as I believe it is, between the owners of accumulated capital and the vendors of labour, it must come by the enlightenment which efforts at co-operative manufacturing give to all those who take part in them. The war between capitalists and workers is an insane and suicidal war, aggravated because the rights of life are too often made secondary to the privileges of wealth. Robert Owen's Socialism was the utterance of one of the many efforts to give life and dignity to labour. Honour, then, his human effort, even if you deny his dogma. I first saw Robert Owen as a Sunday evening lecturer on the platform of the old John-street Institution, about 1848, and it was from the same platform, ten years later, that it became my duty, in consequence of the ill-health of Robert Cooper, to read for Mr. Owen the last speech he ever prepared for delivery at a Freethought meeting. No one, friend or foe, could come in contact with Robert Owen without being most thoroughly convinced of the old man's complete conviction of the accuracy of his views on society, and of his full certainty to the very last that those views would all be realised at no distant date. He was a good, pure, one-idead man, whose long life, from its prime to its close, was one never-ceasing struggle to soften the world's harsh conflict, and to create a new moral world for after-livers.

II.—JOSEPH MAZZINI.

GUISEPPE MAZZINI, the untiring preacher of Italian Republican unity, was born at Genoa on June 22nd, 1805; and he tells us it was in April, 1821, just after the unsuccessful Piedmontese insurrection, that he was first impressed with the idea "that we Italians could, and therefore ought to, struggle for the liberty of our country." When about twenty-two years of age Mazzini commenced his literary career by writing brief book notices for a mercantile journal at Genoa, which journal he made sufficiently political to at length bring down upon it a Government decree of suspension. Vetoed in Genoa by the Sardinian authorities, Mazzini, in a second journal, braved more openly the Tuscan Government at Leghorn; but, after about twelve months, the *Indicatore Livornese*, as the new journal was called, was also suppressed. Induced by his new political associates, Mazzini joined the Carbonari, a secret association, in which the police had usually—as is commonly the case in secret political organisations—sufficient members to betray the whole of the plans of the Society. Betrayed and arrested in 1830, Mazzini was confined for some months in the Fortress of Savona, whence he was ultimately released— the formal evidence against him failing—but was exiled, because the Government were only too sure of his Republican tendencies.

It was while a solitary prisoner in Savona that Joseph Mazzini conceived the plan of *La Giovina Italia* (Society of Young Italy). Intensely national, Mazzini believed that "regenerated Italy was destined to arise the *initiatrix* of a new life, and a new and powerful unity to all the nations of Europe." It is doubtful whether the movements of the Southern and Northern races in Europe have not a distinctness of character which must always be fatal to Mazzini's conception of the *rôle* of Italy. Mazzini rightfully asserted the unity of Italy; but Italian intellect is too poetic and too subtle to be the guide of some of the less musical, but not less thorough, politics of the Teutonic races. From

Italy Mazzini went to Lyons, and in 1831 he joined a forlorn expedition into Corsica, intending to cross thence into the Romagna, where an insurrectionary rising was planned. This expedition failing, Mazzini took up his residence at Marseilles, where he formally founded the Society of Young Italy, to create " an Italy, one, free, and powerful; independent of all foreign supremacy, and morally worthy of her great mission." The statutes declared " Young Italy is Republican and Unitarian. Republican, because theoretically every nation is destined, by the law of God and humanity, to form a free and equal community of brothers; and the Republican is the only form of government that ensures this future. Because all true sovereignty resides essentially in the nation, the sole progressive and continuous interpreter of the supreme moral law. Because, whatever be the form of privilege that constitutes the apex of the social edifice, its tendency is to spread among the other classes, and, by undermining the equality of the citizens, to endanger the liberty of the country. Because, when the sovereignty is recognised as existing, not in the whole body, but in several distinct powers, the path to usurpation is laid open, and the struggle for supremacy between these powers is inevitable; distrust and organised hostility take the place of harmony, which is society's law of life. Because the Monarchical element, being incapable of sustaining itself alone by the side of the popular element, it necessarily involves the existence of the intermediate element of an aristocracy—the source of inequality and corruption to the whole nation. Because both history and the nature of things teach us that Elective Monarchy tends to generate anarchy, and Hereditary Monarchy tends to generate despotism. Because when Monarchy is not, as in the Middle Ages, based upon the belief now extinct in right divine, it becomes too weak to be a bond of unity and authority in the State......... Young Italy is Unitarian, because without unity there is no true nation; because without unity there is no real strength.......The means," say the statutes, " by which Young Italy proposes to reach its aim are—education and insurrection, to be adopted simultaneously, and made to harmonise with each other. Education must ever be directed to teach by example, word, and pen, the necessity of insurrection. Insurrection, whenever it can be realised, must be so conducted as to render it a means of national education."

It is a little difficult, when Mazzini teaches that "insurrection, by means of guerilla bands, is the true method of warfare," to understand how guerilla warfare and educational progress can be consistent. Guerilla warfare is so nearly allied to—and so often results in—mere brigandage that the certain evil seems greater than any possible advantage; and, as a matter of fact, history has most clearly shown that these guerilla bands are more effective for mischief on the enemy than for good to the cause on behalf of which they are arrayed. Mazzini himself teaches that "Great revolutions are the work rather of principles than of bayonets, and are achieved first in the moral, and then in the material sphere." In the programme of Young Italy Joseph Mazzini, who was bitterly opposed to what he called Materialism, affirmed that "the reformation of a people rests upon no sure foundation, unless based upon agreement in religious belief." He declared that "the doctrines of Materialism disinherit man of every noble aim, and abandon him to the arbitrary rule of chance or blind force." Joseph Mazzini was, at the same time, devotedly Republican and religious. He blended his piety with his politics, and regarded Republicanism as God-ordained.

Exile, and some sorrow beyond—a sorrow which he alludes to, but does not state—had given a tone of sadness to his life. Tenacious of purpose, he was fit to be the mainspring of a secret society, but hardly so fitted to be the conductor of any open movement where his views would be subject to contradiction or criticism from his co-workers. . He was grandly thorough in his Republicanism, but he dreamed it for the working men of Italy before he knew what those working men were; and although he made great efforts to educate the people, he never seems to have recognised the fact that the proclamation of a Republic to a people of whom the majority are not prepared for it, is but a small step towards real Republicanism. In Rome he was—when invested with authority—so roughly brought face to face with the bitter truth, that he says "it was put to the vote whether we should not resign our charge the day following. The population, in consequence of the long corruption of slavery, was ignorant and idle; distrustful and suspicious of all things and of all men."

The extension of the propaganda of the Young Italy became rapidly so formidable, that on the representation of the Italian Government, the French authorities, in August,

1832, ordered Mazzini to quit Marseilles, but the order was rendered inoperative by the extraordinary ability with which Mazzini eluded the police, and yet continued most actively his revolutionary work, so that, by the middle of 1833, the Society of Young Italy had become widely extended, if not powerful, through Lombardy, the Genoese territory, Tuscany, and the Roman States. Treason from some, and incaution on the part of others, giving the Government a clue as to the members of the society, many were arrested and put to death.

Mazzini could not help feeling deeply his own share, as the founder of the Association, in the deaths of his co-workers. Four years afterwards he says: "I feel myself a criminal—conscious of guilt, yet incapable of expiation. The forms of those shot at Alessandria and Chambery rose up before me like the phantoms of a crime, and its unavailing remorse. I could not recall them to life. How many mothers had I caused to weep? How many more must learn to weep should I persist in the attempt to arouse the youth of Italy to noble action, to awaken in them the yearning for a common country? And if that country were indeed an illusion, whence had I derived the right of judging for the future, and urging hundreds, thousands of men, to the sacrifice of themselves, and of all that they held most dear?"

Early in February, 1834, an abortive attempt was made to take a column of insurgents, under the command of General Ramorino, into Italy from Geneva. In this column Joseph Mazzini, although the contriver of the expedition, marched as a private soldier. Treachery on the part of the General, and inefficient means of action, caused the failure of the plan; and the defeat almost made Mazzini despair of his whole mission.

The Swiss authorities—compelled by the representations of the European Powers—seized the war stores of the Italian exiles, and menaced themselves with expulsion.

In Berne, where he then took refuge, Mazzini projected the formation of the Society of Young Europe, a combination of Young Italy with two kindred associations, called Young Poland and Young Germany. The ideal of the Association of Young Europe was the federal association of European Democracy under one sole direction; so that any nation rising in insurrection should at once find the others ready to assist it. To this organisation, later in 1834, was added the new Society of Young Switzerland. Writing of Switzerland, Mazzini says : " Since January 1st, 1338, that little people has had neither king nor master. It presents the spectacle—unique in Europe—of a Republican flag floating for five centuries above the Alps, although surrounded by jealous and invading Monarchies, as if to be an incitement and a presage to us all. Charles V., Louis XIV., Napoleon, passed away, but that banner remained sacred and immoveable." The Constitution of the Swiss Republic was regarded by Mazzini as specially defective, in that its Diet, or Central Government, is composed of delegates from each Canton, chosen in each case by the grand *conseil* of the Canton, instead of being directly elected by the people. Mazzini also objected that in the Swiss Diet each Canton has but one vote, irrespective of size, or population, or taxation contribution; and he further objected to the *mandat impératif*, or special instruction to the delegate, as nullifying all spontaneity of thought and conscience. Mazzni justified the Association of Young Europe by affirming that "Liberty is an European right. Arbitrary power, tyranny, and inequality cannot exist in one nation without injury to others." In the middle of 1835 "Young Switzerland" had its journal, *La Jeune Suisse*, and a printing press at Bienne, in the Canton of Berne. The European Governments used considerable pressure to prevent the little Swiss Republic from being continued as the centre for this Republican work, and ultimately a *conclusum* of the Swiss Diet, in 1836, condemned Mazzini to perpetual exile from Switzerland.

In January, 1837, the great Italian conspirator arrived in London. This was a gloomy period in Mazzini's life; exiled, poor, doubting, and doubted, it seemed to himself almost as if his young life had been an utter failure. England gives the shelter of its land to the political exile, but it is a cold shelter if he be a poor or an unknown man; and, until Mazzini's pen had won for him a position amongst English writers, he often knew the extremest bitterness of want. Joseph Mazzini found, too, that although the English nation gave nominal protection to his person, the English Government nevertheless was guilty of the baseness of opening his correspondence, and communicating the contents to foreign powers. That Austria utilised the information communicated to her by Lord Aberdeen's Government, which had tampered with letters addressed to Mazzini by the unfortunate Brothers Bandiera, is now a matter of history. Writing eighteen years later, Mazzini said : " The secret of correspondence is violated in the English Post Office at the present day, precisely as it was in 1844, though perhaps somewhat more rarely." It is certain that in the Irish Post Office letters have been opened by authority during the last few years; and it is also certain that secret police reports have, within the last five years, been furnished in writing by the London Detective Department to the Paris Police. Whether letters are still opened at St. Martin's-le-Grand I have no sufficient means of determining.

The political volcano of 1847-8, shook severely several of the Italian princedoms, and Joseph Mazzini returned to Italy to take part in the struggle which overturned, at any rate temporarily, more than one ducal throne.

On February 9th, 1849—the Pope having fled, and Rome being without any Government—a constituent assembly, chosen by a very large popular vote, and of which Mazzini had been elected member, proclaimed a Republic in Rome. On March 29th, Mazzini, Saffi, and Armellini, were chosen Triumvirs; and on April 25th, the French Republic disgraced itself by landing an army, under General Oudinot, at Civita Vecchia. The story of the siege of Rome, of its heroic defence by Joseph Garibaldi, of its fall at last in July, is too well known to need repeating at length, and is too grand to be pressed into one or two lines. Rome fell, and in July Mazzini was once more a fugitive from his loved Italy.

In 1857 Mazzini endeavoured to organise a general Italian insurrection, and went to Genoa himself to take his part; but although detached risings took place in various parts of Italy, the differences of opinion between the leaders, such as Mazzini, Manin, and Garibaldi, were so great, and the people were so unprepared, that another failure had to be chronicled. Mazzini opposed himself bitterly to the diplomacy of Cavour, who was then endeavouring, chiefly through Prince Jerome Napoleon, to obtain the alliance of France against Austria.

In 1858 Mazzini penned the following words on woman, worthy reproduction, alike from their great merit, and as chronicling this phase of his faith : " Love and respect woman. Seek in her, not merely a comfort, but a force, an inspiration, the redoubling of your intellectual and moral faculties. Cancel from your minds every idea of superiority over her. You have none whatever......Long prejudice, an inferior education, and a perennial legal inequality and injustice, have created that apparent intellectual inferiority which has been converted into an argument of continued oppression. But does not the history of oppression teach us how the oppressor ever seeks his justification and support by appealing to a fact of his own creation? The feudal castes that withheld education from the sons of the people, excluded them on the ground of that very want of education from the rights of the citizen, from the sanctuary wherein laws are framed, and from that right of vote which is the initiation of the social mission......Consider woman as the partner and companion, not merely of your joys and sorrows, but of your thoughts, your aspirations, your studies, and your endeavours after social amelioration. Consider her your equal in your civil and political life."

Mazzini and Mill were alike eloquent pleaders for womanhood, and each deserve woman's tribute of grateful memory.

In 1859 the brain of Mazzini and the arm of Garibaldi effectually moved the peoples of Sicily and Naples, and rousing even the lazzaroni from their lethargy, frightened away Bomba from his Neapolitan Palace. Mazzini and Garibaldi then took entirely different ground, and bitterness arose, which was never cleared away. Mazzini desired Garibaldi to hold the Two Sicilies as Republican, and to strike a blow at Rome for the unity of Italy, while Joseph Garibaldi consented to the annexation of Naples and Sicily to Piedmont, under the rule of Victor Emanuel, and returned to his island home at Caprera, satisfied that his country had advanced one step to the unity, which he, equally with Mazzini, so ardently desired.

It was shortly before this date that I first saw Joseph Mazzini, at his modest lodgings, in Onslow Terrace, Brompton, where he then lived under the name of Signor Ernesti. He was one of the few men who impress you first, and always, with the thorough truthfulness and incorruptibility of their natures. Simple in his manners, with only one luxury, his cigar, he had that fulness of faith in his cause which is so contagious, and by the sheer force of personal contact he made believers in the possibility of Italian Unity even among those who were utter strangers to his thought and hope.

In 1865 the city of Messina elected Mazzini as Deputy to the Italian Parliament; but he refused to take his seat in an Assembly where he would have had to take the oath of allegiance to Victor Emanuel. He said, "Monarchy will never number me amongst its servants or followers. I dedicate myself wholly, and for ever, to constitute Italy one free, independent, Republican nation. I have lived, I live, and I shall die a Republican, bearing witness to my faith to the last."

When in 1870 Mazzini set foot in Sicily, the Government arrested him, and sent him to Gaeta. A general protest went out through Europe, and the imprisonment was not of long duration, but it was yet enough to weaken the already diminished vitality of the oft-disappointed conspirator for Italian Republican Unity.

On the 10th March, 1872, at Pisa, where, under an assumed English name, he had passed five months in almost complete solitude, Joseph Mazzini died; worn out in body and spirit by the forty years' never-ceasing toil for the liberty and unity of his much-loved native land. At his funeral 80,000 men and women met to testify to his truth, to mourn his death. Sentences of death and exile stood unrevoked against him while living. Italy, from that Rome which Mazzini had defended, could not enforce these penal sentences, but it was only her dead son she honoured. Living, she let his broken heart bear undiminished the sorrows of his intense struggle. Dead, a whole population witnessed that the liberty-lesson his life had taught would bear its fruits now the white-haired teacher could no longer use his pen. In seven-hilled Rome a laurel crown was placed by Italy's hand on the head which had bowed to earth in the mighty effort to teach Italia's children how to compass the freedom of their birth-land.

III.—JOHN STUART MILL.

To record the mere life of John Stuart Mill would present little of lasting interest, especially as Mr. Mill never seems to have sought to use his official knowledge of Indian affairs to govern his conduct as a practical politician, after his connection with the East India Company had been determined. It is not so much how he lived as what he thought, not so much what he did as what he taught, that is worth remembering. Born May 20th, 1806, and dying May, 1873, he probably, during the last twenty-five years of his life, influenced, more than any other man, the various thinkers in England and America. As a political economist, a logician, a politician, a metaphysician, the exponent of Utilitarianism, and advocate of woman's rights, he stands in all phases remarkable, in some without superior. In political economy it is his merit to have popularised amongst the people a science which had been generally regarded by artisans as cold and hard, only to be used by the rich against the poor; and it is noteworthy that Mr. Mill won his popularity despite his steadfast maintenance of the Malthusian theory of the law of population.

Mr. Mill clearly distinguished between the laws of production of wealth, which are real "laws of nature," dependent on the properties of objects, and the modes of the distribution of wealth, which, subject to certain conditions, depend on the human will. In this he differed from those who pretend that the distribution of wealth is determined by economic laws, which are incapable of being temporarily defeated or modified by human effort.

As a politician, Mr. Mill affirmed that women were entitled to representation on the same terms with men. He supported Mr. Thomas Hare's scheme for obtaining a more perfect representation of minorities; and, whether or not Mr. Hare's proposal shall ever be embodied in a statutory form, Republicans should remember that thorough respect can never be shown to the decisions of the majority unless the minority are afforded a fair occasion to be heard on all important questions. It is right that the majority should decide, but only on condition that the voice of the minority has full utterance prior to the delivery of the final award. Mr. Mill opposed the ballot, and I avow that I should be pleased if voters could be true and self-reliant enough to dispense with the protection it affords.

Admitting "the irresistible claim of every man and woman to be consulted, and to be allowed a voice in the regulation of the affairs which vitally concern them," Mr. Mill desired to give a plurality of votes to "proved superiority of education," in order to secure "the superiority of weight justly due to opinions grounded on superiority of knowledge."

In his Political Economy Mr. Mill had taught that the

right of freehold proprietorship in land could only be maintained subject to the duty of cultivation; and late in life, as the President of the Land Tenure Reform Association, he propounded a scheme by which the unearned augmentation of rent was to be applied otherwise than to the private aggrandisement of the landlord. The land question in England is yet to become a battle question, serious in character, and uncertain as to its method of solution. Only one thing is certain—viz., that thousands must not be allowed to continue to grow poor and wretched, in order that a few dozen persons may become unfairly, as well as enormously, rich.

In the great American struggle Mr. Mill regarded the course of the Southerners, in all its stages, as "an aggressive enterprise of the slave-owners to extend the territory of slavery, under the combined influences of pecuniary interest, domineering temper, and the fanaticism of a class for its class privileges;" and, therefore, when the upper and middle classes in England expressed pro-Southern views, Mr. Mill arrayed himself with the artisan classes of England on the side of the North.

In philosophy, Mr. Mill affirmed that "the prevailing tendency to regard all the marked distinctions of the human character as innate, and in the main indelible, and to ignore the irresistible proofs that by far the greater part of those differences, whether between individuals, races, or sexes, are such as not only might, but naturally would, be produced by differences in circumstances, is one of the chief hindrances to the rational treatment of great social questions, and one of the greatest stumbling-blocks to human improvement." While describing himself, in the Autobiography published since his death, as one who never had a religious belief, John Stuart Mill was, unfortunately, taught that his heretical opinions "could not prudently be avowed to the world." Now, it is true, he affirms that the time appears to have come in religious matters "when it is the duty of all who, being qualified in point of knowledge, have, on mature consideration, satisfied themselves that the current opinions are not only false, but hurtful," to make their dissent known; " and," he adds, "the world would be astonished if it knew how great a proportion of its brightest ornaments—of those most distinguished even in popular estimation for wisdom and virtue—are complete sceptics in religion."

The effect of Mr. Mill's early teaching is manifested by

a reticence which pervades his writings; a reticence often liable to be utterly misunderstood. Three essays, published since his death—in which the subjects he specially refrained from discussing are treated at some length—make us more completely regret that his silence during life leaves his posthumous utterances, if not contradictory, at any rate deficient in that clearness for which his ordinary writings are so remarkable. Perhaps the most distinct declarations from Mr. Mill's pen, published during his lifetime, were: first, the one in which, in his review of Hamilton, he declared it to be profoundly immoral to teach, with Dean Mansel, that it is man's duty to worship "a being whose moral attributes are affirmed to be unknowable by us, and to be, perhaps, extremely different from those which, when we are speaking of our fellow creatures, we call by the same names." Mill says: "If, instead of the 'glad tidings' that there exists a being in whom all the excellences which the highest human mind can conceive, exist in a degree inconceivable to us, I am informed that the world is ruled by a being whose attributes are infinite, but what they are we cannot learn, nor what are the principles of his government, except that 'the highest human morality which we are capable of conceiving,' does not sanction them; convince me of it, and I will bear my fate as I may. But when I am told that I must believe this, and at the same time call this being by the names which express and affirm the highest human morality, I say in plain terms that I will not. Whatever power such a being may have over me, there is one thing which he shall not do—he shall not compel me to worship him. I will call no being good, who is not what I mean when I apply that epithet to my fellow creatures; and if such a being can sentence me to hell for not so calling him, to hell I will go." The other is in the review of Comte: "Candid persons of all creeds may be willing to admit, that if a person has an ideal object, his attachment and sense of duty towards which are able to control and discipline all his other sentiments and propensities, and prescribe to him a rule of life, that person has a religion; and though every one naturally prefers his own religion to any other, all must admit that if the object of this attachment, and of this feeling of duty, is the aggregate of our fellow-creatures, this Religion of the Infidel cannot, in honesty and conscience, be called an intrinsically bad one."

Occasionally, as in the essay on Utilitarianism, there are

passages in Mr. Mill's writings which a Christian would probably read as meaning more than Mr. Mill intended to convey; and in the two last essays of the latest volume there are several positions conflicting seriously with the ground taken in the first essay.

In 1861, when I fought the authorities at Devonport on the question of the right of meeting, Mr. John Stuart Mill, with whom I had up to that time held no communication, sent me a cheque for £25 towards the heavy costs I then incurred; and in 1868, for reasons which he has himself stated towards the close of his Autobiography, he also subscribed towards the expenses of my election struggle at Northampton.

To show how even his opponents can speak of him, I give the following extract from an official lecturer of the Christian Evidence Society, Mr. W. R. Browne, M.A., Fellow of Trinity College, Cambridge :—" John Stuart Mill was one of the keenest, the clearest, the most influential thinkers of his day. He was also a man much beloved by his friends (Heaven forbid that I should stint a word that can be uttered in praise of the dead !), devoted to the welfare of his fellow-men, regular and temperate in his life, honest, upright, sincere; and he was an utter unbeliever in any form of religion whatsoever. This fault, which was tolerably well known in his lifetime, is made perfectly clear and certain by the volume before us. He was all that I have described, morally and intellectually, either in consequence of, or in spite of, his rejection of all that Christians hold true and sacred. Which of these is the case? There can be no denying that, at first sight, his life makes against the party of religion. I know that it has been felt to be so by many; I have felt it to some extent myself. Can that be true which a thinker so careful and so brilliant—the greatest master, in this age at least, of the science of logic and the laws of evidence—pronounced unhesitatingly to be false?"

Mr. Mill's almost sudden death at Avignon was mourned as a national bereavement. As an able writer in the *Daily News* wrote in the obituary notice, " the full measure of his political influence will not be known until the next generation, when the younger men, who of late, at Oxford and the other seats of learning, have drunk in his doctrines, come in their turn to the front, and assume the task of shaping the nation's destinies."

IV.—CHARLES SUMNER.

ENGLISHMEN need to be reminded that slavery was a vice instituted and fostered in the American colonies by aristocratic and monarchical England. Efforts made by various colonies to check the slave trade were rebuked by the English Government. The barbarism of slavery was the enduring legacy to the West from civilised and Christian England. In the Federation of the United States the right of holding slaves was retained, amongst other State rights, by the Southern States.

As the Republic grew, two hostile elements were distinctly manifested—the one for the abolition, the other for the extension, of the slave power. In 1844 Texas was annexed to the United States by the influence of the Southern members of Congress, and the vast extent of Texan territory promised the Slave States the command of the Gulf of Mexico, and their preponderance as a political party. It was on this occasion that Charles Sumner—known theretofore as a cultivated, eloquent, and rapidly-rising Massachusetts barrister—made his first distinct stand on the side of freedom against slavery. In November, 1845, in a speech in Faneuil Hall against the admission to the Union of Texas as a Slave State, Sumner said: "God forbid that the votes and voices of the freemen of the North should help to bind anew the fetter of the slave." From thenceforward, until the day of his death, Charles Sumner never wavered in the course he had chosen.

Dealing with the matter with the reverence for law, natural to one trained as he had been, Charles Sumner challenged the slaveholders on constitutional grounds; urging that the provisions of the United States constitution, in favour of slaveholding, were merely temporary, and were framed in the expectation that the slave traffic would be abandoned at no distant period. He affirmed that the Congress could, even then, by express legislation, abolish slavery in the district of Columbia, and in any territories; that it could abolish the slave trade on the high seas between the States; and that it could refuse to admit to the Union any new State with a constitution sanctioning slavery;

further, that the people of the United States might, by regular amendment to the constitution, destroy slavery.

In 1851 Mr. Sumner, who was then forty years of age, having been born January 6th, 1811, was elected United States Senator for Massachusetts; and at first he stood at Washington almost alone in his direct pleading for abolition. In 1854, by the Kansas and Nebraska Act, a large extent of fine territory was practically thrown open for competition between free and servile labourers.

Streams of Northern men advocating free soil, and bodies of Southern men, eager to extend slave power, pressed on to the new lands. The Southerners were not, however, content to fight fairly; organised bodies of armed men entered Kansas from Missouri, and controlled the elections with bowie knife and pistol. At the first election of the Kansas Legislature, March 30th, 1855, the revolver and knife were freely used, several unoffending citizens were shot, and the abolitionists, finding themselves overpowered by force, appealed to the Government for protection. Mr. Seward presented to Congress "A Bill for the Admission of Kansas into the Union." During the debate Mr. Sumner delivered, on the 19th and 20th May, 1855, his celebrated speech, "The crime against Kansas," described by the poet Whittier as "a grand and terrible philippic." He said: "The wickedness which I now begin to expose is immeasurably aggravated by the motive which prompted it. Not in any common lust for power did this uncommon tragedy have its origin. It is the rape of a virgin territory, compelling it to the hateful embrace of slavery: and it may be clearly traced to a depraved longing for a new Slave State, the hideous offspring of such a crime, in the hope of adding to the power of slavery in the national government." With almost prophetic voice he added: "The fury of the propagandists of slavery, and the calm determination of their opponents, are now diffused from the distant territory over widespread communities, and the whole country in all its extent; marshalling hostile divisions, and foreshadowing a strife, which, unless happily averted by the triumph of freedom, will become war-fatal, fratricidal, parricidal, war—with an accumulated wickedness beyond the wickedness of any war in human annals."

The speech caused a tremendous sensation through the whole of the South. Previous to its delivery there had been many threats of personal violence against Mr. Sumner; two days after it had been delivered Preston S. Brooks, member of the House from South Carolina, with a gold-headed gutta-percha cane in his hand, came to the seat in the Senate where Charles Sumner sat writing, and, with scarce a word of warning, struck the abolitionist orator a fearful blow, inflicting a severe wound upon the back of the head, repeating the blows until the cane was shivered to pieces, and Mr. Sumner lay bleeding and insensible on the floor of the Senate. The spirit of Southern slave-holding chivalry was well shown. Richmond and Charleston journals praised Brooks for his dastardly blow. Southern clergymen preached in his favour. South Carolina re-elected him as the representative of the State. Southern ladies bought for him a new cane, in lieu of the one which he had destroyed in his murderous onslaught on Charles Sumner. It was nearly five years before the effects of the attack had sufficiently passed away to enable the Massachusetts Senator to plead again for freedom. Perfect recovery was impossible; the shock to the nervous system had been too severe; and Mr. Sumner never ceased to feel the effect of the cowardly attack.

While travelling in Europe to recruit his health, Mr. Sumner, on the introduction of the Duchess of Argyll, had an interview with Lord Palmerston as to the repression of slavery in Cuba, the particulars of which I will give as nearly as possible in Mr. Sumner's own words: "Prompted to it by nearly the last words John Adams used to me before he died, I reminded his Lordship that his own Circular as Foreign Secretary had, in express terms, pledged any Government, in which he was influential, to an abolition policy; and urged on him that Great Britain could, if it would, at any time put an end to slavery in the island of Cuba." "How?" asked Viscount Palmerston. "By simply enforcing the treaty between Great Britain and Spain, which absolutely prohibited all importation of slaves after a fixed date, and provided that any slaves landed in Cuba in contravention of this convention, should be declared free." I added to this that "more than seven-eighths of the slave population of Cuba were under this provision entitled to their freedom." Lord Palmerston was very courteous, but did nothing.

It was in June, 1860, he spoke of "that better day, near at hand, when freedom shall be restored everywhere under the national government; when the national flag, wherever it floats, on sea or on land, with'n the national jurisdiction, will not cover a single slave ; and when the declaration of independence, now reviled in the name of slavery, will once again be reverenced as the American Magna Charta of human rights. Nor is this all. Such an act will be the first stage in those triumphs by which the Republic—lifted in character so as to become an example to mankind—will enter at last upon its noble prerogative of teaching the nations how to live." The story of the election of Abraham Lincoln, the huge war convulsion, the emancipation proclamation, the amendments to the constitution giving the coloured man political equality—this cannot be told here in fitting words.

Sumner is one of the few great warriors for a principle who have lived, not only to witness its emergence from unpopularity and obscurity, but have actually seen victory crown the apparently hopeless effort of their lives.

Charles Sumner, whom I first saw in the autumn of 1873, seemed to feel deeply the charge that he had acted unfairly to England in the matter of the claims arising out of the damage done to United States' commerce by the vessels built for the Southern Confederacy by Messrs. Laird. He said: "I distinguish between the English people, whom I have always regarded with the utmost friendliness, and the English Government. But put yourself in my place. Suppose civil war between Ireland and England; suppose a Member of Congress to build war steamers at Portland under orders from those whom you called the Irish Rebels ; suppose the Government at Washington, duly warned, taking no real steps to stop the vessels ; suppose these vessels coming direct from the American port—and without ever entering an Irish port at all—being fitted with munitions of war, and burning and destroying your merchant vessels ; suppose the builder to sit in Congress, not only without censure, but receiving there constant friendly greeting, and to be treated as a friend by members of the Cabinet—what would be your feelings, Mr. Bradlaugh, as an Englishman, against the America which permitted such a wrong ?"

Charles Sumner died on March 11th, 1874 ; all America felt his loss, and Massachusetts mourned for him as though her dearest son had been taken. At his grave Curtis and Schurz vied with each other in laudations on his life. Amongst those who delivered funeral orations over Sumner was Robert B. Elliott, Senator for South Carolina, who said: "I am a negro, one of the victim race;" and from this oration I take the following: "Fellow citizens, the life of Charles Sumner needs no interpreter. It is an open, illumined page. The ends he aimed at were always high; the means he used were always direct. Neither deception nor indirection, neither concealment nor disguise of any kind or degree, had place in his nature or his methods. By open means he sought open ends. He walked in the sunlight, and wrote his heart's inmost purpose on his forehead. His activity and capacity of intellectual labour were almost unequalled. Confined somewhat by the overshadowing nature of the anti-slavery cause in the range of his topics, he multiplied his blows, and re-doubled the energy of his assaults upon that great enemy of his country's peace. Here his vigour knew no bounds. He laid all ages and lands under contribution. Scholarship in all its walks—history, art, literature, science—all these he made his aids and servitors. But who does not see that *these* are not his glory? He was a scholar amongst scholars; an orator of consummate power; a statesman familiar with the structure of governments and the social forces of the world. But he was greater and better than one or all of these; he was a man of absolute moral rectitude of purpose and of life. His personal purity was perfect, and unquestioned everywhere. He carried morals into politics. And this is the greatness of Charles Sumner: that by the power of his moral enthusiasm, he rescued the nation from its shameful subservience to the demands of material and commercial interests, and guided it up to the high plane of justice and right. Above his other great qualities towers that moral greatness to which scholarship, oratory, and statesmanship are but secondary and insignificant. He was just, because he loved justice; he was right, because he loved right. Let this be his record and epitaph."

V.—LEDRU ROLLIN.

Alexandre Auguste Ledru Rollin was born February 2nd, 1808, when Napoleon I. was in the height of his power. Louis Philippe—after whose flight Ledru Rollin sought from the popular suffrage the post of chief magistrate—was then thirty-five years of age. Louis Philippe at that time an exile, afterwards to be King, and then an exile once more. Poor France! a line of Bourbon Kings ruling for centuries over starved peoples, and ending in a revolt of despair—an attempt for liberty, rendered impossible by bayonets, hired by England from every corner of Europe, and ending in centralised authority and military mania; a one-man rule, without heart or conscience, save such as the lust for power creates, ending in a ruined France, and a Divine-right King restored to his loving people by Uhlans and Cossacks; 1830, and the fallen successor of Louis XVIII. escorted to Cherbourg with much ceremony, Divine-right Monarchy having collapsed by its own feebleness; then, for a little more than seventeen years, Louis Philippe Citizen King. Louis Blanc says: "Charles X. était tombé, parceque son trône reposait sur un principe faux: Louis Philippe est tombé parceque son trône ne reposait sur aucun principe."

Ledru Rollin, who in 1830 became a barrister, won considerable popularity as an *avocat* by his defence of various persons charged with political offences. In 1834 we find his name amongst a muster-roll of the most brilliant names of France, as one of *les défenseurs choisis par les accusés d'Avril*, and the signature of Ledru Rollin appears to a memoir, telling, in terrible language, the horrible story of the slaughterings by Monarchical authority done in the City of Paris, under the Citizen King, on April 14th, 1834.

During the period of O'Connell's great Repeal gatherings in Ireland, Ledru Rollin, who had married an Irish lady, visited his wife's native country, and, being present at one of the monster assemblages, was cheered by the Irish peasantry as a delegate from the Republican party in France.

As Louis Philippe's power diminished, the voice of the Republican advocate made itself heard more distinctly, and his influence was felt over a larger area. At Lille, shortly prior to the end of 1847, he pictured the coming revolution, which, "like the waters of the Nile inundating the land, should sweep away the corruptions and impurities, and deposit the germs of a new and rich life." When the first of the Reform banquets was held at the Château Rouge on July 9th, 1847, Ledru Rollin refused to attend, because—although the toast of the King's health was to be omitted—he apprehended there might still be equally obnoxious toasts. On the morning of February 24th, 1848, Louis Philippe was pressed to abdicate by Emile de Girardin —always the consulting physician to dying governments; in the evening the Monarchy had ceased with the King's flight, and a Provisional Government was chosen, of which M. Alphonse de Lamartine was the nominal head, and in which Ledru Rollin became Minister of the Interior. This Government was in name Republican; but at that date no Republic was possible in France. France was not a country with innumerable municipal centres of political vitality; it was rather a huge watch, with Paris for its main-spring. Whoever controlled Paris, the army, and the telegraphs, controlled France. M. Louis Blanc, in the fourth chapter of his "Histoire de la Révolution de 1848," tells the story how the Republic was proclaimed. Unfortunately, Lamartine, in his own account of his acceptance of the conduct of the Provisional Government on February 24th, shows how easily a few active, earnest men in Paris named the Government which was for a brief space to replace that of Louis XV. The new Minister of the Interior is thus described by his fellow-Republican: "He was well suited to his mission, one entirely of revolutionary propaganda. Quick-witted and penetrating, a political energy tempered by frank and engaging manners, an ardent will, integrity, a vehement desire to assure the success of the Republic, and an oratorical talent of the first class. These were the qualities which Ledru Rollin brought to the accomplishment of his functions, and they were heightened in him by a handsome figure, an imposing stature, and an indescribable magnetism, which, when he spoke seemed to pervade each of his gestures." Lord Normanby, an English ambassador, in his "A Year of Revolution in Paris," thought it right to libel Ledru Rollin, just as former English ambassadors had libelled the men of 1789. Unfortunately for Lord Normanby, and happily for the truth, he published his libels to the world, and there were more newspapers to criticise, and more readers to judge, in 1848 than in the period when Louis XVI. reigned.

On March 5th, by a decree of the Provisional Government, universal suffrage was declared to be the law of France. The law was right; but it should have been demanded by the nation, and voted by the national representatives; the men to whom it was freely given were, in the majority of instances, unable to properly value the right they gained unsought.

Ledru Rollin has been severely assailed on account of an official circular issued just prior to the elections, and addressed to the Commissioners, who acted as his provincial subordinates, directing them to replace the various préfets, sous préfets, and other officials, with persons avowing Republican opinions, and declaring that "all political functions ought to be allotted to men of sure and of Republican principles." Undoubtedly, both Ledru Rollin and Louis Blanc felt justified in using on behalf of Republicanism the centralised authority which had been so long used against it. As a Republican, the exercise of any pressure on the voters was unjustifiable; especially was it unjustifiable when, on April 15th, Ledru Rollin permitted his bulletin newspaper to suggest that, if the result of the elections should prove adverse to Republicanism, a second appeal to the barricades. would be necessary on the part of the Parisian populace. A Republican is bound to submit to the vote of a majority, even if that vote annihilates the Republic. An appeal to force is an appeal to the past; it justifies the conduct of the strongest. When some of the regiments of the National Guards were permitted, if not encouraged, to exact from the officers they were electing a pledge, "that in the event of the new Assembly declaring against a Republic, they would march against the Assembly, and put it down," every teaching of Republicanism was outraged.

A few weeks later, Ledru Rollin, as a member of the Executive Commission, found himself obliged to submit to his colleagues, who gave authorisation to Gen. Cavaignac to use force when the people at the barricades appealed against the decision of the Assembly hostile to the further existence of the Ateliers Nationaux. The bloody days of June were the result of this appeal, and all hope of present Republic was dead. After Ledru Rollin's retirement from the Ministry, he was for a short time *chef du Cabinet* to the Préfet of the Seine; but a strong attack was made upon him, and his popularity became seriously weakened. He was, nevertheless, elected in April, 1849, for Paris, with 129,000 votes.

On June 13th, 1849, Ledru Rollin made an earnest, but ineffectual, appeal in the Assembly against the murder of the Roman Republic by the French army under General Oudinot. The story is told by Joseph Mazzini, how clericalism in France triumphed in inducing the soldiers of one Republic, only just born, to crush the efforts of another Republic struggling into birth.

Forced to quit France, Ledru Rollin was an exile from his native country for twenty-one years. In 1857 he, then in England, was judged *par contumace* for alleged complicity in the attempt by Felice Orsini against the life of Louis Napoleon, but the charge was utterly unfounded, and was probably never even believed by the French police. The only pretence for the use of Ledru Rollin's name in the matter seems to have been that Charles Delécluze, who had established some political associations in France, was known to be in correspondence with the exile; but there was not even a shadow of complicity between Delécluze and Ledru Rollin.

It was in 1857 that I first saw Ledru Rollin, who often consulted me on points of English law during the time of his subsequent residence in St. John's Wood. On one point he was entirely in error: he judged France to be always as he left it in 1849, and was bitterly dis-illusioned when, on his return to Paris in 1870, he found a new generation had grown up with new ideas.

The life of an exile is not a very happy one; the sketch of the career of Joseph Mazzini illustrates this. Ledru Rollin, in his "Decadence de l'Angleterre," says: "Proscribed, we bore with us the sacred right of misfortune, which even amongst barbarians was regarded as a kind of public religion. How has it been respected? We have been each day submitted to insult; the English aristocracy has drawn us about on its journalistic hurdles, denouncing us to its people as convicts escaped from the galleys, as miserable bandits, as the refuse of the sewers of Paris." Ledru Rollin endured exile for nearly twenty-one years.

In 1870, now with whitened hair, and with his heart withered by the exile chill, Ledru Rollin once more returned to his home at Fontenay aux Roses, and was in 1871 chosen by three departments as deputy to the French Assembly, where, however, he at that time declined to sit. A Republican Society in Paris, the Alliance Républicaine, nominated Ledru Rollin as its President; but the hero of 1848 does not seem to have ever regained his old power in Paris.

At his funeral an enormous mass of Parisians gathered. His career had been honest, his devotion had been sincere. While the Empire lasted he had refused it allegiance; he had been loyal to France.

THE lives of Owen, Mazzini, Mill, Sumner, and Ledru Rollin, present several features of likeness. To the whole of these men the clergy were bitterly hostile, for each of them was an apostle of at least some chapter of the gospel of progress. The Welshman, Robert Owen, who taught the communism imperfectly shadowed out by Jesus and his Apostles, was denounced, with more than ordinary fierceness, from nearly every pulpit in England, the Bishop of Exeter encouraging the cry from his place in the House of Lords. The Italian, Joseph Mazzini, the greatest modern preacher of Republicanism, was excommunicated by the Pope, head of a Church always hostile to liberty, and the Italian patriot was anathematised by almost the whole of the Roman Catholic priesthood. The Englishman, John Stuart Mill, had scarcely been lowered into the grave, at Avignon, when the weak-brained and orthodox *Church Herald* yelled out its curses against the scarce-cold form of one who will always rank amongst the chief of Europe's thinkers; when John Stuart Mill was invited by the electors of Westminster to allow himself to be their candidate for election to Parliament, the cry of "heretic" was loudly raised by all sects of Christian preachers, and a

Liberal dignitary in the Church was bitterly assailed because he cast his ballot for the great logician. The New Englander, Charles Sumner, the Abolitionist, was preached against alike from Northern and Southern pulpits; the unfeed pleading of the Massachusetts barrister, on behalf of dark-skinned humanity, was impartially scorned by the sects who pretended to kneel to a common father: and last, though hardly least, in the value of its testimony, the Frenchman, Ledru Rollin's grave—surrounded by the many thousands of men and women who came to honour his civil burial—marked once more the hostility between progress and the Church.

Robert Owen, though he himself died poor, having devoted to popular redemption the fortune he had created, yet lived to see thousands lifted at least a little from their poverty by the practical co-operative efforts which gradually, and after many trials, grew out of his Socialistic theories. The glory of the experiment in infant education, which he first pressed at New Lanark, was, before he died, claimed by the very religious teachers who had so long hindered all education, and who must in time be destroyed by the rescue of children's brains from the control of priestly manipulators. Joseph Mazzini did not die until his much-loved Rome had been proclaimed the capital of Italy, and—though generations of education in liberty and self-reliance will be required to efface the trace of the Divine Bourbon in Naples and in Sicily—yet the lone man's life was not without its fruitful harvest. John Stuart Mill, dying ere his strength was spent, had nevertheless found himself recognised as the thought-maker of his people. Charles Sumner, who had spoken for freedom when angry and brutal men pointed revolvers in his face; who had continued to speak for abolition when the whole continent of America cried out that the speaking was hopeless; who had fallen in the Capitol—at the close of a grand speech against slavery—bathed in his own blood, shed by a felon hand; Charles Sumner lived to see his speech grow into law. And even Ledru Rollin survived long enough to see the Imperial sham fade away, and to hear the very peasantry of France utter their yearning cry for the Republicanism to which he had devoted himself.

It will not be until another age that full justice will, or can, be awarded to the memories of these men. Statues and monuments are readily erected to princes pensioned for the merit accruing from accident of birth, or fortune of marriage; memorial stones are easily found to record great wealth and huge rent-rolls. For the dead who lived for the poor, and died in poverty; for the dead who struggled for freedom, and died worn out in the effort to burst the shackles theretofore worn by others; for the dead who, living, were not known by fashion, nor honoured by wealth; for these the monuments can only be slowly raised, as a new generation inherits, without obstacle, the prizes of social advancement and political freedom, which these dead won with bleeding hearts and wearied brains.

FREETHOUGHT PUBLISHING COMPANY,

28, Stonecutter Street, Farringdon Street, E.C.

The Freethinker's Text-Book.—Part I. By C. BRADLAUGH. Section I., Nos. 1 & 2.—"The Story of the Origin of Man, as told by the Bible and by Science."

Section II., Nos. 3 & 4.—"What is Religion?" "How has it Grown?" "God and Soul."

Each Section complete in itself, with copious Index. Each Number, 6d. Part I., containing the whole four Nos., bound in cloth, price 2s. 6d.

Part II., by ANNIE BESANT.—"On Christianity." Nos. 5, 6, 7, 8, 9, & 10, price 6d. each. Section I.—"Christianity: its Evidences Unreliable." Section II.—"Its Origin Pagan." Section III.—"Its Morality Fallible." Section IV.—"Condemned by its History." Part II., containing the whole 6 Nos., bound in cloth, price 3s. 6d.

History of the Great French Revolution.—A Course of Six Lectures. By ANNIE BESANT. Cloth, lettered, 2s. 6d. Also in six parts—Parts 1 to 5, 3d. each; Part 6, 4d.

Impeachment of the House of Brunswick.—By CHARLES BRADLAUGH. Sixth edition. Price 1s.

The boldest indictment of the present reigning family ever published, with an Appendix on the Civil List.

What does Christian Theism Teach?—A verbatim report of two nights' Public Debate between the REV. A. J. HARRISON and C. BRADLAUGH. Price 6d.

God, Man, and the Bible.—A verbatim report of a three nights' Discussion at Liverpool between the REV. DR. BAYLEE and C. BRADLAUGH.

This is the only debate extant on the purely Socratic method. Price 6d.

Heresy; its Morality and Utility.—A Plea and a Justification. By CHARLES BRADLAUGH. Price 9d.

Verbatim Report of the Trial, the Queen against Bradlaugh and Besant.—Neatly bound in cloth; price 5s., post-free. With Portraits and Autographs of the two Defendants.

Is the Bible Indictable?—By ANNIE BESANT. 2d.

Autobiography of C. Bradlaugh, with Portrait. 3d.

Life of Jonah.—By C. BRADLAUGH. 1d.

The Law of Population: Its Consequences, and its Bearing upon Human Conduct and Morals.—By ANNIE BESANT. 10th thousand. 6d.

On the Being of a God as the Maker and Moral Governor of the Universe.—A verbatim report of a two nights' Discussion between THOMAS COOPER and C. BRADLAUGH. Price 6d.

When were our Gospels Written?—A Reply to Dr. Tischendorf and the Religious Tract Society. By CHARLES BRADLAUGH. Price 6d.

The Existence of God.—A verbatim report of two nights' Debate at Edinburgh, between A. ROBERTSON and C. BRADLAUGH. With a Preface by the late Austin Holyoake. Price 6d.

Cromwell and Washington : a Contrast.— By CHARLES BRADLAUGH. Price 6d.
This is a Lecture which was delivered by Charles Bradlaugh to large audiences throughout the United States.

Five Dead Men whom I Knew when Living.—By CHARLES BRADLAUGH. Sketches of Robert Owen, Joseph Mazzini, John Stuart Mill, Charles Sumner, and Ledru Rollin. Price 4d.

National Secular Society's Tracts.—1. Address to Christians. 2. Who was Jesus? 3. Secular Morality. 4. The Bible and Woman. 5. Secular Teachings. 6. Secular Work. 7. What is Secularism? 8. Who are the Secularists? 9. Secular Responsibility. 7½d. per 100, post free.

My Path to Atheism.—Collected Essays of Annie Besant.—The Deity of Jesus—Inspiration—Atonement—Eternal Punishment—Prayer—Revealed Religion—and the Existence of God, all examined and rejected, together with some Essays on the Book of Common Prayer. Cloth, lettered, price 4s.

Secular Song and Hymn Book.—A Republican and Atheistic Collection for the use of Secular Societies and Secular Homes. Edited by ANNIE BESANT. Cloth, gilt, 1s.

PAMPHLETS BY ANNIE BESANT.

The True Basis of Morality.—A Plea for Utility as the Standard of Morality. Price 2d.

Auguste Comte.—Biography of the great French Thinker, with Sketches of his Philosophy, his Religion, and his Sociology. Being a short and convenient *résumé* of Positivism for the general reader. Price 6d.

Giordano Bruno, the Freethought Martyr of the Sixteenth Century. His Life and Works. A Tract for popular distribution. Price 1d.

The Political Status of Women. A Plea for Women's Rights. Price 2d.

Civil and Religious Liberty, with some Hints taken from the French Revolution. Price 3d.

The Gospel of Atheism. Price 2d.

AND

WASHINGTON.

𝔄 Contrast.

BY

CHARLES BRADLAUGH

LONDON:
FREETHOUGHT PUBLISHING COMPANY,
28, STONECUTTER STREET, E.C.

CROMWELL AND WASHINGTON.

I.—CROMWELL.

OLIVER CROMWELL is probably one of the mightiest amongst England's children. His memory, always fresh, has for its protection no array of statues. A modern Prince has his otherwise undiscoverable goodness prominently recorded in many cities, lest without the stone record all traces of his virtues should be lost; but we can recall Cromwell's greatness without even one marble or granite reminder of his glorious manhood. Statues are now chiefly erected by Englishmen on Utilitarian principles. We build the most monuments to those men who, but for such aids, would perhaps be least remembered.

Oliver Cromwell was born at Huntingdon on April 15th, 1599, just as the reign of Elizabeth was drawing to a close A Royalist from birth until death, Royalist by early association and family tradition, of easy fortunes and fair connections, Cromwell had no special temptation to the adoption of a course of rebellion against the Crown. When about twenty-nine years old he sat in the House of Commons for his native borough of Huntingdon. He owed his seat probably more to the family influence and old estates than to any special merit then manifested; and in this first essay at Parliamentary life Oliver Cromwell has left us very little for record, although the Parliament in which he sat was a great one, and had its stirring scenes. It was the third Parliament of Charles I. Carlyle calls it "a brave and noble Parliament.' This was the Parliament to which his Majesty sent a message, requiring it "not to cast or lay any aspersion upon any Minister of his Majesty," and which forthwith accused and impeached the great Duke of Buckingham. This was the Parliament in which Mr. Speaker Finch tried to stifle speech, and to avoid all Parliamentary remonstrance, by adjourning the House; the only Parliament, as far as I know, in which some of the members held the Speaker in the chair while they, on March 2nd, 1629, voted respectful remonstrances against tonnage, poundage, and other matters.

Denzil Holles, Sir John Eliot, William Strode, and John Selden (who were afterwards fined or imprisoned for their daring) were amongst the most prominent in thus forcibly retaining Mr. Speaker. "Let him go!" cry the King's Privy Councillors. "No," answers Holles; "God's wounds! he shall sit there until it pleases the House to rise." And in all this stir we see no sign of Oliver Cromwell.

Poor Eliot—for his part in this business fined £2,000, and to be imprisoned during the king's pleasure—will make no submission, ask no grace, and the Tower dungeon is his tomb: he comes not out of gaol alive. How many grand men die in the effort to make a country live, and these dead have not even the honour of a grateful memory from the children of those they served so well! Living a day or two too early, they were the forlorn hope, whose bodies helped to fill the ditch, that others might pass more easily to victory and glory. This third Parliament should be memorable if only that gallant Eliot sat in it. It was this Parliament which solemnly declared, in the famous Petition of Right, "That no man hereafter be compelled to make or yield any gift, loan, benevolence, tax, or such-like charge, without common consent by Act of Parliament."

Parliament was soon dissolved; it had only been needed to vote "supply." Not fulfilling this need, it was extinguished, as had been its predecessors. There had already been in this yet short reign two preceding Parliaments, both brief-lived, because they would not vote money without discussing grievances; and now this third Parliament, its members having acted, as the king thinks, like "vipers," is also dismissed. Then, for eleven years, no Parliament in England, and during this space Oliver Cromwell leads apparently a gentleman farmer's life on his lands at St. Ives, near the River Ouse. He had a strong tendency to the fast-developing Puritan spirit of the times; his prominent relatives were Puritans, too; but Cromwell manifested—so far as we can judge—little, or no, inclination to meddle in rising political strife. Yet his very Puritanism counted for something in making him a rebel. Sturdy Puritanism struggled against servile Episcopalian flunkeyism. Mainwaring was made a Bishop by Charles I., and Sibthorp gained preferment in the Established Church, for preaching "that the king might take the subjects' money at his pleasure, and that no one might refuse his demand, on penalty of damnation."

No Parliament for eleven years, and yet the king wants money! and without Parliament he cannot have it. The charges of the king's Government grew more serious in each reign. The Crown lands, once extensive enough for everything, had been given and granted to favourite and favourite's flatterer; now broad acres to this pretty face; now wide baronies to this strong arm; now far-stretching slopes and fertile dales to this proud churchman; until the recipients of royal bounty were sometimes as rich as, or richer than, the kingly donor. Feudal obligations to contribute in peace and war to the maintenance of the royal state, are not, and were not, quite as accurately calculable in their realisable results as would be the proceeds of a modern property-tax. "Forced loans" and "benevolences," then a good source of income, were well enough, if collected from the Jews, whom nobody protected; but when the moneys were sought in the cities, the merchants stood resolutely on their privileges and charters, and obstinately refused to lend or give. "Tonnage and poundage"—which divine-right Charles considered a tax to be levied within his own discretion—was much denied. "Tonnage and poundage" was an imposition upon goods and merchandise exported and imported, and was first granted by Parliament about 1523 to Henry VIII., and the right thus accorded to the sovereign to levy had been renewed in each succeeding reign, until the time of Charles I., when it being proposed in the Commons to limit the right to a single year, the Lords rejected the Bill, and Charles Stuart was left without any statutory right to collect the tax.

It was in 1635 that Oliver Cromwell's cousin, John Hampden, was required to pay ship-money, and refused. According to the old practice, there were military tenures, which bound the landholders in a great part of the kingdom to furnish actual men and arms, or to pay in money their cost. So also the Cinque Ports, and other English seaports, and sometimes maritime counties, had been called upon to furnish a quota of ships for the public service, and there had even been instances of similar demands on inland towns, when piracy was prevalent. Attorney-General Noy, to win favour with the king, and backed by the opinion of a corrupted and time-serving Bench of Judges, sought, under cover of ship-money, to levy taxes from the nation without the authority of Parliament. The first ship-money writ was issued to the City of London and other seaports, in October,

1634, requiring them to provide vessels and armaments to oppose the pirates at sea, and under it £35,000 was obtained from the City of London alone, though not without remonstrance or resistance on the part of the citizens. One Richard Chambers refused to pay, and being committed to gaol by the Lord Mayor of London for this non-payment, Chambers brought an action against the Lord Mayor to recover damages for the false imprisonment. His fight was gallant, but hopeless; for the twelve judges, headed by Lord Chief Justice Finch (the former Speaker), had already given their public opinion that the king might, in his sole judgment, issue such a writ as that under which the ship-money levy was made. On Chambers's trial Mr. Justice Berkely refused to allow his counsel to contest the validity of the writ, declaring "that there was a rule of law, and a rule of government, and that many things which could not be done by the first rule could be done by the other." I expect this man Berkely must have been related to the Governor Berkely, of Virginia, who, in the same reign, declared "free schools and printing to be pernicious inventions of the devil for the spread of heresy and sedition." On a portion of his property John Hampden was required to pay 20s., which he refused. The king sued and won judgment for the 20s., but lost a crown as the final result to the suit. The case was argued on behalf of Hampden by Oliver St. John, who was distantly related by marriage to our Oliver Cromwell. The 25th Edward I., "which forever abrogated all taxation without consent of Parliament," was pleaded, but without avail. Another statute called *de Tallagio non Concedendo*, was urged to like effect, but the judges had pre-determined their judgment. Last, but not least, the famous Petition of Right, "that noble legacy of a slandered Parliament," as Hallam calls it, was brought forward by Hampden's counsel. All to no purpose! Seven judges upheld the ship-money levy against five dissenting. The majority laid down the damnable doctrine that King Charles had absolute power "to command his subjects, their persons and goods, and I say their money too." These were the words of Lord Chief Justice Finch, and he found six judges servile enough to re-echo the slavish formula. Five judges dissented, but only two of them, Justices Croke and Hutton, had the courage to squarely deny the alleged prerogative of the Crown, and to declare ship-money unlawful. Unhappily for them, their names stood already committed in writing to the extra-judicial opinion, concocted by Finch, affirming the king's right to issue the writ, and make the levy. It is said that Justice Croke would have given judgment for the king, the justice being in fear of losing his appointment, but that he was kept on the right side by his wife, "who implored him not to sacrifice his conscience for fear of any danger or prejudice to his family, being content to suffer any misery with him, rather than to be an occasion for him to violate his principles."

Hopeless of obtaining justice from the English Law Courts, and not yet driven by despair to the last desperate appeal to force, many of the Puritan leaders looked across to the New England settlements as a haven of refuge. It is said by Hallam that, "Men of a higher rank than the first colonists are now become hopeless alike of the civil and religious liberties of England; men of capacious and commanding minds, formed to be the legislators and generals of an infant Republic; the wise and cautious Lord Say, the acknowledged chief of the Independent sect; the brave, the open, and enthusiastic Lord Brook; Sir Arthur Hazelrig; Hampden, ashamed of a country for whose rights he had fought alone; Cromwell, panting with energies that he could neither control nor explain, and whose unconquerable fire was still wrapped in smoke to every eye but that of his kinsman Hampden: were preparing to embark for America, when Laud, for his own and his master's curse, procured an order of council to stop their departure." They were to be driven to bay, all loopholes being stopped, all escape being prevented. They turned, and at last the hunted became the hunters.

The litigation with Hampden, from the first assessment to the final judgment, had lasted more than three years; and ship-money was paid less willingly after the judgment, than even while the suit against John Hampden was yet undecided. Passive resistance, when it takes the shape of a general "We won't pay," is very effective. The king needed money; for effectual collection of money he must have a Parliament. London would lend money if a Parliament were summoned, none without; and at last, on the 13th of April, 1640, King Charles's fourth Parliament was assembled, and in this our Oliver Cromwell sat as Member for Cambridge. The duration of this Parliament was of the briefest; it is known as the "Short Parliament," for—not providing money for the king with sufficient rapidity, and providing protest against the Hampden judgment, and criticism against Strafford much too freely—it was dismissed "in a huff, on the 5th of May, after a session of three weeks." Charles I. resolved to get his money without the aid of Parliament, but could not. Ship-money was enforced with greater rigour than before, and brought less profit. Sheriffs who would not levy the tax were fined and imprisoned, but even these fines were not always paid. Loans were asked for, and citizens preferred committal to prison to lending to the king. Merchants' bullion was seized in the mint, and debased coin issued. But all these expedients failed. The king still needed money; London would lend £200,000, but only on condition that a Parliament should be summoned; and, accordingly, on the 3rd of November, 1640, there assembled at Westminster the most notable of all the Parliaments that St. Stephen's has ever known, the "Long Parliament." Instead of being dissolved by the king, it ultimately resolved the king's dissolution. It created a Frankenstein monster in its army, which, at last, under Colonel Pride, weeded out its strength with an array of pikes for weedhooks. It was driven away by angry Oliver Cromwell, but claimed not to be dissolved, and as "the Rump" Parliament it appeared once more to act as usher-in for the restoration of the pious and virtuous Charles II. In this fifth Parliament, Oliver Cromwell again sits as Member for Cambridge, and now gets notice from friend and foe. The friendly words have struggled through the Restoration period with much difficulty; the hostile comments are thick and strong. Thomas Carlyle quotes from Philip Warwick, doubly returned, to sit for Romney and Radnor, but who preferred the latter borough : "I came into the House one morning, and perceived a gentleman speaking, whom I knew not, very ordinarily apparelled, for it was a plain cloth suit, which seemed to have been made by an ill-country tailor; his linen was plain, and not very clean, and I remember a speck or two of blood upon his little band, which was not much larger than his collar. His hat was without a hatband. His stature was of a good size ; *his sword stuck close to his side;* his countenance swollen and reddish, his voice sharp and untuneable, and his eloquence full of fervour." The trait of Cromwell here, which marks the man, is in the seven words, "his sword stuck close to his side." The sceptre of Cromwell was his sword : his sword was his tongue, his pen. Cromwell's will, and Cromwell's sword were alike of a metal which bent little and cut through everything. Lord Clarendon would make out that our Oliver Cromwell, as a young Member, was a blusterer, whose "carriage" was "tempestuous," and "behaviour" "insolent:" and this, even in private committee, where Clarendon alleges that Cromwell replied to Lord Mandevil "with much indecency and rudeness," and in "contrary and offensive" language. It is so easy for a plain man to be rude and indecent to a lord. Our English lords are not to be mauled with rough hands, or pelted with rough words. We have a bankrupt Duke of Newcastle and a bankrupt George Odger. No well-trained mind would think of using the same harsh phrases to the well-housed Duke of Newcastle, in his Clumber Castle palace, that might be fittingly applied to the needy Radical shoemaker, in his poor Bloomsbury home. It is "contrary and offensive" language, even now, to suggest that princes, who live on the country, owe service to it; and I am prepared to admit that Oliver Cromwell, in Parliamentary debate, might have been "contrary," "offensive," "indecent," and "rude," but blusterer he was most surely none. Bluster is the wind-bag weapon of the weak man; the warrior who wears and handles a mace never fights with an air-bladder as his arm of offence. Cowards bluster—those who from the rear shout "Forward," and from a safe distance, and in a crowd, cry "Down with him." But a man like Cromwell, a real man, whose "sword was stuck close to his side," who rode at the head of his troop; who, when the forlorn hope was repulsed, and he was general, went himself "at push of pike" into the breach; he was no blusterer.

The Long Parliament began its work well. It declared ship-money illegal; it annulled the judgment against Hampden; it declared that no tax could be levied on exports or imports, save by common consent in Parliament; it made Parliaments triennial; it abolished the Star Chamber, the Court of High Commission, and several other arbitrary and irregular tribunals; it denied the king's right of impressment for military service; it voted that bishops should not sit in the House of Lords; it impeached and brought Strafford to the block, Charles being cowardly enough to sacrifice his minister as a scapegoat; and on the very day that Strafford's death-warrant was signed, it enacted that this Parliament should not be dissolved without its own consent. To get money, the king assented to this Bill, which in the end proved his death-warrant too. There was some talk even of a Puritan Ministry, with the Earl of Bedford as chief, and Pym, Hampden, and Holles in the Cabinet; but this talk ended in worse than nothing; it only irritated the men, and widened the breach. These Puritans wanted Parliamentary Government; Charles Stuart wanted to be despot, riding England with Parliament as his riding whip. At last, on the 4th of January, 1641, Charles I. determines to stop the daring of Parliament by a blow which shall terrify the most audacious. Pym, Hazelrig, Holles, Strode, and Hampden have been over-daring in their speech, and these the king will punish. So to the House of Commons with a strong armed force enters the king—the Earl of Roxburgh holding open the doors of the House—to seize with his own hands the famous five. But they are no longer in the House. A friendly word of warning had gone before to notify the coming of his angry majesty, and Hampden and the four others are safely within the City walls, where, indeed, all Parliament goes for protection next day, to "consider and advise how to right the House in point of privilege, broken by the king's coming yesterday with a force to take Members of our House." The Parliament, threatened with the sword, takes up the sword to protect itself, and yet with a show of profound reverence for royal authority. It asks the king for permission to raise a militia; it raises the militia without consent, when the request is denied. It vests the command of the militia in persons to be appointed by Parliament, and it prays for the custody of the Tower and other strong places. Its prayer refused, it takes all it can, backing its respectful request with pike, broadsword, and battering ram. And now Oliver Cromwell comes to the front! It is time. He offers to lend £300 to aid the Parliament in reducing the Irish rebellion; he sends down arms to Cambridge; he commences to organise troop 67; he seizes the magazine at Cambridge Castle; and he has prevented the king from getting the University plate, value some £20,000. The king, unhindered by the Parliament, as yet too reverent to touch his sacred majesty's person—has fled from Whitehall to York, on the way gathering an army round him. The queen and the crown jewels have been sent away, to negotiate foreign aid and to raise money abroad.

There is now civil war, not as of old, between rival pretendants for the throne, but of the army of the king and Parliament, against the army of the king. High treason, and yet not enough of Republican spirit to shape the treason into war against monarchy. A strange civil war, in which there are many Parliament men who do not hope to win, many who do not desire to win, and many who do not deserve to win. Captain Cromwell grows daily in his strength, and is soon first in the Cambridge county, and then the eastern counties are associated for common defence, and Cromwell gradually takes the lead; no bigger, braver, or wiser captain being there to stand in front. When there is some defeat, and much terror, Cromwell is firm and unreceding. When lawless troops, in the name of Parliament, do as much wrong to friends as to foes, Cromwell is a stern and strict captain. When cold friends will not find food, forage, and pay for the "God-fearing" "Ironsides," Cromwell's sword pens the requisition which knows no evasion, and must be fully complied with. Cromwell seems daily to grow conscious of his augmenting power, and to play cautiously for more authority: and yet I stand with Cromwell. To re-quote the words attributed to Lord Chatham: "There was ambition, there was sedition, there was violence, but no man shall persuade me that it was not the cause of liberty on the one side, and of tyranny on the other." Lieutenant-Colonel Cromwell is busying himself in fortifying the town of Cambridge against Prince Rupert, in levying "freewill contributions" for the good cause, and in seizing "malignants'" horses; busying himself, too, in riding hard and striking hard, as the need arises, until the Colonel Cromwell is chief of the seven associated counties, with a large force of well-ordered men; "not a man swears but he pays his twelve-pence; no plundering, no drinking, disorder, or impiety allowed." Lord Essex, the Lieutenant-General, grows less, and Colonel Cromwell grows greater, until the big fight comes at Winceby, where, "within half-pistol shot, his horse was killed under him at the first charge, and fell down upon him, and, as he rose up, he was knocked down again by the gentleman who charged him.........but afterwards he recovered a poor horse in a soldier's hands, and bravely mounted himself again," and rides to victory.

Puritan Cromwell is now Governor of Ely; the Cathedral Service does not please him, and so he writes to the Reverend Mr. Hitch, "Lest the soldiers should in any tumultuous or disorderly way attempt the reformation of the Cathedral Church, I require you to forbear altogether your choir-service." Cromwell's will is to be law to Mr. Hitch, even in the regulation of the Ely Cathedral Choristers. The Reverend Mr. Hitch disregarding, next Sunday in walks Oliver Cromwell, his hat on his head, a force at his back, and with a "Leave off your fooling, and come down, Sir," he dismisses poor Mr. Hitch from his pulpit, just as a few years later he dismisses Speaker Lenthall from the House of Commons. The Lieutenant-General Cromwell, early in 1644, finds time to appear in Parliament to complain of my Lord Willoughby, a Parliament General, but one not too well-inclined to see the Parliament over-much-succeeding against the king, and who has "strangely dissolute people about him." And a little later, to Major-General Crawford, the Lieutenant-General Cromwell delivers a sharp reprimand, because Crawford has discountenanced an "anabaptist" Lieutenant-Colonel: "Sir, the State, in choosing men to serve it, takes no notice of their opinions; if they be willing faithfully to serve it, that satisfies. I advised you formerly to bear with men of different minds from yourself.........Take heed of being too sharp, or too easily sharpened by others, against those to whom you can object little, but that they square not with you in every opinion concerning matters of religion." And still a little later—with the extra glory of Marston fight giving further force to his authority—Oliver Cromwell rebukes the Ely Committee for having released some prisoners who had been arrested by some of Cromwell's officers, and forthwith has the released men re-arrested by the warrant of his (Cromwell's) will. The newer soldiers, especially those with strong convictions on religious matter, all inclined to Cromwell. "The man," Baillie says, "is a very wise and active head, universally well-beloved, as religious and stout, being a known Independent, and most of the soldiers who love new ways, put themselves under his command."

After the second battle of Newbury, on October 27th, 1644, there was strife between Oliver Cromwell and his superior officer, the Earl of Manchester. The latter, it was alleged, " does not want to press the king too hard, will not pursue after a victory, does not even wish to fight;" and in December we find Cromwell in Parliament declaring that "it is now a time to speak, or forever to hold the tongue," and urging in effect that these Earls of Essex and Manchester are poor shiftless things, with which it will be indeed difficult to save a nation from ruin. While on the other side it is contended that the firebrand Cromwell has openly avowed that "there never would be a good time in England until we had done with Lords;" and still worse, that "if he met the king in battle, he would fire his pistol at the king as at another." The Scots Commissioners, fearful of Cromwell's growing influence and bold speech, want to learn "whether there be not ground to prosecute Cromwell as an incendiary;" but Cromwell has already too many "Ironsides" to make such a prosecution desirable. And now Lords Essex and Manchester are got out of the army with soft words and flattering distinctions. Sir Thomas Fairfax is Lord-General, and Cromwell is scarcely second.

The self-denying ordinance—which took from all Members of both Houses of Parliament their commands in the army and their civil employments—would, if it had been strictly carried out, have deprived Cromwell of his military position; but Prince Rupert is to be attacked, and who shall be relied on to do it save Oliver Cromwell? Accordingly, "forty days' leave" for his continuance in command being granted, he routs convoys, captures strong houses, and goes on so victoriously, that the leave is renewed for "three months," and at last the "self-denying ordinance" is dispensed with, at least in this case, and the Lieutenant-General Cromwell still remains M.P. for Cambridge.

And now the attempt at any treaty at Uxbridge having failed, the king and Parliament come again to blows on the 14th of June, 1645, when Naseby fight brought Charles and Cromwell very close indeed, and the king's majesty fled. For a moment the daring Rupert seems likely to win, but his cavaliers are better thieves than soldiers, and staying to plunder after their first dashing charge, lose their vantage; and then stern Cromwell, whose "Ironsides" never plunder, drives away Prince Rupert's troopers into disastrous defeat.

Through 1645 and 1646, we find Cromwell continually fighting and growing stronger, capturing Bristol and various strong places, battering forts, and personally doing daring deeds, with a tinge of fierceness, which made his name feared, until the king surrenders to the Scots, and is by the Scottish leaders traded away to the Parliament. Now comes complication of quarrel; Parliament has not only to fight the king, but is also divided against itself; one party thinks the king low enough, the other section would push the man Charles Stuart still harder, even though he fell too low to rise again. With the latter goes the army; with the first ranks the city. City and Parliament Presbyterians would fain disband the army, which has grown too potent through its victories, and at last has marched much too near to London. The army requires its arrears of pay, insists on its "old commanders," and begins to rank itself a power in the State. The king, high with hope, plays army against Parliament, and Scots Commissioners against both. The army appoints "agents," or "adjutators," from each regiment, and Cromwell, though he sits in Parliament, and does not openly side with the growing malcontent spirit, is evidently more inclined to count upon the sword than upon the tongue, and declares to Ludlow that "these men will never leave until the army pull them out by the ears." The army petitions, and marches nearer London, and now the Lieutenant-General Cromwell goes to Saffron Waldron to see "the army disbanded," which does not disband, but, on the contrary, and probably by Cromwell's connivance, seizes the person of the king, not altogether too unwilling to be so seized. There is some thought in Parliament to arrest Cromwell, but no opportunity. He now plainly sides with the army, and it marches still nearer London, and demands not only its arrears of pay, and redress of other grievances, but claims also "a settlement of the peace of the kingdom, and of the liberties of the subject." On the one side Presbyterian Parliament and London; on the other, the army, drawing closer to the city walls, with Oliver Cromwell its real commander, and with the king in its midst, his majesty vainly hoping that the contending parties may destroy each other, leaving him the master. Hallam says that the royalists "seem never to have comprehended that many active spirits looked to the entire subversion of the monarchy. The king, in particular, was haunted by a prejudice, natural to his obstinate and undiscerning mind, that he was necessary to the settlement of the nation." Nor was Cromwell, nor were his followers, irrevocably hostile to the king. Soon after the capture of the king by Cornet Joyce and his troopers, they declared, "we do not see how there can be any peace to this kingdom, firm or lasting, without a due provision for the rights, quiet, and immunity of his majesty." Unfortunately for himself, Charles Stuart irritated even the portion of the army well disposed to him by his utter deceitfulness.

For a little time there is compromise between the Presbyterian and Independent factions, and an effort is made to limit the duration of the Parliament by its own vote, in which effort Oliver Cromwell is beaten by a small majority only. The king keeps a sort of prisoner's state in Hampton Court Palace, which serves as a not unpleasant gaol, until all negotiations fall through, and on the 11th of November, 1647, he absconds from Hampton Court. His Majesty's flight had been hastened by the discovery—through the interception of letters to the queen—of the worse than double part that his insincere kingship was playing. The army had been provoked at the notion that they had been tricked by the king. Fifth-monarchy men began to menace the king's person; and in the army the levelling spirit, which had threatened Parliament, turned also, for an instant, its angriness against Oliver Cromwell, who quickly, and without mercy, trampled out the mutinous spirit, the leader being shot as a warning to prevent other want of discipline.

The king is a prisoner in Carisbrooke Castle. The Scotch, who not long since delivered him into bonds, now march, or threaten to march, into England, to obtain his majesty's release. The very hope encourages Presbyterian royalism in Wales, which bursts out in royalist risings; but Cromwell burns one place, starves another, and generally terrifies the Welshmen into quiescence; even if he does not win them to the complete abandonment of the now utterly-ruined monarchy. The Scotch threatening is at last real invasion. Duke Hamilton has crossed the border with heavy forces, and is coming southward, Preston way, with a huge and straggling army stretching miles backward, like some unwieldy serpent. Cromwell, hurrying out of Wales, and over the Lancashire and Cheshire hills, throws himself on this Londonwards marching army, breaks its back, stamps on its tail, and pounds its fangs into impotence. With the rout at Preston commence the funereal ceremonies for Charles Stuart; to be delayed for a scant space, while in his turn Oliver Cromwell crosses the Scottish border in pursuit of Hamilton's broken men; but coming to an end at Whitehall on the 29th of January, 1649.

The theory of divine-right rule was exploded for ever in England on that day. The divinity which doth hedge around a king proved no barrier to the headsman's axe. There had been an effort in the Presbyterian Parliament to save the king, and, in December, a majority of 129 against 83 had voted that "his majesty's concessions in the treaty of Newport are a ground of settlement." On the second day after this vote, on the 6th of December, 1648, Colonel Pride's regiment of foot paraded under arms in Westminster Hall, and Colonel Rich's regiment of horse stood in the Palace Yard outside. Pride's purge is applied to the House of Commons. Those who are against the army, may not go in, but must get them gone. The sword is stronger than the law. Lieutenant-General Cromwell has hurried up to town: the minority has become majority, and Charles Stuart is "convicted, attainted, and condemned of high treason." Here it is not fair matter to discuss regicide at any length; killing kings is poor work and useless work. Republics are not created by carving off the head of a monarch; they can only grow gradually in the development of peoples into a grandeur of stature higher than tinsel kingcraft knows. Regicide is weak work, for it is mostly the vengeance of an indignant people, for a wrong which was only possible while that people participated or acquiesced in the perpetuation of the wrong. I am against beheading kings, as a matter of policy; it is only chipping off an unimportant morsel of the monarchy; but I am still more against killing kings, as a matter of principle, for I object entirely to capital punishment. Punishment can only be lawful—that is, moral; that is, useful—when it has for its end and aim the prevention of the recurrence of crime, not only in the criminal, but also in the society to which the individual culprit belongs. Punishment which is only vengeance for past offence is itself crime, and it brutalises those by whom, and amongst whom, the vengeance is carried out. I am against killing kings, for I am against the right of society to take human life; but while capital punishment obtains in any country, I know no reason that the headsman's axe should be blunted and turned from a king's neck. The law should see no distinction of person in any citizen, unless, indeed, it tempers itself with tenderness to the poor-born, the weak, the starved, and the ignorant. I do not understand the cant of warped humanity, which sheds a tear for the royal martyr, and has, nevertheless, dry eyes for the scores of thousands, whom the royal murderer pushed to death and ruin by his crime, his folly, or his impotence.

On the 19th of May, 1649, it is solemnly declared that England is "A commonwealth or free state, and shall from henceforth be governed as a commonwealth and free state, by the supreme authority of this nation, the representatives of the people in Parliament, and by such as they shall appoint and constitute officers and ministers under them for the good of the people, and without any king or House of Lords." Alas! paper decrees do not make commonwealths, and England as yet is hardly full enough of men to continue a government "without any king." An uncrowned king has already commenced to reign by the force of his own grand will. Charles Stuart is indeed dead, but there is not even the hope or shadow of a possible Republic in England. The one-man rule is more potent than ever; but it is now the rule of a real, resolute man, not that of a mere irresolute royally-born puppet; an Oliver Cromwell wields power, not a Charles Stuart. The uncrowned king governs with a steel sceptre, but he governs for England; Charles Stuart misgoverned for the king. Oliver Cromwell is tyrant, not Republican; but his heart is, despite the lust of power, a patriot's heart, and he uses a giant's might to build his country's glory and its strength. He knows no mercy, no toleration, for episcopal royalism, or mass-saying adherents to the monarchy. He is law and judge, and his verdict is fiercely severe.

Poor Ireland was for, and was against, Charles I., and now is nearly all in arms for Charles II. And so in Ireland, the Lord General Cromwell acts with a Puritan mercilessness of judgment against these misguided Papists. The Irish page is a bloody one—"One could pity this poor Irish people; their case is pitiable enough." But Cromwell does not torture the captive, nor strike the fallen. To the foe in arms, and counting high his strength, fierce fight, no truce, no peace, no mercy. To the foe on his knees, abandoning his arms, all manner of protection and fairness, save one—no shadow of toleration for Rome. The freedom of worship, claimed and taken for Independents, was denied to Romanists. "I shall not where I have the power, and the Lord is pleased to bless me, suffer the exercise of the mass where I can take notice of it. No, nor in any way suffer you that are Papists, where I can find you seducing the people." When the Lord General Cromwell landed, nearly all Ireland was united against the Commonwealth, and had declared for the young Charles II. Two cities alone, Dublin and Derry, and they besieged, still held for the Parliament. In less than twelve months Oliver Cromwell had burned and trampled out all resistance, and, save the city of Waterford, had captured in turn every strong place. No plundering, no murder, no violence permitted;

but when the fight comes, and Tredah summoned will not cede, Cromwell himself has to lead the fresh assault: then no mercy, no pity, all the garrison are put to sword. And more than one Tredah in this twelvemonths' history!

"A train of favouring events, more than any deep-laid policy," says Hallam, "had now brought sovereignty within the reach of Cromwell. His first schemes of ambition may probably have extended no farther than a title and an estate, with a great civil and military command in the king's name. Power had fallen into his hands because they alone were fit to wield it; he was taught by every succeeding events his own undeniable superiority over his contemporaries in martial renown, in civil prudence, in decision of character, and in the public esteem which naturally attached to these qualities." And this from Hallam, hostile, it must not be forgotten, to our Cromwell. The wine of power is an intoxicating draught. The taste grows with the drinking. It is easy now to condemn Cromwell for taking power, but who is there who—having dared to lift the glass to his lips when each drop was bitter—would have the courage to turn away the goblet when the hour of triumph came, and the whole contents seemed sweet and pleasant, and the world, with loud shouts, acclaimed the drinking? It requires a hero's might to leave the won prize ungrasped, and this Cromwell was only a man. A grand man, it is true, as men are measured in these peddling days.

Hardly is Ireland roughly smitten into sullen peace before Scotland again calls for similar chastening. Charles II. has there become a covenanted king; has signed a public declaration acknowledging his late father's sins, and his own errors, which he filially puts to the account of evil training. On the 26th of June, 1650, "Oliver Cromwell, Esq., is made Captain-General and Commander-in-Chief of all the forces raised, or to be raised, by authority of Parliament, within the Commonwealth of England," and in a few more days is on the march to Scotland, where he has to match himself against cool and cautious General David Lesley, who is too strongly intrenched to be attacked safely on his own ground, and who will not leave his chosen lines. Here for nearly two months, with a little poor skirmishing, until Oliver Cromwell and his men get short of supplies, and David Lesley is much worried for his over-caution by kirk committees and royalist civil dignitaries, and battle is given at Dunbar; and on the 3rd of September, 1650, "the Scotch army is shivered to utter ruin." The day before the battle the Scotch were sure of victory, and Cromwell deemed defeat possible. The fight at Dunbar was not his choice, "we were necessitated," he writes Ireton. The day after the battle his view has changed; he now writes, "the kirk has done their do," and so they had. There is yet more fighting to be done, but it all goes one way. At last, as a desperate effort, the Royalist Scots' march southward, carrying with them their young king, and Cromwell hurries after. Through Lancashire, past Shrewsbury to Worcester, where some rest is taken, goes Charles II. Through Northumberland and Yorkshire, and by way of Nottingham, comes Cromwell; and on the 3rd of September, 1651, a year to a day from Dunbar fight, comes the battle of Worcester, where too there is another utter rout, and the young king is a fugitive, without the shadow of an army.

Ten weeks after the battle of Worcester the Long Parliament voted that it would cease to exist on the 3rd of November, 1654. "But why," asks the army, "should there be still three years delay?" And then there are difficulties about the new representation, and on these the army officers and the Parliament are by no means agreed. The army desires to shut out the possibility of a Presbyterian majority, and the Parliament hopes to prevent any other. It is thought by many officers that the Rump Presbyterian Parliament desires to keep its power, and continue its existence. These difficulties grow into dangers, until on the 20th of April, 1653, the Lord-General Cromwell, in plain black, but with a company of musketeers close at hand, goes into the House, and sits him down for about a quarter of an hour, and then, with an "I will put an end to your prating," calls in the musketeers, and dissolves the Parliament by the sole warrant of his will. After a brief two months, by the same warrant of his will, and by no other law, Oliver Cromwell issues his summonses for a National Council, to which come 138, selected by him as members for various counties. This Council, called by some the Little Parliament, by others the Barebones Parliament, is greeted on the 4th of July, 1653, by Oliver Cromwell, in a speech wherein he declares that in the "Act for a Representative," brought forward in the Parliament he had just dissolved, "plainly the intention was, not to give the people a right of choice," but "was only to recruit the House, the better to perpetuate themselves," and "truly, I say, when we saw all this, having power in our hands, we could not resolve to let such monstrous proceedings go on." This "Little Parliament" worked vigorously for five months, doing in that time some good service to the State, and then resolved, "That the sitting of this Parliament any longer, as now constituted, will not be for the good of the Commonwealth, and that, therefore, it is requisite to deliver up unto the Lord-General Cromwell the powers which we received from him."

On the 16th of December, 1653, "a council of officers, and other persons interested in the nation," nominated Oliver Cromwell Lord Protector of the Commonwealth of England, Scotland, and Ireland. "Through a gross and glaring evidence," says Hallam, "of the omnipotence of the army, the instrument under which he took his title accorded to him no unnecessary executive authority. The sovereignty still resided in the Parliament, he had no negative voice in their laws."

On the 4th of September, 1654, was assembled the first Protectorate Parliament duly elected by the nation. This Parliament wants to discuss too freely; for it discusses the very right and authority of the Protector himself; but only for a week, for on the 12th of September the Parliament House is locked up and guarded with soldiers, and the Members are all invited to attend his Highness in the Painted Chamber, and there he, Oliver Cromwell, tells the assembled Commons "that he would sooner be rolled into his grave and buried with infamy" than throw away the Government, and that, until they all acknowledge his position as Lord Protector, he says, "I have caused a stop to be put to your entrance into the Parliament House." Some submit at once, some more submit to-morrow, some—as Bradshaw, Hazelrig, Thomas Scott, Major Wildman—will not submit at all. Non-submission avails nothing; those who will not submit may have no entrance, no voice, but may get them home, or go whither they will, save into the Parliament House.

The Lord Protector's Government is certainly of the most despotic; but says one, "it makes England more formidable and considerable to all nations than it has ever been in my days." Cromwell looks to Virginia; deals sharply with Spain; refuses to sign the French treaty until some show of justice is done by the Duke of Savoy to the Protestants "of Lucerna, of Perosa, and St. Martin;" and generally marks himself as a live head for England.

There are plots against Cromwell's life, a reward is offered by Charles II. of "virtuous life and blessed memory," of £500 a year to any one who by "sword, pistol, or poison," shall kill "the base mechanic fellow, named Oliver Cromwell," and this reward is offered "on the word and faith of a Christian king." There are men too more dangerous, because more honest, who seek Cromwell's life, because they regard his power as paralysing all hope of liberty. And there is a Parliament which has so reluctantly recognised his chieftainship that it cumbers and hinders his Government by its resolutions and red-tape provisions for limiting his authority; so that on the 22nd of January, 1655, Cromwell makes it a last long speech, of which the peroration is: "I think it my duty to tell you that it is not for the profit of these nations, nor for the common and public good, for you to continue here any longer"; and Parliament is dissolved, even before the five calendar months are yet run out during which it is provided that Parliament shall not be dissolved. Cromwell construes the month to be but four weeks, and he wears a sword that would, if need be, measure a hour to have only fifty minutes.

Parliament had voted the Protectorate elective by 200 voices against 60, and although compelled by Cromwell to admit his personal might unquestioned, had resolutely debated and examined every other article of the instrument of Government, under which the Protectorate had been created. Parliament dissolved, Cromwell governs by a pure military despotism, dividing England into ten districts, presided over by Major-Generals, nominated by himself. These Major-Generals levy heavy taxes on disaffected persons, their authority being, that it is by Cromwell's will. Duties on merchandise having been levied in excess of law, by Cromwell's authority, and a Mr. George Cony, on whom the tax had been enforced, having made suit at law against the collector, Cromwell sent Cony's counsel to the Tower, while the Lord Chief Justice Rolle retired from the bench rather than give judgment against the Protector.

And yet after his fashion, and as between individuals, Cromwell dealt out a rude justice, and in all matters other than those which touched the firm maintenance of his Government, was equitable in his dealings as chief-magistrate of the land. He filled the benches with wise and able judges, and, outside the one question of his personal rule, he governed well for the country which he held in the grip of his iron gauntlet. In all matters, even of minor appointments, he would have his way, and writes to Mr. Secretary Thurloe : " I have not the particular shining bauble for crowds to gaze at or to kneel to, but—to be short—I know how to deny petitions, and whatever I think proper for outward form, to 'refer' to any officer or office, I expect that such my compliance with custom shall be looked upon as an indication of my will and pleasure to have the thing done."

On the 17th of September, 1656, a fresh Parliament is summoned of about 400 members, and of these Cromwell, against all law, prevents nearly ninety persons from taking their seats. The men excluded have been duly elected, but some are too Republican, some few too Royalist, and Cromwell will have none of them. Under this Parliament the major-general system is abolished with Cromwell's consent, and some slight show of constitutional Government presented. At last, on the 31st of March, 1657, the House of Commons present to Cromwell their petition and advice that his Highness, the Lord Protector, may be pleased to adopt the title "king." Irate major-generals and stern Puritan officers have already remonstrated and urged upon his highness the danger of even seeming to covet any such title. And Cromwell, he will, and he will not, become king. For himself, he is far stronger with the Lord Protector's staff than he would be with the king's sceptre; but then the crown, should he take it, would pass to his son by custom. So he refuses, in view of army opposition, but not too peremptorily, for he still hopes and wishes to wear the crown, if it may be done without too much war with his old Ironside following. In discussing whether or not he shall take the title, he uses no grand thought of right or plea of duty ; it is a shambling, hesitating, argument, with none of the thoroughness of Cromwell in it. "I suppose it will have to stand on its expediency," he says, and so it does, and being judged by Cromwell to be not expedient, is at last refused. On the 8th of May his Highness says : " I cannot undertake this Government with the title of king," and so keeps the Government as Protector, with such new advantages and stipulations as Parliament sees fit to give and make ; and on the 26th of June, 1657, Oliver Cromwell, now more formally recognised as Protector by the English Parliament, is solemnly installed in his Protectorship, in Westminster Hall, with grand State ceremony, and Parliament is prorogued until January, 1658, when it meets again with two Houses as of old, Lords and Commons. But into the Commons House now the excluded Members may (by terms of the Petition and Advice) enter if they will but take the oath, and they, or at least some of them, do take the oath, and entering range themselves in sturdy opposition. For ten days there is discontented debate in Parliament, with at least the echoings of disaffection outside; and on the 4th of February, therefore, Oliver Cromwell makes his last speech to the two Houses, saying: "You have not only disjointed yourselves, but the whole nation.........it hath not only been your endeavour to pervert the army while you have been sitting, but some of you have been listing of person by commission of Charles Stuart to join with any insurrection that may be made. And what is likely to come upon this, the enemy being ready to invade us, but even present blood and confusion?.........And if this be the end of your sitting, and this be your carriage, I think it high time that an end be put to your sitting. And I do dissolve this Parliament! And let God be judge between you and me." And now for a brief seven months governs alone again Oliver Cromwell, and on the 3rd of September, 1658, dies.

Oliver Cromwell dead, the Protectorate was dead too. It had never been a Government created by the people, it was the work of one resolute man. During the storm-strife provoked by Charles Stuart's arrogant imbecility, Cromwell had taken the helm of the State ship, and had navigated her, roughly but safely, through tempest, fury, and dangerous passages. But he had allowed none other of the crew to study navigation, nor to share with him the piloting; and when the rudder slipped from his hand, palsied by death, the poor Protectorate bark drifted to wreck, because none had been trained to fill his place. Cromwell's was a one-man rule, a pure despotism. Two thousand years earlier he would have been carried into Rome on the shields of his soldiers, and saluted "Imperator." Cromwell was no Republican; but he was a grand Englishman, who pushed to the front by virtue of his sturdy thoroughness, and who did mighty service for the nation whose authority he took, whose power he wielded. One with whom he dealt roughly said of him: "One could bear a little with Oliver Cromwell, though contrary to his oath of fidelity to the Parliament, contrary to his duty to the public, contrary to the respect he owed to that venerable body from whom he received his

authority, he usurped the functions of Government. His
merit was so extraordinary, that our judgments, our passions,
might be blinded by it. He made his way to empire by the
most illustrious actions; he had under his command an army
that had made him a conqueror, and a people that had made
him their general." The author of a fine history of "Democracy," recently published in Massachusetts, describes Cromwell as "hypocrite in his religion, a fanatic in his politics, and
a despot in his rule." That he was "a despot in his rule," is
true; that he was a "fanatic in his politics," I see no evidence. Clearly a monarchist, he trampled on the monarchy
and accepted a Government without a king; was content
with a Protectorate with one chamber, equally content with
a Protectorate with two chambers. Having overthrown the
king, would have accepted himself the kingly title, had it
not been for the dangerous opposition of men who were
alike fanatics in politics and religion. Whether Cromwell
was, or was not, a "hypocrite in religion," is harder perhaps
to decide, and I may not be the best one to express an
opinion. Many great leaders have professed themselves
God-sent, and even I, who would always regard such a
profession as utterly untrue in fact, am not prepared to say
that the utterer is necessarily a hypocrite. Hindostan gave
us recently a great leader claiming to be god-sent. The
Moslem, twelve centuries ago, had his Mohammed. That
Cromwell was a "fanatic" in his religion is, I think, more
easily proveable; and that he was, at any rate, in the last
eleven years of his life "a hypocrite" in his politics, is, I
think, capable of demonstration. But, despite all this, he
was a man of huger stature and of mightier will than any other
who lived in his age. He made the haughty Spaniard bend;
forced Mazarin to be tender to Piedmontese Protestants;
compelled the sturdy Dutchman to admit England's supremacy; and made his brief page of power dazzling with the
glory of his grand rule. He died, and the night of his life
was without starlight; his grave without honour afforded no
shelter to his bones. A people whom he had overmastered
became again willing servants to the dynasty he had ex-
pelled. Sole ruler of his race, his sceptre fell as his coffin
was lowered. The might of his manhood had offshoot in
no breast. The Captain is dead, and the wind and waves
urge the helpless ship to ruin, for amongst the crew none
dares take his place.

II.—WASHINGTON.

On the 22nd of February, 1732, nearly three-quarters of a century after the death of Cromwell, George Washington was born at the family homestead on Bridges Creek, on the Virginia side of the Potomac River. Washington was the offspring of a royalist family of estate and position, and his early associations with the friends and relatives of Lord Fairfax were calculated to increase his feeling of reverence for Monarchical and aristocratic traditions. When yet only nineteen years of age, George Washington was appointed Major and Adjutant-General of the Virginian Militia, and before he was twenty-two was charged with a most difficult and dangerous mission to those of the Indians and French then united in arms against the English Colonists, and also to the tribes of Indians who had not yet committed themselves to open hostilities. In this mission he exhibited much prudence, firmness, and devotion, coupled with admirable tact and self-possession.

In April, 1754, Washington fought his first battle with a small French force; and writing to his brother in the flush of the excitement, says how he "heard the bullets whistle." His first campaign ended most disastrously, his command having, after hard fighting, to surrender to a very superior force; but Washington received, nevertheless, the thanks of the House of Burgesses of Virginia for the bravery he exhibited.

In 1755 a great expedition, under General Braddock, having been organised against the Indians, Washington's talents were utilised by the English commander, who appointed Washington as a volunteer aide-de-camp, but only partially adopted the advice given by the young Virginian. The utter disregard by Braddock of part of Washington's information was attended by most fatal consequences; for the English general led his troops into an ambuscade of Indians and Frenchmen, against which he had been warned, where the English regulars were literally cut to pieces, and Braddock himself was mortally wounded. In this sad business Washington distinguished himself alike for his courage, his modesty, and his wisdom; and when, a little later, the Colony of Virginia raised special forces to defend its boundaries against attacks from the French and Indians, Washington was, with the full assent of his countrymen, appointed Commander-in-Chief of the Colonial forces (somewhat against the wish of Governor Dinwiddie, who behaved with coldness and ungraciousness to the Virginian militia-man). The position of the young Commander-in-Chief was further embarrassed, by the fact that any officer holding a commission from the king refused to obey orders from an officer whose commission was only signed by the Governor; and we find Washington journeying to Boston in the hope to get himself and officers put upon the regular establishment, with commissions direct from King George III. It is useless now to speculate on what might have been the result on Washington's military future had his request been complied with. Luckily for the struggles for independence, his demand in this respect was refused. Theodore Parker, speaking of his severity as a military disciplinarian at this period, says: "From natural disposition, he loved the exercise of power. But he was singularly careful to defer to the civil authority when possible. If the right was doubtful, the conscientious young soldier left it to be exercised by the magistrate, not by the military arm. This is to be noted, because it is so rare for military men to abstain from tyranny." Washington's position was a very painful one; he had to defend a wide-stretching frontier against a wily and savage enemy, and this with an utterly inadequate force, badly supplied with munitions of war. He was thwarted and snubbed by Governor Dinwiddie, and nearly all his requests for necessaries in the conduct of military operations were disregarded. Washington's health entirely broke down under these varied annoyances, and he ultimately resigned his position. Having been elected to the House of Burgesses of Virginia, he took his seat in 1759, being greeted on his entry to the Legislature by the special thanks of the House for the services he had rendered. To these thanks Washington could make no reply; his talents were not those of the orator. Self-possessed in face of danger, he was unnerved amidst his friends by the praise thus publicly tendered to him.

In the House of Burgesses George Washington was not, therefore, at first a conspicuous figure, save as the soldier who had earned its thanks prior to his installation. There is, however, a storm rising through the land which shall so endanger the liberties of the citizens, and excite their wrath, that a man of Washington's stature cannot long be overlooked. The Navigation Laws enforced by England against the Colonies had entirely excluded the Colonists from trade with foreign countries; had subjected the trade between the various Colonies to heavy duties, and had either totally prohibited, or imposed prohibitory restraints on, all Colonial manufactures thought likely to interfere with the manufacturing interests of the mother country. Much discontent and dissatisfaction had been produced, especially in New England, by the operation of the Navigation Laws; and in 1760 this feeling of discontent was aggravated by an attempt made in Boston to collect, under writs of assistance, duties on foreign sugar and molasses, which had been smuggled into Massachusetts. Those writs of assistance were resisted before the law courts as unconstitutional, the question being argued so eloquently by the famous James Otis, that it is said that all his hearers went away ready to take up arms to resist the enforcement of such writs. The litigation on these writs of assistance was really the first potent step in the struggle for independence—the beginning of the great American Republic.

At the conclusion of the French war, the most active efforts were made by the British men-of-war, acting under stringent orders from the Home Government, to suppress the clandestine trade theretofore carried on with the Spanish Colonies. To this the New England men replied by resolving not to purchase British fabrics, and the home trade was in consequence much diminished.

In 1764 the ill-advised Ministry of George III. sought to levy taxes in the Colonies, and in 1765 the famous Stamp Act was passed. Washington, who had hitherto been a devoted royalist, and had shown himself submissive to all the procedures of the Home Government, now denounces "this unconstitutional method of taxation." The resistance to the Stamp Act was so great that it was repealed on the 18th of March, 1766; and Washington then writes that all "who were instrumental in procuring the repeal are entitled to the thanks of every British subject, and have mine cordially." So that in the spring of 1766 Washington not only regarded himself as a British subject, but actually raised no objection—perhaps saw no objection—to the clause of the repealing act—so much impeached by Henry, Otis, Franklin, and the Adamses—which declared that "the king, with the consent of Parliament, had power and authority to make laws and statutes of sufficient force and validity to bind the Colonies and people of America, in all cases whatsoever." Those who contended for principles in America still protested against this clause, but Washington took no part in the protest. He remained quietly at Mount Vernon attending to his plantation. Year by year the attitude of the Home Government grew more menacing, and the dissatisfaction in the Colonies grew more marked. In 1767 a variety of duties were enacted for collection in the Colonies. To prepare for a possible struggle "armed negotiators," in the shape of two regiments, were sent from England to Boston to protect the Commissioners of Customs. The inhabitants of the Bay State City resolved, in towns' meeting, that the king had no right to send troops thither without the consent of the Assembly, and quarters were refused to the troops, who were thereupon billeted in the State House, in Faneuil Hall, and other public buildings. The resistance offered in Massachusetts encouraged others. Washington in 1769 writes to his friend George Mason: "At a time when our lordly masters in Great Britain will be satisfied with nothing less than the deprivation of American freedom, it seems highly necessary that something should be done to avert the stroke, and maintain the liberty which we have derived from our ancestors. But the manner of doing it, to answer the purpose effectually, is the point in question. That no man should scruple, or hesitate a moment, in defence of so valuable a blessing, is clearly my opinion; yet arms should be the last resource."

In 1769, on the proposition of Washington, the burgesses of Virginia—following the example of the northern Colonies—pledged themselves neither to import nor use any goods, merchandise, or manufactures taxed by Parliament. Washington adhered rigorously to this, and strictly enjoined his London agent not to ship him anything subject to taxation.

In 1770 Lord North became Prime Minister in England, and he abandoned all the duties levied in 1767, save one, the right to a tax on tea, which he reserved, "to maintain the Parliamentary right of taxation." "A total repeal," he said, "cannot be thought of till America is prostrate at our feet." This tea tax, if it had been collected, would have produced not quite £300 a year. England spent £139,521,035 in the vain endeavour to enforce the tax!!

EARLY in 1773 Lord Dunmore was appointed Governor of Virginia, and despite the hostile feeling arising between the Colonists and the Government, Washington appears to have been on the most friendly and intimate terms with the Court Party, until the arrival in Virginia of the news of the monstrously mad and vindictive policy adopted by Lord North—a policy which it is now clear was actually strongly urged and enforced by George III.—by which the port of Boston was to be closed and its commerce entirely ruined. The whole of Massachusetts determined to stand by Boston, and the query now was, Would the other Colonies stand by Massachusetts? Washington offered to "raise one thousand men, and subsist them at my own expense, and march myself at their head for the relief of Boston." General Gage had encamped his infantry and artillery on Boston Common, and the cry went round the whole country to break off all intercourse with Great Britain, until the colony was restored to full enjoyment of all its rights; and further, to renounce all dealings with those on this American side, who should refuse to enter into a similar compact. On the 18th of July, 1774, a meeting was held in Fairfax County, at which a committee was appointed, with Washington as chairman, to draw up resolutions, which state first the illegal conduct of the British Government; covenant not to import or hold intercourse with England or any colony, town, or province refusing to agree to the plan adopted by the General Congress; then recommend a petition to the king, "lamenting the necessity of entering into measures that might be displeasing; declaring their attachment to his person, family, and Government, and their desire to continue in dependence upon Great Britain." The attachment to the person of "mad George" may be passed by as a phrase of fashion, and even when we remember that his family included the lustful and lying George IV., the corrupt and brutal Duke of York, the niggardly and paltry William IV., and the bestially immoral Duke of Cumberland, it must not be forgotten that the "family" was then very young, and the "attachment" was probably for the good qualities which the Royal Family might have manifested had their lives been reversed, and their vices passed for virtues.

On the 3rd of September, 1774, a General Congress of

fifty-one deputies, delegated from the various Colonies, assembled at Philadelphia (Georgia alone being unrepresented). It was from this Congress that the famous address was sent to England which won such high praise from the lips of Chatham. On his return from this Congress, the eloquent Patrick Henry was asked whom he considered the greatest amongst the men assembled there. He replied: "If you speak of eloquence, Mr. Rutledge, of South Carolina, is by far the greatest orator; but if you speak of solid information and sound judgment, Colonel Washington is unquestionably the greatest man on that floor." Even yet Washington—irritated as he and his friends had become by aristocratic misrule—had no sort of disposition to advocate any separation from the mother country. Writing to Captain Mackenzie as to Independence, he says: "I am well satisfied that no such thing is desired by any thinking man in all North America."

It is worthy notice that the struggle in England, out of which Cromwell grew into power, and that in America, which ended in the elevation of Washington to the chief magistrature, had each its inception in the denial of the right claimed by the king and his ministers to levy taxes without the consent of the taxed. It was not, says Washington, "against paying the duty of 3d. per pound on tea....... No, it is the right only that we have all along disputed." Although Washington appears to have been opposed to some of the extreme measures of resistance advocated by a strong party of the Eastern men, yet so soon as a definite course was resolved upon, he went loyally with the majority; and he wrote to his brother, "It is my full intention, if needful, to devote my life and fortune to the cause."

The crisis soon came; General Gage detached a body of regular troops to destroy some provincial military stores at Concord, Massachusetts. At Lexington Green these troops fired on the local yeomanry, and before night a large body of English troops had been literally chased into the City of Boston by the "minute men," who ran, gun in hand, from their industries, to revenge the blood recklessly shed on the road to Concord. The Massachusetts yeomen, in their indignation, blockaded the English army within the limits of Boston, and the second Philadelphia Congress shortly afterwards appointed George Washington Commander-in-Chief of the insurgent army, now assembled in front of the Bay State City. Washington—who had in no fashion sought the appointment, and whose nomination had been unanimous—when he accepted the position, added : " But lest some unlucky event should happen unfavourable to my reputation, I declare that I do not consider myself equal to the command I am honoured with. As to pay, I beg leave to assure Congress that, as no pecuniary consideration could have tempted me to accept this arduous employment, at the expense of my domestic ease and happiness, I do not wish to make any profit of it. I will keep an exact account of my expenses. These, I doubt not, they will discharge, and this is all I desire." Adams, in a letter written at the moment, praises highly the conduct of Washington, " a gentleman of one of the fairest fortunes upon the Continent, leaving his delicious retirement, his family and friends, sacrificing his ease, and hazarding all in the cause of his country. His views are noble and disinterested."

There is a tree at Cambridge—an old elm—where it is noted that Washington assumed his high command; and the first time I halted under the tree I tried hard to picture to myself the variously accoutred, roughly-dressed, badly-armed array of agriculturists which had so shut into Boston the well-drilled, well-armed, and highly-trained regular troops of the British Monarchy. The great fight at Bunker Hill—in which the gallant though unsuccessful attempt to fortify a position which would have commanded every portion of the City had shown the sturdy stuff of these New England " minute" men—had taken place prior to Washington's assumption of command. What army he found was to him very disappointing. Tired of merely watching the British forces, many of the newly-enrolled troops had returned to their farms, which sorely needed cultivation; and instead of 20,000 men supposed to be in camp, Washington only found there about 14,000 fit for service, and many of these without muskets or ammunition. The only troops presenting any appearance of drill or fair equipment were those from the small colony of Rhode Island. Theodore Parker says : " The camp was full of jealousies, rivalries, resentments, petty ambitions ; men thinking much for themselves, little for their imperilled nation." Washington desired to force General Howe into general action, but, on taking stock of the gunpowder in the stores, found that the whole supply of powder would not provide nine cartridges per man.

In the American, or "Continental," army, as it was called, there were many divisions of opinion and interest. Some of the New England officers were personally indisposed to co-operate with the Virginian gentleman, whom they found much too aristocratic for their home-spun fancies. To quote the words of Washington himself: "Confusion and discord existed in every department, which in a little time must have ended either in the separation of the army, or fatal contests with one another." While Washington was organising his troops, and slowly obtaining for them the necessary military equipment, he had the constant fear that the British army might be able to take advantage of the disorganisation in the newly-raised levies he commanded. But General Gage and General Howe were content, while waiting for reinforcements, to thunder away from Bunker Hill batteries, while keeping their troops within their own works; the Americans, from want of powder, making but scant reply to the noisy cannonade.

The delay in the siege produced many embarrassments. Men who were brave enough in a fight would not patiently wait, doing nothing, in front of this fortified city, while their farms went to ruin. Enlisted for one year only, many would not re-enlist at all. Those who did manifest willingness to re-enlist would only serve under officers of their own choice; and men from one Colony, as Connecticut, would not serve under Rhode Island officers. In a letter written at this juncture Washington says: "I find we are likely to be deserted at a most critical time......Our situation is truly alarming.....Could I have foreseen what I have experienced, and am likely to experience, no consideration upon earth should have induced me to accept this command." It must not be forgotten that the position of the men was not of the most enviable kind. "The first burst of revolutionary zeal had passed away; enthusiasm had been chilled by the inaction and monotony of a long encampment." No regular commissariat, and nearly all comforts absent. "The troops had suffered privations of every kind—want of fuel, clothing, provisions. They looked forward with dismay to the rigours of winter, and longed for their rustic homes and family firesides." Throughout the Colonies much more was expected from Washington than he was able to perform, his available force was over-rated, and his motives for inaction mis-construed. "I know," writes Washington on the 10th of February, 1776, "the unhappy predicament I stand in; I know that much is expected from me ; I know that, without men, without arms, without ammunition, without anything fit for the accommodation of a soldier, little is to be done, and, what is mortifying, I know that I cannot stand justified to the world without exposing my own weakness, and injuring the cause by declaring my wants; which I am determined not to do further than unavoidable necessity brings every man acquainted with them...... My own situation is so irksome to me at times that, if I did not consult the public good more than my own tranquillity, I should long ere this have put everything on the cast of a die. So far from my having an army of 20,000 men well armed, I have been here with less than half that number, including sick, furloughed, and on command, and those neither armed nor clothed as they should be. In short, my situation has been such that I have been obliged to use art to conceal it from my own officers...... To have the eyes of the whole Continent fixed with anxious expectation of hearing of some great event, and to be restrained in every military operation for want of the necessary means of carrying it on, is not very pleasing, especially as the means used to conceal my weakness from the enemy conceal it also from our friends."

Ultimately, as every one knows, the regular army of England evacuated Boston, beleagured by "an undisciplined band of husbandmen," and General Howe and his well-equipped legions sought safety in the warships from the persevering advances of Washington to the reduction of the Bay State City.

Convinced that "no accommodation could be effected with Great Britain, on acceptable terms," and that "a protracted war was inevitable," Washington now sought to force upon Congress the need for enlisting an army disposable for the whole war, and available in any portion of the continent. While his energetic remonstrances produced some improvements, there was still much left to be desired. The base of operations was changed from Massachusetts to New York State. Now, to a much larger degree, than when near Boston, Washington felt the effects of treachery; one plot nearly cost him his life, his very body-guards having been corrupted. Those who were the most willing agents of Monarchy and Toryism were found amongst the Quaker families, one of which, for its cowardly rascality, still receives from the British Government a pension of £4,000 a year.

On the 4th of July, 1776, Independence was declared in words; but a severe reverse, sustained by Washington on Long Island, made many persons despair of its realisation. The troops he had under him in this campaign were very ill-equipped. "Many of the yeomen of the country, hastily summoned from the plough, were destitute of arms, in lieu of which they were ordered to bring with them a shovel, spade, or pickaxe, or a scythe straightened and fastened to a pole." The effect of the defeat on Long Island was shown in the wholesale return to their farms in Connecticut alone of more than 4,000 men. Despite all this, Washington always presented a firm face to the enemy, even when himself nearly heart-broken, by the disregard of his entreaties by Congress, and by the indisposition shown by the several Colonial Governments to second his exertions, and comply with his requirements.

In September, 1776, the difficulties of his position, and the defection of some of his troops, seem to have rendered Washington desperate, and in some of the frays he risked his life needlessly. His natural calm, however, soon returned, and though evidently very doubtful as to the possibility of ultimate victory, he now recommenced those series of careful manœuvres which so embarrassed the English and German generals to whom he was opposed. General Washington had the danger of his position considerably heightened by the conduct of General Lee and General Gates. The first a brave and ambitious soldier, who aspired to the chief command, and who regarded Washington's star as on the wane, actually withheld reinforcements from Washington's crippled forces, when the latter was retreating through the Jerseys after the British successes at Fort Washington. The second (Gates) about the same time pleaded ill-health as an excuse for avoiding a command, so that he might go to Philadelphia to intrigue against Washington before the Congress.

If not entirely disregarding, at any rate in no fashion publicly noticing, the hostility of Lee and Gates, General Washington gave courage to his army, and restored the sinking spirits of the American Colonists, by a most brilliant dash at the Hessian quarters at Trenton, where, with actually inferior forces, he created an utter panic amongst the British troops. Just after the Trenton victory there is a fine illustration of the slender thread on which hung the future of American Independence. Several of the regiments wished to return home; only enlisted for one year, their term of service had expired, their pay was in arrear, their presence was indispensable to Washington, at any rate for a short time, and by the offer of a bounty of ten dollars per man, they were induced to agree to stay for six weeks; but there was no money in the pay-chest, and the poor, penniless men could not rely on promises of future payment. Washington had to borrow £150 to enable him to pay the most pressing, and thus temporarily kept his forces together.

At the close of 1776 Washington was invested by Congress with almost dictatorial powers, and in acknowledging the resolution of Congress, he says: "I find Congress have done me the honour to entrust me with powers, in my military capacity, of the highest nature and almost unlimited extent. Instead of thinking myself freed from all civil obligations by this mark of their confidence, I shall constantly bear in mind that, as the sword was the last resort for the preservation of our liberties, so it ought to be the first thing laid aside when those liberties are firmly established." Washington was true in letter and in spirit to this promise. No enticement of ambition made him waver for one moment in his fidelity to the trust he had accepted.

Although Washington possessed nearly absolute authority, he seems to have been extremely reluctant to use it, and often permitted Congress to interfere, and to make appointments and arrangements which were neither consonant with his views nor with the dignity of his position. This is of course open to the criticism, that had Washington been less wise, it might have been very difficult for him to have held together the Eastern men, some of whom honestly seemed to entertain the notion that despite his professions Washington was really aiming at the establishment of a military rule.

The surrender of General Burgoyne, and the division under his command, to General Gates in the north; and the repulse of the army under Washington at Germantown, gave room for some of the disaffected to revive the intrigues hostile to the Commander-in-Chief. General Gates not only omitted to report to George Washington the surrender by Burgoyne, but actually corresponded secretly with dissatisfied officers in Washington's camp to induce them to cabal against their chief. The glorious achievements of Gates were compared with the disasters which attended

Washington in this campaign. It was overlooked that Gates —who was afterwards utterly ruined by his defeats in the South—was only carrying out Washington's original far-seeing plan of operations, and with a very large force at his command, aided by a generally favourable spirit in the part of the country where his military operations were conducted, while Washington had an inferior force weakened by troops he had detached to aid Gates—which troops General Gates now withheld from his Commander—and was in a lukewarm State, where many were disaffected to the American cause. Washington himself says that "General Gates was to be exalted on the ruin of my reputation and influence." The American army had great difficulty in obtaining provisions; in some places where the inhabitants had provisions and cattle, they denied them to General Washington, and preferred taking their cattle and food to Philadelphia, where the English army gave them higher prices.

In 1778 Washington writes: "For some days past there has been little less than a famine in the camp; a part of the army has been for a week without any kind of flesh, and the rest three or four days. Naked and starving as they are, we cannot enough admire the incomparable patience and fidelity of the soldiery." Philadelphia was occupied during the winter by a British army 20,000 strong, provided with every comfort; while Washington was at Valley Forge, besieging the city after a fashion, with not more than 5,000 men, in sadly wretched plight, sometimes without ammunition to serve its cannon. At last General Howe resigned the command of the British army to Sir Henry Clinton, by whom Philadelphia was evacuated, under orders from the Home Government.

Now came the effect of the treaty concluded by Franklin, between France and America, in the aid of a French squadron and French funds. This French contingent rather increased the temporary difficulties of Washington as Commander-in-Chief, although the general effect of the French alliance was to render the British prospects in the Colonies one of the gloomiest character. George III. was wicked enough, personally, to encourage the barbarous employment of Indians; and scalping, ravishing, and burning were amongst the means ineffectually resorted to by an anointed king to win back the affections of his subjects. The English Church and English landed aristocracy, by public addresses, encouraged their king in his cruel obstinacy, and the war to subdue the Colonies was to be carried on in despite of the failures already experienced. In America the French alliance had at least one bad effect; many deemed that the war would now cease at once; that there was, therefore, no necessity for continuous supplies to the army; for long drills or great preparations. The several Colonies were unwilling to comply with military requisitions, which they thought had now become needless, and General Washington found himself exceedingly embarrassed, and his popularity endangered by his persistence in requiring the means for continuing a long, arduous, and costly struggle; and at the close of 1778 he writes: " Our affairs are in a more distressed, ruinous, and deplorable condition than they have been since the commencement of the war."

Difficulties in the internal condition of the army, and its relation to the various States, may be best illustrated by the case of the Jersey Brigade, in which, in 1779, the officers —who complained that they could get no pay, and that their families were starving—refused to march unless their arrears were first discharged. Here Washington acted with great tact as well as with great firmness; and while entirely denying the right of the officers or men to utilise their military position, he at the same time pressed Congress and the State Legislature to deal more patriotically with their defenders in the field.

For weeks at a time the army was on half allowance of food, sometimes without meat, sometimes without bread, sometimes without both. Congress being destitute of the power of levying general taxes, the State Governments were each severally charged with the duty of supporting their own quota of troops to the army. This naturally resulted in great inequality and discontent. Some States furnished their troops amply with pay and clothing; some States were niggardly in these respects; and some States were so neglectful as to leave their troops practically destitute, producing in these latter a more discontented and mutinous spirit from the contrast with their more favoured brethren.

To remedy this disastrous condition of things increased powers were sought for Washington, but any augmentation of his already large authority was strenuously objected to by some of the best men. It was urged, " that his influence was already too great; that even his virtues afforded motives for alarm; that the enthusiasm of the army, joined to the kind of dictatorship already confided to him, placed Congress and the United States at his mercy."

In the middle of 1780 matters came to a crisis. Two Connecticut regiments turned out in armed meeting, resolved to march home, " or at best to gain subsistence at the point of the bayonet." Suppressing this mutinous outbreak with considerable difficulty, Washington found it nearly impossible to get bread for his famishing soldiers, and in a spirit of deep despondency he wrote : " I have almost ceased to hope." Yet when the English commander, informed by his spies of the condition of Washington's forces, marched to attack the American troops, he found that Washington's great personal influence was enough to arouse their patriotism and unite their ranks ; and instead of a discontented and disorganised rabble, the British were confronted by a compact and well-ordered, though badly-equipped, army, before whom the English forces retreated, despite the superiority on the royalist side.

In 1780 Washington seemed at the end of his resources. He writes : "I see nothing before us but accumulating distress. We have been half our time without provisions, and are likely to continue so. We have no magazines, nor money to form them; and in a little time we shall have no men, if we have no money to pay them." The Pennsylvanian troops mutinied in 1781, and compelled Congress to treat with them. Encouraged by this, a part of the Jersey troops also revolted; but Washington, here close at hand, sternly stamped out this revolt. A striking feature connected with these mutinies by the American troops against Congress is, that the mutineers nevertheless remained faithful to the American cause, and made prisoners of agents sent to them with money and promises from the English camp.

In October, 1781, the war was practically decided by the surrender of Lord Cornwallis at Yorktown ; and it is needless to dwell here at any length on the closing scenes of a struggle which terminated on the 20th of January, 1783, by the signature of the treaty at Paris.

The army, as in the case of the Commonwealth struggle, was now a power in the land. The pay of officers and men was in arrear; they had many grievances ; the future conduct of affairs was doubtful; there was a suggestion of—if not an absolute attempt to organise—a military government. One veteran officer took upon himself to suggest to Washington that "the title of King would be attended with some material advantages." Washington replied without hesitation that no event in the war had given him so much pain as "your information of there being such ideas expressed in the army," which "I must view with abhorrence and reprehend with severity." With the army General Washington had a most difficult task. Their grievances were real, and to the Congress at Philadelphia he represented these in the strongest terms. To the army itself he was sternly firm in forbidding any use of their military force in support of their claims against Congress.

At last, on the 23rd of December, 1783, at Annapolis, having first in methodical fashion settled up his pecuniary accounts—and without one farthing pay or profit or recompense for his military services—George Washington relinquished the authority the nation had entrusted to his hands, and retired to private life without a stain on his shield, unhesitatingly disregarding those allurements of power which would have been irresistible to a weaker man. It is noteworthy that the total amount of Washington's account—including £1,982 10s. for secret service—was only £19,306 11s. 9d., and this was from July, 1775, to December 28th, 1783. In General Washington's own private book there is an entry that he was a considerable loser from items that, "in the perplexity of business," he had omitted to charge. No claim was ever urged by him to have this deficiency made up.

In 1785, the Assembly of Virginia, by an unanimous vote, gave to Washington a number of shares, value about 40,000 dollars, in two schemes connected with the navigation of the Potomac and James Rivers. Washington, who had resolved not personally to accept any valuable reward, asked and obtained the permission of the Virginian Legislature to apply the gifts to objects of a public nature, and ultimately the value was devoted to educational purposes.

The conclusion of the struggle with the mother country left the many, discontented with the burdens and troubles of the war, a full opportunity for the expression of their dissatisfaction. The Government had little or no effective authority now that the war was concluded, and martial law no longer prevailed. "The confederation," writes Washington, "appears to me to be little more than a shadow without the substance, and Congress a nugatory body, their ordinances being little attended to." Colonel Henry Lee having applied to George Washington to use his influence with the people, the latter thus replied from Mount Vernon: "You talk, my good Sir, of employing influence to appease the present tumults in Massachusetts. I know not where that influence is to be found, or, if attainable, that it would be a proper remedy for the disorders. Influence is not government. Let us have a government by which our lives, liberties, and properties will be secured, or let us know the worst at once. There is a call for decision. Know precisely what the insurgents aim at. If they have real grievances, redress them if possible; or acknowledge the justice of them, and your inability to do it at the moment. If they have not, employ the force of the Government against them at once. If this is inadequate, all will be convinced that the superstructure is bad and wants support.............Let the reins of Government be braced and held with a steady hand, and every violation of the constitution be reprehended. If defective, let it be amended; but not suffered to be trampled upon whilst it has an existence."

Something had to be done to bind the independent Colonies together. "A government," says Marshall, "authorised to declare war, but relying on independent States for the means of prosecuting it; capable of contracting debts, and of pledging the public faith for their payment, but depending on thirteen distinct sovereignties for the preservation of that faith, could only be rescued from ignominy and contempt by finding those sovereignties administered by men exempt from the passions incident to human nature."

On the 25th of May, 1787, a Congress assembled at Philadelphia, of which George Washington was appointed President. After several months of doubtful, and sometimes bitter, discussion and uncertainty, this Congress published the Constitution of the United States of America. Of this Constitution Washington writes to Lafayette that, while not free from defects, "the general Government is not invested with more powers than are indispensably necessary to perform the functions of a good government," and 'that these powers, as the appointment of all rulers will forever arise from, and at short stated intervals recur to, the free suffrages of the people, are so distributed among the legislative executive and judicial branches into which the general government is arranged, that it can never be in danger of degenerating into a monarchy, an oligarchy, or an ristocracy, or any other despotic or oppressive form, so long as there shall remain any virtue in the body of the people."

Under the New Constitution the first Wednesday in January, 1789, was appointed for the election by the people of their first President, and the vote was unanimous in the choice of George Washington.

III.—THE CONTRAST.

Though in many respects occupying positions of similar character, no two men could be more dissimilar than Oliver Cromwell and George Washington. The first, as is shown by his life, grew into a ruler of men by the force of his own character and by the warrior skill he manifested, and this in spite of the leading spirits of his age. The second became the chief magistrate of a newly-made nation by the force of the times, by the suffrages of men with intellects clearer, and even bolder, than his own, and because of the thorough faithfulness he had shown to the cause to which he had most disinterestedly and unselfishly devoted himself. Cromwell made his will the law for the nation, and used his sword to enforce the law. Washington accepted the will of the majority, which had entrusted him with authority, as the law which he was bound to obey. Cromwell played the army, and especially his Ironsides, against the Parliament. Washington submitted most completely to Congress, and refused to side with the dissatisfied army when it wished to rely on its weapons to enforce the redressal even of its just grievances. Neither Cromwell nor Washington were really Republicans. Cromwell, though destroying the Monarchy, never ceased to be Royalist, and took himself the throne—uncrowned, it is true, save by the trooper's helmet, in which he had fought his way to the right to wield the Protector's sceptre-staff. Washington, wrestling against a far-away and blundering Government, amidst men with more vigorous politics than he had learned, went with the stream, and became Republican *malgré lui*—that is, he accepted the form, and honestly strove to adopt the spirit from the grander brains who gave to the world the famous Declaration of Independence. Washington made a better man than Cromwell. Cromwell was a bigger man than Washington. Washington rejected the mere whisper of a crown, and indignantly condemned the suggestion, even before it had found clear shape of utterance. Cromwell created the spirit which formally presented to him the kingly dignity for acceptance, and he weighed the glittering bauble regretfully in his hands before he put it aside as an ornament scarcely valuable enough to wear, as against the danger of weakness it brought to the wearer.

There can be few men more thoroughly true and honourable than George Washington. History tells of *no* other man that you may rank in the same line, with Oliver Cromwell. Washington has many statues, for the century which has marched over his grave has freshened each year the laurel-wreath with which the giant child-Republic crowned its foster-father. Oliver Cromwell has few or no monuments. The country to which he devoted his virility has seen his bones rattle in gibbet chains, and for two hundred years has, on its knees, thanked God that hollow, tinsel, lying, lustful, Stuart was restored to rule England, in lieu of this fierce, sturdy, Puritan man, whose soul inbreathed power only because the power carried England's standard higher.

A fitting emblem for Oliver Cromwell is presented by the grandly glorious Western sunset. Still mighty in the fierceness of its rays, few eyes can look steadily into the golden radiance of that evening sun; the strongest must lower their glances, dazzled by its brilliance. Every cloud is rich with ruddy gilding, as if the mere presence of that sun made glorious the very path it trod. And yet, while one looks, the tints deepen into scarlet, crimson, purple, as though that sun had been some mailed warrior, who had gained his grand pre-eminence by force of steel, and had left a bloody track to mark his steps to power. And even while you pause to look, the thick dark veil of night falls over all, with a blackness so cold, complete and impenetrable, as to make you almost doubt the reality of the mighty magnificence which yet has scarcely ceased. In the eventide of his life's day such a sun was Cromwell. Few men might look him fairly in the face as peers in strength. His presence gives a glory to the history page which gilds the smaller men whom he led. And yet Tredah and Worcester, Preston and Dunbar, and a host of other encrimsoned clouds, compel us to remember how much the sword was used to carve his steps to rule. And then comes the night of death—so thickly black that even the grave cannot protect Cromwell's bones from the gibbet's desecration.

And not unfittingly might the sunrise, almost without twilight, in the same land, do service as emblem for George Washington. He must be a bold man who, in the mists and chill of the dying night, not certain of its coming, would dare watch for the rising sun. And yet, while he watches, the silver rays, climbing over the horizon's hill, shed light and clearness round; and soon a golden warmth breathes life and health and beauty into blade and bud, giving hope of the meridian splendour soon to come. George Washington was the morning sun of a day whose noontide has not yet been marked—a day of liberty rendered more possible now that slavery's cloud no longer hides the sun; a day the enduring light of which depends alone on the honest Republicanism of those who now dwell in that land where Washington was doorkeeper in Liberty's temple.

Printed by ANNIE BESANT and CHARLES BRADLAUGH, 28, Stonecutter Street London, E.C.

AND THE

COMING STRUGGLE.

BY

C. BRADLAUGH.

(THIRD EDITION.)

LONDON:
FREETHOUGHT PUBLISHING COMPANY,
28, Stonecutter Street, E.C.

PRICE TWOPENCE.

LONDON:
PRINTED BY CHARLES BRADLAUGH AND ANNIE BESANT,
28, STONECUTTER STREET, E.C.

THE LAND, THE PEOPLE, AND THE COMING STRUGGLE.

THE growth of the Agricultural Labourers' movement in England, the increasing agitation for the repeal of the law of hypothec in Scotland, and the wail from ruined farmers in the Lowlands, all serve to show that it will be on the Land Question that that large section of the English aristocracy which regards the preservation of territorial rights and privileges as essential to good Government will shortly have to encounter a stronger force, and to cope with a wider movement, than has been manifested in England during the last 200 years. It is in connection with the Land Question that thoughtful working men are commencing to look for a speedy solution of some of the most difficult problems as to the more striking evils of modern society.

So long as skilled labour in mine or factory could easily earn the means of purchasing grain from foreign lands, men remained comparatively quiescent, while the native landholders usurped power and avoided obligations. To-day labour struggles despairingly against reduced wage, and to-morrow's outlook is still more gloomy. While wages are decreasing, the cost of living is augmenting. House rent in England and Wales alone has increased from £36,575,600 per year—which it was in 1846—to £80,726,502—which it had become in 1873—a growth of more than thirty-four millions of pounds in twenty-seven years, all paid by the poor to the rich. The annual income from land, including mines and minerals, has increased, since 1698, from a little over £6,000,000 to about £200,000,000.

The bulk of the land is in the hands of comparatively few persons, and these monopolise the House of Lords, and materially control the House of Commons. In Scotland, 171 persons own 11,029,228 acres of land, and 409 other persons own other 3,876,980 acres, that is, 580 persons own 14,906,208 acres. In England 773 persons own 8,219,468 of acres, making that, in England and Scotland, 1353 persons own more than twenty-three millions of acres.

In too many cases these landholders treat their freehold rights as of infinitely more importance than the happiness of the peasantry of the neighbourhood. Ancient footpaths are closed, common rights denied, game preserving and rabbit breeding carried on to the point of crop annihilation, county members nominated and returned as if the title to the freehold carried with it monopoly of political right; and a most contemptuous indifference is shown as to the condition of the tiller of the soil, or, what is even worse, there is a mockery of charity, to remedy in small part the evil which the very charitable gentry have themselves created.

For the last 163 years this landed aristocracy has been the real governing class, superseding the Crown, and, until 1832, entirely controlling the people.

During this time—viz., from 1714—the standing army has been built up, and the National Debt has been almost entirely created, while Imperial taxation, and the rent-rolls of the few privileged ones, have enormously increased; thus the burdens of Imperial and local taxation have been shifted from the shoulders of the landholder to those of the labourer. For since, with the accession of the Brunswick family to the English throne, the monarch, excluded even from the political councils of the nation—at first because he could not speak the language of his subjects, as in the case of George I.; then because of his indifference, as in that of George II.; and then because of his oft-recurring insanity, as in that of George III.—has been practically reduced to a mere costly show puppet, it is impossible for the student of our history not to remark how the landed aristocracy have utilised their possession of political power for the transference from their own shoulders of the bulk of the local and Imperial taxation.

Amongst the agricultural classes, pauperism has become more permanent and more widespread, and certain classes of crime and misery have more prevailed, as the land monopoly has become more complete.

The agricultural labourers of many English counties, and notably of Dorset, Wilts, Gloucester, Norfolk, Suffolk, have, from bad and insufficient food and shelter, so degenerated, that their state is a disgrace to any civilised country in the world. The *Westminster Review* urges, on the evidence of Mr. Simon, Medical Inspector, that rather more than one-half of our Southern population are so badly fed, that a class of starvation diseases, and a general deterioration of mind, must result. In Berkshire, Oxfordshire, and Somersetshire, insufficiency of nitrogenous food is the average.

Landowners, in the large majority of instances, and this whether the proprietor be Whig or Tory, regard their tenants as bound to follow the politics of their freeholder, and as fairly liable to ejectment when malcontent.

Mr. Latham, a magistrate of Cheshire, before the House of Commons' Committee, said that "it was the evil of property that a man considers that he owns not only the property itself, but that he owns the souls of the tenants also."

The Duke of Buccleuch, not content with the influence which his vast holdings in Scotland give him, has actually followed the practice of manufacturing voters, by granting to certain persons feu rents or freehold rent-charges, to qualify them for county voters, and this to such a glaring extent as to excite popular indignation. This fabrication, however immoral, is held to be legal, although, since the grant of the rent-charges, his Grace has actually sold to a railway company a considerable portion of the property charged. This Duke of Buccleuch, in his Wanlockhead mining works, in Dumfriesshire, employs a number of wretched lead miners, who sometimes do not see five pounds in actual money from year's end to year's end, being constantly in debt to the overseer's shop. They are badly paid and tyrannically dealt with.

In Wales, because at the general election in 1868 the advantage was "won by the Liberals, through the votes of the freeholders and leaseholders of cottages, the landlords," says the *Westminster Review*, "enraged at their defeat, proceeded to wreak their vengeance upon those of their tenants who had presumed to vote in accordance with their convictions." Mr. Harris, a gentleman of independent means in Cardiganshire, "believed that as many as 200 notices to quit had been served in Cardiganshire alone, at Lady Day after the election. He was himself aware of from thirty to thirty-five served upon tenant farmers, in some cases where the families had been 200 years upon the estates; in others where considerable sums had been laid out by the farmers in improving their farms, which, as the law now stands in England, they have no means of recovering."

In Ireland you have a landlord—perhaps like the late Most Noble the Marquis of Hertford—constantly residing out of the country, having no sympathy or connection with his property, except that of sucking it as dry of vitality as the law permits him. At election times, "his lieutenant, the agent, armed with notices to quit, and backed by the police, is sufficiently formidable. Threats of eviction (and more than half a million evictions have taken place in Ireland during the last thirty years), distresses, and demands for immediate payment of rent, large arrears of which are usually due," assail the voter. "It has long been the practice in Ireland for the landlords to collect together their tenants who are voters, to place them upon cars, and send them in a body under the agent to record their votes at the polling-booth. These parties of voters are frequently escorted by detachments of police and military, on the alleged ground that there is fear of their being prevented by violence from going to the polling place: it is observable that these escorts are always asked for by the landlords or their agents, never by the voters themselves." General MacMurdo, who commanded a brigade in Ireland at the 1868 election, admitted, before the House of Commons' Committee, in answer to Mr. Gathorne Hardy, that these voters are practically prisoners, one of whom would not be allowed to go away even if he desired, until he had been escorted to the polling-booth.

Under the feudal system in England, bad as it was, there were no seignorial rights without a declaration of corresponding duties—the vassals gave their services, and in return the lord apportioned them land, and gave them some sort of protection; but now the lord claims the land as his own freehold, without any admission of obligation accompanying the ownership, and regarding himself as unduly taxed if any fiscal imposition touches his pocket. In many cases, in order to relieve themselves from the burdens of supporting the poor, the great proprietors have ordered the wretched cottages of the labourers working on their lands to be destroyed. The tillers of the soil cleared out from a noble landowner's domains get shelter how they can, in hovels in bad condition and dearly priced, where they are huddled together, as the following picture, taken from the Parliamentary Blue Book, shows:—"Modesty must be an unknown virtue, decency an unimaginable thing, where, in one small chamber, with the beds lying as thickly as they can be packed, father, mother, young men, lads, grown and growing up girls—two and sometimes three generations—are herded promiscuously, where every operation of the toilette and of nature—dressing, undressing, births and deaths—is performed by each within the sight or hearing of all; where children of both sexes, to as high an age as twelve or fourteen, or even more, occupy the same bed; where the whole atmosphere is sensual, and human nature is degraded into something below the level of the swine. It is a hideous picture, and the picture is drawn from life."

In Scotland, even under the old semi-barbarous, but patriarchal, system of clanship, the land was treated as the property of the entire clan—so much so, at any rate, that the chief of the clan had no power, under penalty of death, to alienate any portion of the land without formal authority of the clan given in solemn assembly, and the meanest member had privileges in connection with the cultivation of the soil.

In Ireland, the old Brehon laws as to the land are more clear and distinct than on most other topics. Each member of the local society or tribe had a life interest in the land of the society; and when he lost it by death, or by quitting the tribe, a new partition of land was made, so as to prevent too large a portion falling into the hands of any one holder. And yet, after generations of progress, we find that at the passing of the Church Disestablishment Act the land was practically in the hands of a few large families, who consider that they are entitled to hold the soil without any sort of consequent liability to provide for the lives or to ensure the happiness of the inhabitants. Under the provisions of the Irish Land Act, 1871, and of the Church Disestablishment Act, some facilities are now offered in Ireland to small tenants to become landowners, and under the second Act 4000 proprietaries, averaging twenty acres, have been created, and 6000 similar freeholds are said to be in course of purchase. Unfortunately, no similar possibility exists in any other part of the United Kingdom.

The land is constantly increasing in value, or, at any rate, a higher rental is exacted by the freeholder, and yet there is no corresponding contribution from the landowner towards the imperial burdens; on the contrary, the landowner shifts the fiscal burdens on to the labourer.

In illustration of this, the territorial incomes for England and Wales alone amounted, in 1800, to £22,500,000; in 1810 they had increased seven millions; in 1850 they had swollen to £41,118,329; in 1861 they had grown to

£54,678,412; to-day, including mines and minerals, they exceed £198,000,000; while the land-tax, which in 1800 was about £2,032,000 per annum, is now reduced by redemption to about one-half that amount.

Since the date of the usurpation of power by the territorial aristocracy—viz., since the accession to the throne of the House of Brunswick—land has, according to the *Westminster Review*, increased in value in Great Britain to a startling extent. Our taxation is constantly and fearfully on the increase; in 1842 it was, without the charge for the Kaffir war, under 57 millions; in 1877 it overtops 78 millions—an increase of 22 millions in twenty-eight years.

Out of this taxation, in this country, less than one-seventy-seventh portion of the burden falls on land. In France, land, prior to the Franco-Prussian war, bore one-sixth of all imperial burdens; in India, nearly one-half of the taxation falls on the land. To make the contrast more striking, we may point out that twenty-five years before the accession of the House of Brunswick, land paid nearly two-thirds of all the imperial taxes, the rents received by the aristocracy being then only the tenth part of what they are to-day. And these rents, which have grown tenfold in two hundred years, for what are they paid? For the natural fecundity of the soil, which the owner seldom or never aids. It is for the use of air, moisture, heat, for the varied natural forces, that the cultivator pays, and the receiver talks of the rights of property. We shall have for the future to talk in this country of the rights of life—rights which must be recognised, even if the recognition involves the utter abolition of the present landed aristocracy. The great rent-takers have been the opponents of progress, they have hindered reform, they kept the taxes on knowledge, they passed combination laws, they enacted long parliaments, they made the machinery of parliamentary election costly and complicated, so as to bar out the people. They have prevented education, and then have sneered at the masses for their ignorance. All progress in the producing power of labour has added to the value of land, and yet the landowner, who has often stood worse than idly by while the land has increased in value, now talks of the labourer as of the lower herd which must be checked and restrained. As Louis Blanc says: "The general wealth and population are susceptible of an almost indefinite increase, and, in fact, never do cease increasing; commerce demands for its operations a territorial basis wider and wider; towns are enlarged, and new ones built; the construction of a railway suddenly gives to this suburb, to that district, an artificial value of some importance. All this combines in a manner to raise the value of land."

These land monopolists, too, are ever grasping; they swallow common lands and enclose wastes, relying on their long purses, the cost of legal proceedings, and the apathy of a peasantry ignorant of their rights and unable to perform their duties.

The *Westminster Review* says that no less than 7,000,000 acres of commons have gone to increase the already large estates of adjoining proprietors during the last 200 years— all, be it remembered, since the landed aristocracy have, under the present reigning family, wielded full parliamentary power—all taken during the time that the imperial national debt had risen from about £52,000,000 to that enormous sum, of which we still owe upwards of £750,000,000 in England, besides our debt in India, being estimated at over £120,000,000 more. Side by side with this increased taxation, and upon these huge estates, we find an unimproved—if not an absolutely deteriorated— farm population. The parliamentary blue-books of 1867 describe the population round Mayhill as seeming " to lie entirely out of the pale of civilisation; type after type of social life degraded almost to the level of barbarism." In Yorkshire we are told of the "immorality and degradation arising from the crowded and neglected state of the dwellings of the poor."

In Northamptonshire some of the cottages "are disgraceful, necessarily unhealthy, and a disgrace to civilisation." In a Bedfordshire parish "one-third of the entire population were receiving pauper relief, and it seemed altogether to puzzle the relieving officer to account for the manner in which one-half the remainder lived." In Bucks the labourer has to " pay exorbitant rent for a house in which the ordinary decencies of life become a dead letter." So we may go through all the eastern, southern, south-western, and most of the midland rural districts, until the repetition grows as nauseous as it is hideous.

The wages of this wretched agricultural class varied before the union of agricultural labourers from 7s. to 15s. per week, wage of 10s. to 12s. per week being the most common, out of which a man had to pay rent, and feed, clothe, and educate himself and his family. Children were sent into the fields to work sometimes before they were seven years old, often before eight years, and nearly always about that age. Even now, in Somersetshire and Dorsetshire, agricultural labourers' wages average about 11s. per week. Lord Walsingham claimed them at from 13s. to 15s. The Prince of Wales pays 13s. And with education thus rendered practically impossible, we find the organs of "blood and culture" taunting the masses with their ignorance. We allege that the mischief is caused by those who exact so much for rent, and waste so much good land for pleasure, that no fair opportunity for happy life is left to the tiller of the soil. While the condition of the agricultural population is as thus stated, it cannot be pretended that sufficient compensation is found in the general prosperity of the artisan classes. Probably there are at this moment in England and Wales more than half-a-million able-bodied paupers—that is, men able to work, who cannot get work in a country where millions of acres of land fit for cultivation lie untilled.

In Plymouth, in 1870, one out of every fifteen persons was in receipt of pauper relief; and we fear that throughout England and Wales it would be found that, at the very least, one in every twenty is in the same position, while, in addition, many thousands struggle on in a sort of semi-starvation misery. During the last half-dozen years the figures have been improved by the restrictions on out-door relief, but the improvement is but a surface-polish. At Cardiff the most fearful revelations have been made before the Parliamentary Commissioners as to the state resulting from the folly or criminality of some of the large capitalists. In this part of Wales, by paying wages at long intervals, men who were sometimes justices of the peace and large landowners, in 1870 compelled their labourers to ask advances as of favour when they were really entitled to payment as of right. Then, by a dexterous evasion of the Truck Act, the men were forced to a "tommy shop," where the advance was made in goods instead of cash. Men swore before the Commissioners that it was with the greatest difficulty they could get a few shillings of ready money, and that, to obtain it, they were often compelled to re-sell the goods forced on them at a loss. The shop being sure of its customers, the women have been kept waiting for nine hours for their turn, and have had to assemble two, and sometimes four, hours before the opening of the shop, this even in the winter weather; and, in two or three cases, have been known to wait outside all night, and this through rain and storm, to secure a good place when business should commence, so that they might get the food they were unable to obtain elsewhere, and without which the breakfast meal could not be got. We wonder what kind of homes they can possess which can be left for nine hours, and what is done with the young children! The cruelty inflicted upon the women themselves by such a necessity is scarcely credible. One woman had not "seen money for twelve years," being constantly in debt to the shop. The same woman on oath said : "I went once when my son-in-law was ill, and I wanted only two or three shillings, and I begged and cried for it, but do you think I could get it? No!" Nay, it was proved that when a collection was made for a funeral, as the bulk of the workers were without money, the cashier entered the amount subscribed by each man in a book. Five per cent. was charged for cashing the list, then any amount due from the deceased's family to the shop was taken out, and even then part of the balance had to be taken in goods. Deductions were made week by week for the doctor, who was paid by bill at the end of the twelve months, and the men had no means of knowing the amount paid.

Nor is the state of things just described confined to Wales. In Scotland a companion picture may be traced. In the lead mines belonging to His Grace the Duke of Buccleuch, near Elvanfoot, in Lanarkshire, the miners have been treated more like serfs than free labourers. Young men of from eighteen to twenty were stated in 1870 to be working for 10d. a day; and while the nominal wages are 14s. to 16s. per week, or £36 8s. to £41 12s. per annum, for the ordinary working men, a horribly clever system of infrequent payments, occasional advances, a "tommy shop," and a complicated system of accounts, has so entangled the men that their pay for the year is said to range from £25 to £35. The Duke of Buccleuch is more careful of his game and his salmon than he is of his lead miners. About twelve months before the first edition of this pamphlet was issued, not far from Hawick, a poor woman, with a child at the breast, was sent to gaol for being in possession of a salmon for which she could not account. The child died whilst its mother was in gaol; but the Duke of Buccleuch's interest in the salmon fisheries was maintained.

In the *Liverpool Mercury* it was alleged that the wickedly-fraudulent truck system—here, too, cunningly disguised to evade the Truck Act—also prevailed in the Wednesbury district. And yet the noble lords and high-minded gentlemen who thus grind down the poor, and who, by cheating their labourers, demoralise honest labourers into cheats—will preside at pious gatherings, and talk about saving the souls of those whose lives they are damning. Or these born legislators will denounce trades union outrages—these high-minded men, who draw scores of thousands out of the muscle and heart of their wretched workpeople, and then endow a church, and listen to a laudatory sermon preached by the local bishop.

We affirm the doctrine laid down by Mr. Mill and other political economists, "that property in land is only valid, in so far as the proprietor of the land is its improver," and that "when private property in land is not expedient, it is unjust;" we contend that the possession of land involves and carries with it the duty of cultivating that land, and, in fact, individual proprietorship of soil is only defensible so long as the possessor can show improvement and cultivation of the land he holds. And yet there are—as Captain Maxse shows in his admirable essay published in the *Fortnightly Review*—in Great Britain and Ireland, no less than about 29,000,000 acres of land in an uncultivated state, of which considerably over 11,000,000 acres could be profitably cultivated.

There are many thousands of labourers who might cultivate this land, labourers who are in a semi-starving condition, labourers who help to fill gaols and workhouses. To meet this let the legislature declare that leaving cultivable land in an uncultivated state is a misdemeanour, conviction for which should give the Government the right to take possession of such land, assessing it by its actual return for the last five years, and not by its real value, and handing to the proprietor the amount of, say, twenty years' purchase in Consolidated 3¼ per cent. Stock, redeemable in a limited term of years. The land so taken should not be sold at all, but should be let out to persons willing to become cultivators, on sufficiently long terms of tenancy to fairly recoup the cultivators for their labour and capital, and these cultivators should yearly pay into the National Treasury, in lieu of all other imperial taxes, a certain proportion of the value of the annual produce. This tenancy to be immediately determinable in the event of the improvement being insufficient, and extensible on evidence of *bonâ fide* improvement of more than average character.

All land capable of producing food, and misused for preserving game, should be treated as uncultivated land. The diversion of land in an old country form the purpose it should fulfil—that of providing life for the many—to the mere providing pleasure for the few, is a crime. The extent to which the preservation of game has been carried in some parts of England and Scotland shows a reckless disregard of human happiness on the part of the landed aristocracy, which bids fair to provoke a fearful retribution. Paragraphs in the newspapers show how almost tame pheasants are driven to the very muzzles of the guns, to be shot down by royal butchers, who have not even the excuse of sport in their wholesale slaughterings.

It is calculated that for the deer forests of Scotland alone nearly two million acres of land—some of it the choicest pasture, much of it valuable land—is entirely lost to the country. Two red deer mean the displacement of a family, and it is, therefore, scarcely wonderful that we should learn that much of the Duke of Sutherland's vast estate is a mere wilderness.

Country members who shun the House of Commons while estimates are voted, and go to dinner when emigration and pauperism are topics for discussion, crowd the benches of St. Stephen's when there is some new Act to be introduced for the better conviction of poachers without evidence, or for the protection of fat rabbits, which eat and spoil crops, against lean farm labourers, who, having not enough to eat, pine alike in physique and intellect.

The Game Laws are a disgrace to our civilisation, and could not stand twelve months were it not for the overwhelming influence of the landed aristocracy in the Legislature. The practice of game preserving is injurious in that, in addition to the land wasted for the preserve, it frequently prevents proper cultivation of surrounding lands, and demoralises and makes criminals of the agricultural labourers, creating for them a kind and degree of crime which would be otherwise unknown.

Poaching, so severely punished, is often actually fostered and encouraged by the agents of the very landholders who sit as Justices of the Peace to punish it. Pheasants' and partridges' eggs are bought to stock preserves; the game-keepers who buy these eggs shut their eyes to the mode in which they have been procured, although in most instances it is thoroughly certain how they have been obtained. The lad who was encouraged to procure the eggs, easily finds that shooting or catching pheasants gains a much higher pecuniary reward than leading the plough-horse, trimming the hedge, or grubbing the plantation. Poaching is the natural consequence of rearing a large number of rabbits, hares, partridges, and pheasants, in the midst of an under-paid, under-fed, badly-housed, and deplorably ignorant mass of agricultural labourers. The brutal outrages on game-keepers, the barbarous murders of police, of which we read so much, are the regrettable, but very natural, measures of retaliation for a system which takes a baby child to work in the fields, sometimes soon after six years of age, commonly before he is eight years old, which trains all his worst propensities, and deadens or degrades his better faculties, which keeps him in constant wretchedness, and tantalises him with the sight of hundreds of acres on which game runs and flies well-fed, under his very nose, while he limps ill-fed along the muddy lane which skirts the preserve—game, which is at liberty to come out of its covert and eat and destroy the farmer's crop, but which is even then made sacred by the law, and fenced round by carefully-drawn covenants.

An agricultural labourer (with a wife and family), whose weekly pittance gives him bare vitality in summer, and leaves him often cold and hungry in winter, in the midst of lands where game is preserved, needs little inducement to become a poacher. Detected, he resists violently, for his local judges are the game owners, and he well knows that before them he will get no mercy. The game watchers are armed with flails, bludgeons, and firearms; the poacher uses the same brute argument. Indicted at the Assize he goes to the county gaol, and his wife and children go to the union workhouse. Imprisonment makes the man worse, not better, and he is confirmed into the criminal class for the rest of his life, while his family, made into paupers, help to add still more to the general burdens of the country.

In the agricultural districts, offences in connection with the Game Laws are more numerous than those of any other class. Men suspected of inclination for poaching are easily sent to gaol, for cutting a twig or for nominal trespass, by magistrates who, owning land on which game is reared, regard it as most wicked sacrilege that hungry labourers should even look too longingly across the hedge.

In this land question the abolition of the Game Laws must be made a prominent feature.

The enormous estates of the few landed proprietors must not only be prevented from growing larger, they must be broken up. At their own instance and gradually, if they will meet us with even a semblance of fairness, for the poor and hungry cannot well afford to fight; but at our instance, and rapidly, if they obstinately refuse all legislation. If they will not commence inside the House of Parliament, then from the outside we must make them listen. If they claim that in this we are unfair, our answer is ready—

You have monoplised the land, and while you have got each year a wider and firmer grip, you have cast its burdens on others; you have made labour pay the taxes which land could more easily have borne. You now claim that the rights of property in land should be respected, while you have too frequently by your settlements and entails kept your lands out of the possibility of fulfilling any of the obligations of property, and you have robbed your tradespeople and creditors, because your land was protected by cunningly contrived statutes and parchments against all duty, while it enjoyed all privilege. You have been intolerant in your power, driving your tenants to the poll like cattle, keeping your labourers ignorant and demoralised, and yet charging them with this very ignorance and degradation as an incapacity for the enjoyment of political rights. For the last quarter of a century, by a short-sighted policy, and in order to diminish your poor-rates, you have demolished the cottages on your estates, compelling the wretched agricultural labourers, whose toil gave value to your land, to crowd into huts even more foul and dilapidated than those you destroyed. We no longer pray, we argue—we no longer entreat, we insist—that spade and plough, and sickle and scythe, shall have fair right to win life and happiness for our starving from the land which gave us birth.

To the landowners in the House of Peers we say:—It is on the land question, my lords, that the people challenge you, at present in sorrow and shame. Take up the matter while you may, and do justice while yet you can. The world is wide for you to seek your pleasure, the poor can only seek life—where death finds them—at home. Give up your battues, your red deer, your black game, your pheasants, your partridges; and when you see each acre of land won by the fierce suasion of hardy toil to give life and hope to the tiller, in this you will find your recompense.

You few, who lock up in your iron safes the title-deeds of more than half Scotland's acreage, I plead to you; forget mere territorial pride and power, and be generous while you may, for the day is near when your pride may be humbled, and your power may be broken.

For you, lords of Erin's fertile soil—you who have wrought her shame and made her disaffection—you who have driven her children across the broad ocean to seek for life—even for you there is the moment to save yourselves, and do good to your kind. Thoughtful workmen will try to gradually win your land by law, hungry paupers may suddenly wrest it from you in despair; you may yield it now on fair terms, and grow even richer in the yielding. England is growing hungry, empty bellies make angry faster than heads reason, and the Land Question cannot stand still.

The struggle—if you compel it, landlords of Great Britain—will be one in which the landless will claim political power, and use it as a weapon, as did their French brethren eighty-five years ago.

At present by gradual concession, you may even win a meed of praise for generosity of conduct, and you may avert for generations that appeal which hunger has always prompted, when pride and power have been deaf to the cry of a nation. At present you have prestige to aid you; use it for good, while you can, for once let the storm-wind of popular indignation turn against your rank and position, and your peerage-prestige will be like a rotten reed on which to lean.

To-day the arbitrament is in your hands, and we pray a just deliverance. To-morrow—if to-day you do nothing—it may be your turn to pray, while your judges may be too hungry to listen. To-day you make the law; use it for human right; for it may be that if you do nothing, to-morrow the law will unmake you, as penalty for having worked and permitted so much wrong against your poorer brethren.

AMERICAN POLITICS.

BY CHARLES BRADLAUGH.

To deal with American Politics with any pretensions to fairness, it is necessary to consider several points, often overlooked by critics, and some of which are peculiar to the United States of America. The most important of these are as follows :—

1. The enormous extent of its territory, stretching from the Atlantic to the Pacific; from the great lakes to the Gulf of Mexico: supplemented by Alaska, or Russian America, and containing in all about 3,510,978 square miles. Its diversities of climate and physical character, and these so extreme that, even excluding Alaska, you find in the North the vegetation of an almost arctic region, while in the South you have "the luxuriant foliage of the tropics."

Grand mountain ranges, like the Alleghany, the Rocky Mountains, the Coast range, and the Sierra Nevada; huge fresh-water lakes, larger in their total extent than any others known in any country in the world, and a river valley drained by the Missouri—Mississippi, for nearly 4,500 miles. The widest diversities of food, climate, and soil, each and all affecting most materially the social and political character and conduct of the various persons of foreign birth or foreign parentage, subjected to these influences.

2. The rapidly-increasing population, to-day numbering more than 40,000,000; in 1860 numbering only 31,183,000. The fact that this increase differs in character from that of any other country in the world. In most of the old and settled countries, all increase in population is from the excesses of births over deaths. In the United States of America the increase is in chief the result of immigration, and is only in very small part due to the preponderance of births. It is perfectly true that in many of the British

Colonies the augmentation of population is by the immigrant stream, but there is a wide distinction between the effect of that stream on political affairs in the British Colonies, and of the influx of immigrants in the United States.

Nearly all the accessions of population to Canada, New Zealand, Australia, and British Columbia, are of emigrants from the British Isles. They speak the language of the people amongst whom they come to dwell; they are already acquainted with the habits, literature, and traditions of the people with whom they are to associate. The new comer and the old colonist have almost the same national feelings and interests; the same general views on religious and social questions. In the United States, on the contrary, the increase is from diverse races, with distinct and often opposing traditions, with national associations generally hostile to those held by the people amongst whom they are to live, with strange tongues and contrary habits, and with creeds which can never amalgamate, but which must extinguish or be extinguished. English, Russian, German, Swede, Italian, Pole, Wallachian, French Canadian, French, Chinaman, Dane, Norwegian, all jostle together in the New World; where they have to struggle for existence; the Chinaman at one end of the country is now to have the Esquimaux at the other; all are to be governed under the constitution of the United States Republic. And yet critics in English journals amuse themselves with leading articles illustrative of America and its shortcomings, written by men whose highest qualification is that they write in the sublimest ignorance of the subject on which they treat.

Of these new comers to America, the large majority have little or no interest in the form of the government under which they are to dwell. They have, for the most part, left the country of their birth because food was scant, and mouths many. Some of the immigrants are too old even to acquire the language of the country of their adoption, and there are not a few who place obstacles in the way of the instruction of their children in the tongue in which is administered the law of their new homes. There are Pennsylvanian Dutchmen who have gone through generations of residence in the Quaker State, and who to this day conserve a barbarous patois, the relic of their native tongue. There are French Canadians, and these a rapidly increasing element, who will not, when adults, learn the English language, and whose priests (Roman Catholic), probably to prevent heresy, do their best to hinder the education of the children. Through Maine, New Hampshire, Massachusetts, Connecticut, and Rhode Island, you find this French Canadian stream. The signs, painted in French, in front of many shops, evidence the illustration here given. Thus you have a population increasing vastly every year, and at present not betraying the slightest interest in the political conduct of the country where it obtains the means of existence.

There are Germans, arriving even in greater numbers than the English, who, when they come into newly-settled lands as in Wisconsin, Minnesota, or Iowa, sometimes continue to speak little or nothing but their own language. These have journals of their own, printed in German, some, as the *Staats Zeitung*, of very wide circulation, and who by mere diversity of user of tongue are kept to a great extent apart from their fellow citizens. Even in great cities they often dwell in large bodies by themselves. "Germantown," or "little Germany," is a well-known description for the suburb of many a good-sized city from Buffalo westward. The Germans have amongst them men who are able political leaders, notably Carl Schurz, who, but for the fact of his foreign birth, might well hope to attain the Chief Magistrates' seat. Yet it is no easy task to identify with the political life of the country a mass of men, thinking in a strange tongue, whose home life has had in it no training for political citizen duty. Here they are not rallied by a religion of Fatherland, they have no other interest at first in the country than the estimate of next year's crop. The life is new, the land is new. At home they have been governed, and it is hard for the one taught under a paternal "blood and iron" monarchy, all at once to realise that here, in this United States, it is the duty of each man to govern himself, and of all to help to govern one another. The struggle for mere existence is so absorbing to the immigrant settler that the political national vitality is of slow growth, and there is, therefore (amongst many hundreds of thousands of new comers for the first few years), an utter indifference as to who "runs" the Federal or State Government. There are no traditions dear to the newly-arrived man associated with his future home; the page of his adopted country's history has to be read when he can find leisure, in a language which he has often to learn, laboriously or reluctantly, at a period of life when the child's aptitude for being taught has long since departed.

3. The United States of America differ, further, from all other countries in having within their confines an aboriginal race, who seem on the road to extermination—a race protected nominally by treaty with, and by authority of, the Federal Government, in territory which is not subject to ordinary United States law; a race which does not seem to be amenable to the influences of civilisation, except so far as "civilisation" tends to utter annihilation. Here I speak of the Indians—the "red" men, who once owned the whole vast expanse of North America, but whose descendants now number not more than some 25,000 persons. The political difficulty is here one of the soil—*i.e.*, whether a few can hold land which the vigorous and hungry many press for. Not reckoning the various Indian reservations in other States and territories, there is the Indian territory lying between Arkansas on the east, New Mexico on the west, Kansas on the north, and Texas on the south. Here you have 55,000,000 acres of land, with a rapidly-decreasing population, to-day numbering about 15,000 human beings. To these, "a mere handful," the whole territory is preserved by treaty as long as "river runs and grass grows." If treaties make enduring barriers, the Indian would be safe enough against the swelling tide from the Old World. But coal crops up to the surface for many miles, and the Indian does not work it. The land is rich in metal, which the Indian does not mine. It is not in his nature to search the bowels of the earth with slow and painful strokes; he loves to roam its surface. The soil is a fruitful one, but is left by the Indian comparatively untilled. The Old World empties the white race from out its bosom, and they look too greedily over the Indian borders for the period to be very long, ere the pressure of population shall burst the treaty limits, and drive the red man from his last retreat in the West. In the North-east no trace of the pure Indian scarcely exists.

In Maine the Indian is gradually disappearing by amalgamation with the "superior" race. The money originally devoted in the East to the education of the Indian finds at Dartmouth College only one to teach, and he not of pure Indian blood. At Oldtown it is easy to see that, despite the law which declared void all marriage between the white and red races—the mingling of bloods is ending in the entire destruction of the aborigine by the Teuton. Yet, while the solution is certain, the problem is one not free from grave questions, all to be considered when estimating American politics.

The lawlessness which is prevalent in parts of Western Askansas, Southern and South-Eastern Kansas, Texas, and Eastern New Mexico, is a natural result of the existence of this Indian territory, wherein ordinary civil authority is powerless. No doubt the difficulty has been aggravated by the anti-slavery struggle fought out on these borders, in the worst spirit, by the worst men; and on the cessation of which struggle even, had its too long-enduring mischief in the presence of those remnants of the guerilla fighters from both sides, who had become too much corrupted by war to again settle down into peaceful citizens.

4. The existence in the United States of America of 4,500,000 human beings, not indigenous to the soil, until recently treated as mere chattels, and who enjoy now nominal political rights, with the disadvantage in very many cases of having been utterly unfitted for political duty by their whole life surroundings. Throughout North and South Carolina, in Virginia, Tennessee, Georgia, Alabama, and Louisiana, the negro has for nearly 100 years been treated as if he were a kind of superior cattle; and although the fifteenth amendment did, five years ago, give a paper political equality to the coloured man, no one can doubt that it would—even under favourable and peaceful conditions—require several generations of average school training, several generations of practice in self-reliant effort, several generations of participation in self-government, to even give the coloured race the possible chance of making the best of the organisation they inherit. Much more difficult is this negro problem, embittered as it is by the conduct of those long-resident in the South, who, by the warmth of the climate, and the habits of their fathers, have been unfitted to cope with their Northern or Western brethren in the struggle for life. Still more difficult of solution is this negro problem, encumbered as it is by the rascality of some who, really caring nothing whatever for the negro, seek to use his vote as a means of winning power for their party or place for themselves. Terrible enough is this negro problem, even for those who have their hearts sternly set against slavery in all its forms.

The fearful war-struggle in America broke down legal slavery; but it did not win, it could not win, the Southern planter to co-operate with the Northern merchant, or manufacturer, or farmer, in the work of elevating the newly-enfranchised man. The result of a war may crush, but it does not convince; the defeated party. The pro-slavery men in the South, who organised the armed Kuklux conspiracy immediately after the war, and who now organise the White League, represent an element which will never cease to oppose the recognition of the equality before the law of the negro race. I do not in this brief space do more than allude to the purely ethnic question, and yet without considering this, it is impossible to treat American politics except in the most superficial manner.

The Civil Rights Bill, to which Charles Sumner attached so much importance, and which he intended should remove all obstructions to the gradual raising of the coloured man, has been robbed of its most important and most valuable provision—viz., the School clause. Mr. G. S. Boutwell, in a recent speech in the Senate of the United States, said: "When the children of the white people and the black people are compelled to go into the same schools, sit upon the same forms, accept the same teachers, study the same books, become rivals in education and in the pursuits of life, you will have a community that will believe practically in human equality. Therefore it is that that provision which has been stricken out of the Civil Rights Bill in the other House is of more consequence than all the other provisions of that Bill." Draper says: "That while the Slave States existed as a political power, they were forced by the necessities of their position to impose a forced ignorance on the low elements of their society." It is only by insistance on the most complete facilities for negro education that permanent improvement can be hoped.

Hitherto in America there have been two great parties—Republican and Democratic; and one of these, the Democratic party, has suffered severely, first, from its identification with the pro-slavery movement and the Southern rebellion; and, second—and more recently—from the fact that the men convicted in New York City of misdealing with, and misappropriation of, the city moneys were elected by the Democratic vote, which in that city has an overwhelming majority, nearly the whole Irish vote being cast for the Democratic ticket.

Candidly, I do not think that the Democratic party ought to be condemned entirely for the sin of slavery; nor do I hold that the Republican party ought to be credited with the original virtue of abolition principles. Unfortunately for the Democratic platform, the affirmation of State rights involved the perpetuation of national wrongs. The English Monarchy had planted slavery more or less throughout the thirteen colonies, but especially in Maryland, Virginia, North and South Carolina, and Georgia. The slavery so planted had been enforced, preserved, and encouraged by direct acts of the Home Government. When the several colonies became independent States, they conserved—unfortunately for themselves—the fatal privilege of retaining their negro brethren in bondage. The privilege of slave-holding became a State right; and in the Southern States the climatic conditions helped to give colour to the notion that it was a social necessity. The affirmation of State right identified the Democratic party with the maintenance of the curse of slavery in those States respectively which refused to vote for abolition.

In judging American politics an Englishman should at least remember two things : first, that slavery was a legacy left by the English Monarchy to the new Republic; and next, that when the great American people had at last determined to free themselves from the shame and disgrace of the slave blot on the American escutcheon, it was the English aristocracy and land-owning interest which, while making profession through the world of a policy of universal emancipation, nevertheless gave its sympathy to the slave-holding South, and permitted without protest the building in, and issue from, its ports of war vessels to be used against its ally the North, though that North had then, by the force of events, become pledged to the abolition of slavery.

In declaiming, too, against corruption in New York State, it should be especially borne in mind by English critics that the controlling voting power of the city of New York was thrown into the hands of a large mass of men who, in the country of their birth, had been debarred from any wholesome political activity, whose fathers had for generations been absolutely deprived of political life, and who had personally suffered the severest want. These men, to escape death by starvation, left their own shores absolute paupers ; and the country of their adoption has had to pay some of the penalties attending the early practice of full political right by a mass of men not yet educated to the consciousness of their duty.

New issues are now raising in the United States, and neither the platform of the Republican party nor that of the Democratic party seems to me to make full provision for facing the serious points involved. One of the most grave is the approaching conflict between Labour and Capital, a conflict which will now be aggravated by the presence in the large cities, such as New York, Boston, Philadelphia, and Chicago, of very large bodies of men either entirely without employment, or unable to earn enough to obtain decent food, clothing, and shelter. Very many of these men—especially the recently-arrived Germans in the West—hold extreme Socialistic theories, and do not regard the Government of their newly-adopted country with even the habit-reverence which does much to restrain the inhabitants of old countries. They have many of them quitted Europe with exaggerated ideas of the value of labour in the New World, and without any notion of the smaller purchasing power of money. Many of them are unprepared to go out of the range of civilisation, and they, therefore, stick close to some great centre of population. Some find themselves and their families absolutely unequal to the task of battling in the open country with a climate more severe than that of their native land. They prefer the shelter a crowded city apparently offers, and they forget the bitter disadvantages it involves. These poor men, crowded together in rich cities where they are strangers, grow to regard the suffrage rather as a weapon of offence against the capitalist class, than as a means of performing a common duty in carrying on the Government of the country.

The gatherings in New York City, and the menaces in Chicago, are the outward exhibitions of a terrible undercurrent of discontent, resolvable all into one sentence, Dear food, dear lodging, and poor wages. The politician who grapples boldly with this labour question will need a firm courage and clear head; the party which avoids the question must certainly be ruined.

Another difficult problem in United States politics is presented by the claim of the Western pork and grain-raiser to have his produce cheaply transported to the Eastern markets. In the fertile Mississippi valley, produce may be raised sufficient for the whole population of Europe. In the great West and the North-West, the soil yields readily of its abundant richness, but the cost of transport to the consumer's door is often so great as to entirely devour the farmer's hard-earned profit.

The protest of the cultivator against the railroad owner has resulted in those Grange associations now thickly scattered through the West, and which, if they gave their temporary allegiance to either party, might easily determine a Gubernatorial, or even a Presidential, election.

That the Grangers have legitimate grievances cannot be disputed, but that the remedy is to legislate down the charge for railway transport is not so clear. No railway company can or will carry at a freight rate which does not meet the cost of permanent way, provide for payment of servants, and furnish some interest on capital. While there are many inconsistencies, and probably some extortions, in the charge for conveying produce, the real remedy will probably be found, partly in the utilisation of the great Mississippi as a pathway to the sea, and partly in the creation of more industrial centres in the agricultural States, so as to bring the consumer closer to the means of subsistence. Railway companies in Europe only construct railways to meet the needs of population already settled. Railways in the United States are built into wilds where there is no population, to provide an iron track for the conveyance of future settlers. The railway monopolist in the East, and his customers in the West, are likely to be arrayed on different sides in a political struggle, unless indeed much forbearance be shown by the leaders of both parties, and unless wise statesmanship can teach each side its common interest and duty.

In America the Roman Catholic question, which is just now so agitating the Old World, is of extreme importance. America has no State Church, and amongst the various and conflicting religious bodies, the Roman Catholic Church stands out prominently, not only as the richest and most complete organisation, but also as having more rapidly increased in numerical strength than any other body. Probably nearly one-fifth of the population of the United States are now Roman Catholics. I am inclined to doubt whether this increase is not a little more nominal than real. I do not regard it as showing an addition to the general strength of the Roman Catholic body. It is nearly all the result of immigration of Irish, Germans, and French Canadians. The latter are the most superstitious, the most ignorant, and the least disposed to permit themselves or their children to be educated; but they are also fortunately the fewest. The two former occupy a very different place. The Germans are, as a body, extremely indifferent on religious matters, and are strongly inclined, when they give themselves any trouble at all, to favour Rationalistic views; and the American-Irish—that is, children American-born of Irish parents—are figuring so well in the common schools that as long as the education is unsectarian it only needs in addition to be made compulsory, and the political future of the United States would be perfectly safe-guarded from danger, from this source at any rate. And I avow that I do regard the overwhelming predominance of the Roman Catholic Church in any country as an element of grave hostility to Republican institutions. Roman Catholicism maintains the principle of authority not derived from the people; as against the right of private judgment, and the constitution of government by the exercise of individual suffrage. I do not mean by this that it is the duty of a Republic to legislate against the Roman Catholic Church; on the contrary, I conceive it to be the duty of a Republican Government to ensure to all its citizens the fullest liberty and protection in religious matters, permitting to each and all the profession of faith the individual judgment inclines to, securing, to each and all, the fullest right of dissent and nonconformity without penalty or disability. The law should secure free Church in free State, and should protect, equally with the believer, the man who makes work his worship, and who refuses to kneel at any altar.

I am not unaware that Father Hecker, a really admirable man, and his able co-workers in New York, make a very strong plea that the Catholic in America can be a consistent and intelligent citizen of a Republic, and if I pass their plea here in silence, it is from no want of respect for the men, and most certainly in no contempt of their ability.

One evil in the practice of American politics is the habit which has grown up of changing most, if not all, of the lower government officials on the election of each President. All thinking Americans regret this; it is no necessary consequence of the constitution, and there is little doubt that at an early period a President will be found who will revert to the line of conduct observed by the earlier occupants of the Presidential chair, who only displaced officials for actual misconduct.

Another evil is the abstention in some States and cities of many of the best educated men from the performance of their political duties. This has been especially so in New York

City, but is not, I think, so much the case in Massachusetts. I believe, too, that this is an evil which originally arose from the Southern pro-slavery influence on the Democratic party, and that the future will show a vast improvement under this head.

For the information of many who have addressed me questions on the subject, I beg to add the following rough sketch of the American political machine.

The United States of America contains 37 distinct States, and also the territories of Colorado, Wyoming, Dacotah, Montana, Oregon, Idaho, Washington, Nevada, Utah, Arizona, and New Mexico. Each State has its own law courts for administration of State laws; its House of Representatives and its Senate for internal legislation; also its executive, headed by the State-Governor, who is the supreme executive magistrate within the limits of the State. In describing Massachusetts constitution I present a fair notion of the several constitutions of the other States, although there are many minor differences. The Governor, who must be a resident freeholder, is chosen annually by manhood suffrage. The vote is by ballot. He is commander-in-chief of all State, naval, and military forces, and has the sole right of resorting to force against the enemies of the State; but he cannot, of his own authority, order State troops outside the limits of the State. He has absolute power of pardoning criminals convicted in the States courts of offences against the State law. With the consent of his councillors (who are elected by the people) he nominates all State officers. No moneys are paid from the State treasury except on his warrant. In the event of the death of the Governor, the Lieutenant-Governor, likewise chosen by popular vote, succeeds to his office. All the several States and territories are alike subject to the constitution of the United States. The United States has at Washington[1] its House of Representatives, who are elected for two years, in the proportion of at least one representative to 30,000 inhabitants, by the people of their several States. Every representative must be twenty-five years of age, must have been seven years resident in the United States, and must be an inhabitant of the State by which he is elected. The Second Chamber, or Senate, contains two senators from

---

[1] Washington is the seat of Government; its inhabitants have no votes.

each State. These senators are elected for six years, but are nominated one-third every second year, and are chosen by the vote of the Legislature of the electing State. A senator must be resident in his State, must be thirty years of age, and have been for nine years a citizen of the United States. The Senate has the power on impeachment to try and condemn the various Federal officials, including the President of the United States. The Senate and the House of Representatives are together Congress, and they have the power to levy and collect taxes, to borrow money on the credit of the United States, to coin money, regulate foreign commerce, declare war, maintain an army and navy and militia, but no army appropriation can be made for more than two years. The executive power is vested in a President elected for four years. The President is chosen by an electoral assembly, chosen by popular vote from each State, equal in number to the whole number of Senators and Representatives entitled to set in Congress from such State. The President must be native born, must be at least thirty-five years of age, and must have been fourteen years resident in the United States. The President and Vice-President cannot both be inhabitants of the same State. The President is commander-in-chief of all military, militia, and naval forces. He can pardon all persons convicted of offences against the United States laws, except those convicted on impeachment. He can make treaties, subject to the concurrence of two-thirds of the Senate. He nominates, and, if approved by the Senate, appoints, all ambassadors, consuls, judges, and other officers, whose appointment is not specially provided for.

Each of the severally-named territories has its own government, legislature, and law courts, under act of Congress. These territories send delegates to the Congress at Washington, but with limited authority.

PRICE TWOPENCE.

Printed and Published by C. WATTS, 17, Johnson's Court, Fleet Street, London, E.C.

TAXATION:

HOW IT ORIGINATED,

AND

WHO BEARS IT.

BY

CHARLES BRADLAUGH.

LONDON:
FREETHOUGHT PUBLISHING COMPANY.
28, STONECUTTER STREET, E.C.

LONDON:
PRINTED BY ANNIE BESANT AND CHARLES BRADLAUGH,
28, STONECUTTER STREET.

TAXATION:

HOW IT ORIGINATED, AND WHO BEARS IT.

In ancient times, in this country, the ordinary expenditure of the sovereign, as representing or wielding the executive power, was made up of Crown rents, feudal dues of various natures, prisage—a right the king claimed of taking to his own use and at his own valuation as much as the king had occasion for—of all merchandize belonging to merchant strangers, and sometimes merchandize of native-born merchants, out of every ship importing the same; and butlerage, a similar exaction applied to wine. These prisage and butlerage exactions were at first a mere sort of uncertain extortion by force, and were taken by some feudal lords, as well as by the Crown; but in time they became a prescribed or customary levy, payable by native merchants and by merchant strangers in different proportions; and the exactions having been at first taken in kind, were at last commuted into a money payment, and were called "tonnage and poundage," being so much per ton on wine, and so much per pound on other goods. The word "customs" in ancient time seems to have covered many customary payments and dues, regal, feudal, and ecclesiastical, but became gradually restricted until it was at last limited only to the duties payable to the king upon the importation, exportation, or carriage coastwise of various articles. In the reign of Richard I. an import duty on wine, called "prise," was payable to the king and was accounted for to the Exchequer. In the reign of John import duties are mentioned on wood, salt, and fish, and export duties on wool and leather. The first parliamentary authority we can find for the exaction of a customs duty is in 1297, when the community of the realm granted to Edward I., in aid of his war with France, a customs duty of

40 shillings for every sack of wool, and 5 marks for every last of leather, exported, for the space of two or three years, if the war should last so long. There must have been earlier parliamentary grants than this, but we cannot trace them. When the grant of 1297 was made, the king declared that he would take no fresh custom of the nation without its common consent, but that he reserved the right to continue to collect the "old customs duties," said to have been granted before that time, of half a mark for every sack of wool, and a mark for every last of leather. The duties of "tonnage and poundage" were generally granted to the king by one and the same Act of Parliament, and were called the subsidy of tonnage and poundage. Some of the kings claimed the right to levy tonnage and poundage at their own will and discretion, and by their own authority, but this was from the 16th century forward almost always contested by Parliament. It was in 1629 that what Carlyle calls "a brave and noble Parliament" held the Speaker in the chair until remonstrances had been voted against the king's claim to collect tonnage and poundage by his own writ. It was this same Parliament which declared: "That no man hereafter be compelled to make or yield any gift, loan, benevolence, tax, or such like charge, without common consent by Act of Parliament." Prior to this declaration forced loans and compulsory benevolences were extremely common, and the Jews were especial and unpitied sufferers.

In the early times the customs were let or farmed by the Crown to collectors for a cash purchase-payment, or as a recompense for services rendered, or as a reward to a favourite, or to secure, and as a repayment of, a loan, previously made or then agreed to be made, to the king. In 1329 the entire customs of England were farmed for £20 a-day, Sundays excepted, the total amounting to £6,260 a-year. In the year 1400 the customs were let for £8,000 a-year. In the year 1650 they averaged £500,000 per annum; in 1800 they were £8,144,380; in 1876 they amounted to £20,341,502, or, with the excise, to £48,641,321 per year.

The practice of farming customs ceased in 1671, when the collection was transferred to a board of commissioners. For extraordinary war expenditure, the old military tenures involved special charges on the landowners, but these feudal obligations slowly disappeared, and subsidies and aids by Parliament were gradually substituted for them. In 1635, in consequence of the reluctance of Parliament to vote any subsidy until certain grievances had been redressed, an effort was made by King Charles I., while no Parliament was sitting, to levy a tax called ship-money by his own writ, without any concurrence or sanction of Parliament, and the courts of law affirmed the king's right to make this levy; but in November, 1640, the Long Parliament declared ship-money illegal, and enacted that no tax could be levied on exports or imports save by the common consent of Parliament. Amongst ancient direct taxes was one of hearth-money, which does not, however, appear under this name as a statutory tax until 1662, when Parliament granted two shillings per year to Charles II. for every firehearth or stove. This hearth-money was voted as a compensation for the suppression of the Court of Wards, and of other feudal tenures. Hearth-money was finally abolished in 1689, on the resolution of the House of Commons "that the said revenue cannot be so regulated, but that it will occasion many difficulties and questions, and that it is in itself not only a great oppression to the poorer sort, but a badge of slavery upon the whole people, exposing every man's house to be entered into and searched at pleasure by persons unknown to him."

Several poll-taxes were from time to time enacted; the first we can find is in 1377, of 4d. per head for every man and woman above 16. The aristocracy paid higher rates, a ducal head being rated at £6 13s. 4d. The Wat Tyler rebellion grew out of resistance to a poll-tax. The last poll-tax was enacted in 1698, but some collection of arrears was continued for a few years later. There have been several very absurd direct taxes. In 1723 there was a papist tax, and in 1695 taxes were levied on weddings, burials, bachelors, and widows. In 1710 and 1718 two shillings a ton duty was laid on coals in order to build some new churches, and afterwards to provide for the clergymen.

Whenever extraordinary funds were necessary for the purpose of carrying on a war, or for any other special object, Parliament made an extraordinary grant as an aid or subsidy. These subsidies were a specified proportion—as a tenth or fifteenth—of the nominal income; or a special duty for a limited period upon wines or goods. The most usual aid to the king was the grant of a fifteenth, and was at first rather a substitution for the feudal revenue payable by the landowner to the king. By the 14th Edward III., statute

1, cap. 20, A.D. 1340, a ninth and a fifteenth were granted for the wars in Scotland, France, and Gascony. The ninth lamb, ninth fleece, and ninth sheep were to be taken for two years, and the ninth part of all goods and chattels in cities and boroughs. Foreign merchants not dwelling in cities and boroughs, and other people dwelling in forests and wastes, were to pay one-fifteenth. Poor cottiers, and those living by bodily travail, were exempt.

The last grant of a tenth and a fifteenth appears to have been made in the reign of James I., and the last subsidy was in the reign of Charles II. The land-tax grew out of these subsidies, the king complaining that the aristocracy defrauded him by under-rating their incomes.

A land-tax should in every country be the chief source of internal revenue. In India land pays to-day a very large proportion, nearly one half, of the total taxation. In France, before the late war, land paid one-sixth of all the taxation. In England, on the accession of George I., it paid two-fifths of the total taxation; to-day land bears less than one-seventy-eighth part of the national burdens.

Land to-day is assessed at the rate of 4s. in the £ on a valuation made in 1692. Under this assessment land paid, in 1798, £2,037,627 net, and the gross annual value of land was then stated at £22,500,000. In 1877 the land-tax realised, gross, £1,084,889, and the parliamentary return gives the gross annual value of land, including mines and quarries, for 1873, at £198,275,717. At the rate of 4s. in the £—thought fair by the landowners themselves eighty years ago—the land-tax alone ought to amount to £39,655,143, or about half the present total of our extravagant taxation.

This unfairness in the land-tax will scarcely be wondered at when it is known to what an enormous extent land is owned by persons who are either members of the House of Lords or of the House of Commons, and when it is considered how few persons own a large proportion of the whole area of the United Kingdom. The total area of the United Kingdom is 77,635,182 acres, and of this 38,875,522 acres are owned by 2184 individuals, of whom 421 persons own no less than 22,880,775 acres. Can it be wondered at that land-laws are unfair when it is remembered that nearly every one of these landholders speaks or votes in one or other of the legislative assemblies either by himself or by his nominee. The land valuation of 1692 was certainly imperlect, and some have urged that it was purposely and fraudulently understated. This valuation was adopted without challenge by William Pitt in 1798; he had, however, the grace to say that his measure for the nominal land-tax of 4s. in the £ was not intended to prevent a future Parliament from augmenting the tax. So far from augmenting the amount, we have the fact that the land-tax to-day represents throughout Great Britain a most unequal and ridiculously low figure. The accountants of the Liverpool Financial Reform Association have made a careful analysis of the land-tax as it is paid, and the land-tax as it ought to be paid, and it appears from this calculation that—entirely omitting the value of mines, quarries, iron works, and other real properties transferred to Schedule D in 1866—the highest land-tax paid is in Suffolk—5½d. in the £; in many counties the tax is less than 1d. in the £, and in some less than one farthing in the £. In Lancashire the land-tax is half-a-farthing in the £, and in Scotland three-sixteenths of a 1d. The general average of the land-tax throughout the United Kingdom is 1d. and five-eighths of a 1d. per £.

The contention in this essay will be that the landholding class, being practically the legislating class, with a monopoly of one House, and, until 1832, with absolute control of the House of Commons, have gradually shifted from off the land the fiscal burdens which land ought not only to bear, but which would be less oppressive if levied on land than they are when borne by labour.

While the tax-levying Parliaments were composed—as in the first half of the seventeenth century—of the persons who actually paid the taxes, the votes were small and hard to carry through the House of Commons. Now the votes are large, and pass much too easily. Joseph Hume is dead, and no one bears his mantle.

It ought, however, to be remembered that Members of the House of Commons are not sufficiently encouraged and supported by their constituents on questions of financial reform. Members are derided for "cheeseparing" and "nibbling at the estimates," and yet it is only by close investigation of each separate item and by attempted restriction of each disbursement that any permanent economy can be hoped for. Voters should carefully watch the conduct of their local members when the estimates are being discussed, and should, when necessary, hold meetings and send in petitions to give weight to the voice of the man who represents them in Parliament.

The gross taxation for 1877 amounted to £80,099,051; in 1848 it was £59,323,465; in 1837 it was £49,878,124; in 1706 it was £5,691,000. It is submitted that the increase during the present reign, and especially during the last twenty years, has been unduly extravagant, and it is urged that, unless the increase be stopped, and a marked reduction be effected, revolution must result from this enormous increase of the people's burdens.

The increase in our home expenditure during the present reign has been nominally about £29,250,000, but has been really almost £31,000,000, allowing for the lesser charge in 1877 for the interest and management of the National Debt.

The first item in our National Expenditure consists of the charge for interest and management of our National Debt amounting to £27,992,833 14s. 7d.

I agree with Mr. Dudley-Baxter that a national debt is a national evil. It is a mortgage of the earnings of generations unborn—a mortgage created by the Parliament of the nation—a mortgage on earnings in which Parliament has no property. Parliament, and the Government maintained by its authority, have not even the right of ownership of the actual earnings of the living citizens, much less has either Parliament or Government any right of ownership in labour not yet existing. It has only a protectorate and limited jurisdiction over the vast aggregate of existing property, and over the living workers, whose economies constitute the capital—and the ability to create the capital—of the country. No Government has justification for the creation of national debt, save "in case of great emergency, with which the State is otherwise unable to cope," and then only if it may be fairly maintained that those who are to be called upon to bear the burden shifted from the borrowing generation will enjoy benefits which would be impossible, save for the borrowing. The creation of a national debt is only justifiable when the money is expended on public works which increase the productive ability of the nation, or so facilitate commerce as to render actual produce more available. Mr. Baxter says: " Owners of property that was not in existence at the time of the loan, and workers who have inherited no property at all from their borrowing ancestors, are obliged by this law of public credit to pay interest as to the amount of which they have had no discretion, and to deprive themselves of comforts, and even necessaries, for the cost of services in which they have no share, and probably have derived no benefit. Such a power as this transfers a burden from one set of workers and property to a materially different set of workers and property, and inflicts a great deal of hardship, and often of injustice, upon future generations—more particularly on the poor among them. Hence the power of borrowing ought only to be exercised on the clearest necessity, and with the utmost economy." And, further:. "The unnecessary or extra portion of war expenditure, occasioned by the adoption of borrowing, is capital unnecessarily diverted from productive investments, and spent on unproductive objects. Instead of being employed in trade or industrial undertakings, or improvements, adding a new annual produce to the net income of the nation, this capital becomes a pensioner on the old net income of the country. It is like taking an army of artificers and agricultural labourers from their workshops and fields, to maintain them, and their children after them, without labour, upon the taxes. An unproductive debt, by its absorption of useful capital, prevents improvements, hinders the growth of industrial capital, and stunts the development of a nation; while, at the same time, to meet the necessity of paying interest, it imposes additional taxation, and lessens the margin of tax-bearing power of the nation." The whole of the debt owing to-day by Great Britain is the unpaid balance of money borrowed for war expenditure. To-day we owe about £776,000,000; we have spent for wars alone, during the last 180 years, £1,555,421,160, and this without reckoning the cost of borrowing, and without calculating the interest paid on the money borrowed.

The total military and naval expenditure during the war in Ireland and against France, 1688 to 1697, amounted to £36,876,203.

During the war from 1702 to 1713, called "the war of the Spanish succession," the total cost for army, navy, and ordnance was £66,279,292. It was at this time that the increase of our standing army commenced, and the system of subsidising foreign Powers and hiring foreign troops originated.

The naval and military expenditure during the war with Spain, from 1718 to 1721, came to £11,399,324.

Between 1739 and 1748, we had the "war with Spain (right of search) and Austrian succession," and in those years spent for fighting £62,077,642. When the treaty of peace was made at Aix-la-Chapelle, the right of search was not even referred to.

The "seven years' war" was nominally 1756 to 1763, but really involved military expenditure over eleven years, at a cost of £104,611,374.

The war which severed the connection between the North American colonies and the British monarchy—the war which served to create the Republic of the United States of America—necessitated a total outlay of £139,521,035.

The war with France—nominally commencing in 1793, but really commencing with the signature of the secret arrangement in 1791 (concurred in by George III. and the Tory Government), by which the various Continental Powers, parties to the secret treaty of Mantua, agreed to invade France, in order to overthrow the Constitution—made up the enormous total of £989,636,449, when the expenditure ended in 1817. So that if we had not joined in the conspiracy to enable Louis XVI. to break his oath, we should now have had no debt, and France might possibly have escaped the Reign of Terror.

The Crimean war cost £116,053,151, for the maintenance of the Turk at Constantinople and the prevention of Russian war vessels in the Black Sea. The first result has enabled the Sublime Porte to borrow English money, and to misgovern and maltreat Bulgarian, Bosnian, and Herzegovinian peasants. The Russian diplomatists have since persuaded the English Government to abandon the second result, despite the blood and treasure lavished to secure it.

Some contend that it is unjust to include, as I have done, the whole expenditure for army, navy, and ordnance during war years; but I submit that I should be justified in adding to the above items all increase of the annual charge of the public debt, and all interest paid on money borrowed towards defraying the war expenditure. If this were done, the total cash wasted for and through war, during the last 180 years, would not be less than £2,000,000,000.

Our Military Expenditure.

The second item is for our army and navy, £28,186,117, and of this the army cost us altogether £16,820,716, being nearly double what it cost us in 1852, while the navy cost us £11,364,383, as against £5,849,916 in 1852. Omitting the items for army purchase and localization of forces, the cost of the army for last year was £15,421,356. For this we had a supposed effective force of 96,275 men, with a total muster-roll of 132,884 men of all ranks. The German army, on a peace footing with 420,000 men of all ranks, costs as nearly as possible the same sum as does the English army, although the latter has 287,000 less men. In the British army we pay the salaries of a large number of gentlemen as nominal colonels of regiments, which these titular commanders sometimes never see; the salaried colonelcy is occasionally the reward of merit to a tried warrior of foreign lineage who has done this country the honour of associating himself by marriage with our Royal Family. The increase in the peace cost of our army has been very terrible. In 1871 the cost was £13,430,400. In 1847 our army, militia, commissariat, and ordnance cost £9,061,233, everything included; showing the outrageous addition in twenty years of £7,775,000 per annum to the one item of military expenditure. Compare this with the cost of the army in 1792, just prior to the great continental wars, and the total then for Great Britain and Ireland was £2,410,212, or about one seventh of the army expenditure for 1877.

Estimates are so wonderfully framed that it is possible some inaccuracies may be found in these figures; if so, the inaccuracies will only be of form and not of substance. Without regarding any increase for war, our peace establishment for the army for 1878 is to cost £15,595,800, and for this, unless we denuded Ireland of her garrisons, we could probably not collect and have ready in the field within two months more than 50,000 men. It is true that we have in the three Indian presidencies 60,000 men, but we dare not remove these at the risk of an immediate rebellion. Divine service in the army costs £49,300; and as each officiating clergyman for his share of this sum has to devote about two hours per week to each regiment, it can hardly be said that religion is too cheaply provided for. As the Gospel does not make all soldiers good, the expenditure for military punishments comes to £28,600. The total charge for the militia is £1,287,753; and the yeomanry cavalry, whose availability for war will be evident to the meanest capacity, cost £74,400. The most famous achievement of the yeomanry cavalry was in 1819, at Peterloo, and the recollection of this should endear that branch of the service to all real Radicals. It is sometimes pretended that the Duke of Cambridge foregoes some of the salaries attaching to the numerous colonelcies he holds, but in the foot note to the statement on the estimates of his salary of £4432 as Commander-in-Chief, it is expressly stated that this is "in addition to the full pay" "of the military ranks" "held in the army." When commissions in the army were sold, there was a regulation price, and every officer selling his commission used to pledge his word of honour that he did not receive, and every officer purchasing gave a pledge on honour that he did not pay, more than the regulation price. It was always well known that the whole system was a farce; that more money was always demanded and paid; and that the amount varied according to popularity or otherwise of the regiment. When the practice of promotion in the army by purchase was abolished, there was actually provision made for paying compensation to officers for these fraudulent "over-regulation prices;" the amount apportioned for 1878 under this head is £29,200.

Revenue Departments.

The cost of collection of our customs and inland revenue might be much lessened if direct taxation were made the rule. Almost all earnest financial reformers seek to substitute direct for indirect taxation. Indirect taxation is a levy of revenue by taxes on the transit of merchandise, on articles of food, on the raw materials used in manufacture, and on the process of manufacture. Direct taxation is here intended to mean the levy of revenue by a tax on income. There are, of course, various direct taxes of obnoxious character which would be utterly impolitic. Indirect taxation is objectionable, because, in the end, the pressure of it always falls most severely on the mass of the consumers, and the richer tax-payers manage to transfer their burdens with interest to the poorer and ultimate purchasers. Indirect taxation is always a hindrance to industrial enterprise. It encourages smuggling, fraud, and perjury, and compels the maintenance of a strong force for the detection and punishment of the crime it creates. The governing classes, and those who are opposed to economy, will naturally object to direct taxation, for its very simplicity makes each taxpayer unpleasantly and immediately conscious of every increase in his fiscal burdens. Almost all local taxes are direct taxes, and when all imperial taxes are direct there will be less opportunity of annual increase in our expenditure without a vigorous protest. Men and women ought to pay taxes for the preservation of their property, their liberty, and their persons, but the severest pressure of tax ought not to come upon those whose wage is insufficient for the decent maintenance of themselves and their families. In 1849 the Liverpool Financial Reform Association issued some most able tracts dealing with the questions of direct and indirect taxation. Since that date very many indirect taxes have been entirely abolished, but there is still enough of indirect taxation remaining to make the following passage worth reproducing from the Financial Reform Tract, No. 3:—

"On a careful examination of the sources whence the public income is derived, the Association are astonished to find how completely the taxation is laid on the trade and industry of the country. Contrasted with the accounts of the expenditure, it divides the community into two distinct classes: one, those who pay; the other, those who spend the taxes. The former comprises the great mass of the population, all who labour and produce the wealth of the nation; the other, the favoured few who from accident of birth or connections are exempt from the necessity of toil; and who seem on that account (for no other reason can be discovered in the examination of official documents, but the fact that such is the exemption) to be relieved from the duty of contributing their fair and proportionate amount to the pecuniary requirements of the state."

It is, of course, just to add that—thanks to men like Joseph Hume, John Bright, Richard Cobden, and last but most certainly not least, William Ewart Gladstone—much change for the better has been made since 1849 in the imposition of our national taxation.

Public Works and Buildings.

In the expenditure, under the head of "Public Works and Buildings," there are some items to which special attention should be drawn. 1st. Palaces in the personal occupation of Her Majesty, which cost £12,397 last year, and for which £12,158 are asked for 1878. £5454 is charged in addition for palaces partly in the occupation of

Her Majesty. 2nd. £3357 is the bill for repairs, *inter alia*, to the apartments of Her Royal Highness the Duchess of Cambridge in St. James's Palace, but including also rent of stables for Her Royal Highness in Brick Street, Piccadilly. This is in addition to the pension to the duchess, which will be found given under the head of " Payments to the Royal Family." Why the nation should pay the Duchess of Cambridge's stable rent is a mystery which poor and hungry taxpayers would do well to clear up. 3rd. The repairs for 1878 to Marlborough House, the residence of the Prince of Wales, for 1878, are estimated at £6450 ; the actual charge for last year under this head was £4100. 4th. There are items amounting to £45,907, in 1877, for diplomatic and consular buildings, which shall be dealt with later, together with the other items for foreign office services.

Expenses of Public Departments.

The House of Lords nominally cost, in 1877, for salaries and similar expenses, £47,053, but this does not include £6000 further charged on the Consolidated Fund for the Lord Chancellor, making a total of £53,053. The House of Commons, including a sum of £5000, also charged on the Consolidated Fund for the Speaker, costs £61,649. Warming, ventilating, lighting, dusting, and general looking after both Houses of Parliament, comes to £21,130. This is a total for Parliament—without reckoning payments to counsel who draw Parliamentary Bills—£115,832. This is a fairly large outlay for a Parliament in which there is no payment of members, except of the speaker and chairmen of committees. The Foreign Office costs £83,400, one notable item in which total is the salary of £1250 to the Chief Clerk, who is at the same time in receipt of £794 2s., being compensation granted to him for abandoning against his wish and will the illegal and extremely profitable practice of levying black mail on the salaries of Foreign Office *employés*, who were compelled to employ him as their agent to receive their salaries. The Lord Privy Seal's Office figures for £2807, a not unreasonable yearly stipend for acting merely as a " gilt figure-head." This was the office recently held by the Earl of Beaconsfield, from which he professed to gain no emolument, but from which he actually received the full salary, until public attention was drawn to the matter.

Secret Service.

There are two items, one of £10,000, charged on the Consolidated Fund, and the other of £24,000, in the Civil Service Estimates, for Secret Service Money. These are items which ought to be erased from our national expenditure. The usually accurate "Financial Reform Almanack" for 1878 gives the sum for Secret Service in the Civil Service Expenditure at only £14,000, but this is an error, the sum is £24,000, making £34,000 in all.

The House of Commons ought to insist on the nation knowing whether this amount is disbursed at home or abroad. If the sum is only paid to supplement official salaries, it should be voted openly. If it is employed for bribery, or in pursuance of dishonest work, it should not be voted at all. About 250 years ago the House of Commons committed a Secretary of State to the Tower for refusing to give information as to the alleged disposal of Secret Service Moneys, and the House only released the, at first, obstinate offender on his making full submission and furnishing complete accounts. To-day the House of Commons is too subservient to Ministers to do anything half so bold.

Foreign Office Expenditure.

Without reckoning diplomatic pensions or allowances, but including diplomatic and consular buildings, our Foreign Office Service costs in all for the current year £567,205, and this, not including special missions such as that of the Earl Rosslyn to Madrid to attend the marriage of the King of Spain, which cost £3200, or the Duke of Abercorn's journey to Rome to invest the new King of Italy with the insignia of the Order of the Garter, the charge for which is £5500. First, in point of expenses and, possibly, also in the prospect of future mischief, come our legations and consular expenses in China and Japan. The charges of the embassies—£9460 for China, and £5660 for Japan —compared with the extravagant totals, are apparently comparatively moderate. The total charge for the United States embassy to China is £6100, including in this all contingencies; while to the £9460 which our embassy cost have to be added the items for legation buildings, legation guards, &c., amounting to several thousand pounds more. The United States embassy to Japan, including all expenses comes to £3000; our embassy costs £5660, without reckoning the costly additional expenditure. What good our ambassador is to us in China at all is not very clear, as a good Consul-General would do all the real work; but this is only the commencement of a long series of items for the Celestial Empire. The consular services in China amount to £50,664, and those for Japan to £27,772, while the legation and consular buildings come to an additional £15,948, with £2674 for rents, or a round total for our representation in China and Japan of £112,178. It should be borne in mind by taxpayers that many statesmen and their advisers have in recent times suggested the possibility of the extension of English territory in China and Japan.

Diplomatic and consular representation in Persia, where there are only two consulates, costs us £10,085, and the embassy buildings at Teheran are continually figuring in the estimates. Last year they cost £1938. This is one of the cases where a costly embassy is worse than useless. The Shah was a rather uncomfortable visitor, and seems a most expensive acquaintance. If we desire any benefit from the embassy it would be interesting to have such benefit clearly recorded.

Turkey costs us for its embassy no less than £11,345, for embassy and consular buildings, £4,628, and for consulates, after deducting the fees acknowledged and returned, £20,287. For this huge outlay we get the worst of all returns—absolute misrepresentation by our officials to the Turks of the state of English feeling, and to England of the condition of Turkish misrule. If it had not been for the correspondents of the *Times* and *Daily News* during 1876, we should have been absolutely without reliable information as to what was happening in Bulgaria and Bosnia. Our present ambassador is A. H. Layard, who, when he was the English minister in Madrid, actually did all he could to prevent the abolition of slavery in Porto Rico, and plotted actively with Marshal Serrano to overthrow the Republic temporarily established under Castelar. Marshal Serrano travelled through Spain to Santander disguised as the servant of and in company with the English Ambassador, and thus escaped arrest. Turkish embassies are not, however, expected to do special work, and there is a Danubian Navigation Commission which costs us £3,000 a-year, and a Turco-Persian Boundary Commission for which we pay £2,000 a year. Last year there was a special service in

Montenegro, at an expense of £650. The United States embassy to the Ottoman Porte costs for everything £5,600; our embassy, not including legation buildings, costs more than double.

Many of the petty continental legations have been swept away during the last 25 years, and there are several more which ought also to be abolished. The Chargé d'Affaires at Coburg, and his brethren in Wurtemburg, Darmstadt and Dresden, might well be spared, our consuls being most certainly sufficient for all useful purprses.

The eccentricities of disbursements in the Foreign Office department are very wonderful. Vice-Consuls in small places are found receiving more pay than vice-consuls in larger towns. Consuls in important ports receive often lesser salaries than consuls in ports of little or no consequence. Sometimes consuls receive less than vice-consuls. No sort of reasonable explanation can be given for such anomalies.

We now come to the items for superannuations, retired allowances, and gratuities for charitable and other purposes, or in plain words to the Pension List.

We who are Radicals do not object to pensions given for real service; nor do we object to large pensions, if the service rendered to the nation has been equivalent. The retiring pensions to our common-law and chancery judges are generally well, sometimes even hardly, earned, and none of them should be grudged. We do object to all pensions corruptly obtained, or granted without equivalent national service; we object, especially, to hereditary pensions, and we contend that Parliament has the right to cancel an improperly received pension without having either the legal or moral obligation to make any compensation to the deprived pensioner.

In the list of payments on behalf of the nation, for the year 1876, appears a pension of £843 as paid to the Duke of Grafton. This pension is a compensatory annuity paid to the Duke of Grafton on the abolition of a legal sinecure conferred on the first Duke of Grafton, who was the son of Charles II.

The modest £843 per annum — received as compensation for ceasing to perform certain supposed legal services, actually never performed—is but a very small proportion of the amount still really paid by the nation to, or on behalf of, the Duke of Grafton. King Charles II.—of pious and virtuous memory, for whose restoration to the Crown of England a grateful and devout people until very lately repeated a thanksgiving service, which was officially printed in the Common Prayer Book—in his desire to provide sufficiently for his offspring, gave to his son, the Duke of Grafton, the right of levying and taking prisage and butlerage duties on all wines brought into England, with the exception of such wines as should be imported within the jurisdiction of the Duchies of Cornwall and Lancaster. In 1797 it was estimated that the Duke of Grafton received from this source alone about £7,500 a-year. In 1806 under 43 George III., c. 156, and 43 George III., c. 79, the prisage and butlerage privileges of the Duke of Grafton were purchased for an annuity of £6,870 payable to the Duke of Grafton and his heirs male. This annuity was nominally extinguished by the redemption, as to a part, in 1809, and as to the remaining part, in 1816. In 1809 the Duke of Grafton received £49,133 11s. 8d., and in 1816 he received £86,435 7s., or together £135,568 18s. 8d., as the compensation for no longer taking prisage and butlerage on wines.

It would of course have been utterly unreasonable in a rich country like Great Britain—where in 1877 Paisley weavers are averaging 10s. per week all the year round, where a Herefordshire labourer gets eight shillings per week, and where Lord Walsingham proudly boasts that agricultural labourers' wages average 13s. to 14s. per week—to expect a man of the merit and services of the great Duke of Grafton to exist on a wretched pittance of £7,500 a-year, and, therefore, on the 22nd October, 1673, by Royal Letters Patent his loving father Charles II. created a further hereditary pension of £9,000 a-year, which somehow got reduced in 1856 to £7,191 12s., which latter sum was all that the Duke of Grafton then received for that particular pension. This sum of £7,191 12s. was also nominally extinguished in 1856 by the payment to the Duke of Grafton of the further sum of £193,777 13s. 2d.

There was still another pension received by the Duke of Grafton. This last pension appears to have been originally charged upon the Post Office Revenues as a pension of £4,700 a-year to Lady Castlemaine. Unfortunately, on

this point authorities conflict, for in 1663 the whole revenue
of the Post Office was apparently given to the Duke of York.
Perhaps the accounts of the General Post Office were then
as elastic as were the notions of the duties attaching to
letter carriers, for we find "Fifteen couple of hounds"
passing through the post, "going to the King of the Romans
with a free pass," and we also find delivered without charge
by the General Post Office, "Two servant maids going as
laundresses to my Lord Ambassador Methuen;" and, last
but not least, safely and gratuitously transmitted by the same
patient Post Office "Dr. Crichton, carrying with him a cow
and divers other necessaries." Post Office regulations at
present hardly include the foregoing curiosities. In 1857
the sum received by the Duke of Grafton for this special
pension amounted to £3,384 a-year, and for the extinguish-
ment of this he was paid a still further sum of
£91,181 17s. 7d. If these composition sums are totalled,
they amount to £420,528 9s. 5d., and this vast total has
helped to swell our national debt, and the nation, in fact,
pays the interest on it until this very day. By removing
the three several pensions of £3,384, £7,191 12s., and
£6,870 from the surface of the pension list, the grievance
has been dexterously hidden without having been redressed.
A permanent charge has been created equal to the interest at
£3 5s. per cent. on about £450,000, or, in round figures, nearly
£15,000 per year, which is the sum the Duke of Grafton
still costs the country for pensions which do not appear on
the face of the Finance Accounts. Besides the above-
mentioned commuted pensions, the post of Remembrancer
of the Court of First Fruits was, under Charles II., made
a patent place for ever, and was conferred upon the family
of the Duke of Grafton, and it is from this source that the
£843 is derived. If "high wage" helps to drive away
trade, as the landowners and capitalists say, it would be
interesting to know their opinion on the value of the Duke
of Grafton as a stimulant to commerce.

William Henry Fitz-Roy, sixth and present Duke of
Grafton, owns 7,316 acres in Buckinghamshire, 8,458 acres
in Northampton, 13,642 acres in Suffolk, and 2,784 acres
in Banff. We shall be glad to hear from any of our readers
the wages paid to agricultural labourers on his several
estates. His Grace is a Whig in politics.

After speaking in strong terms of the origin of these
Grafton pensions the author of the Financial Reform

Tracts, No. 2, published by the Liverpool Financial Reform Association, says: "Many generations have since succeeded each other, but no Duke of Grafton has yet arisen with sufficient honour or patriotism to refuse to profit by the wickedness of his ancestors, and to reject money taken, without requital, from the honest earnings of the industrious poor."

Another pension which the country continues to pay practically, while theoretically relieved from the burden, is one of £19,000 per year to the Duke of Richmond. On the 18th December, 1676, Charles II. granted to the Duke of Richmond and his heirs 1s. per chaldron on all coals exported from the River Tyne, and consumed in England. On the 5th July, 1799, this burden on poor colliery workers and coal consumers, known as the "Richmond Shilling," was changed into a permanent pension of £19,000 per year, which pension was nominally extinguished in 1825 by a payment of £490,833 11s. 6d. paid in three instalments. Charles Henry Gordon Lennox, sixth and present Duke of Richmond, owns 17,117 acres of land in Sussex, 69,660 acres in Aberdeen, 150,950 acres in Banff, 12,271 acres in Elgin, and 27,400 acres in Inverness. In Sussex we know something of the wretched earnings of the farm labourers, but we shall be glad to have more precise details from any of our Sussex readers. All names will be considered as strictly confidential. His Grace is a Tory, and is Lord President of the Privy Council; his official salary is £2,000 per annum.

Before we quit this Richmond Pension there is one most scandalous feature requiring notice. The heirs of Sir Thomas Clarges at present receive £800 per year on the pension list. This pension is an extremely puzzling one. Originally, in 1676, Sir Thomas Clarges, his heirs and assigns, had a charge on the 1s. per chaldron coal duty granted by Charles II. to the Duke of Richmond. In 1799, by some process of government manipulation, while the Tories were in power, the Clarges annuity was taken off the shoulders of the Duke of Richmond and placed on the backs of the British taxpayer. The effect of this was that the great Duke of Richmond twenty-six years later actually received a huge money compensation for this £500 a-year, to which he had no right, while the country, having thus paid the principal monies to the Duke, continues to pay the annuity to the Clarges family. The pension though nominally paid to the heirs of Sir Thomas Clarges turns out to be really paid to Lord St. Vincent, who also receives a further sum of £3,000 per year. The £3,000 is made up of two pensions granted to the famous Admiral St. Vincent, of whom the present Viscount is heir, but I cannot make out why Carnegie Robert John Jervis, third Viscount St. Vincent, should also receive the Clarges pension.

In 1662 a pension of £1000 a year was granted in perpetuity by Charles II. to the Earl of Kinnoul. George Drummond Hay, eleventh Earl of Kinnoul, and Viscount Dupplin, a Conservative peer, still receives on account of this pension £676 4s. per annum. This Earl of Kinnoul owns 12,577 acres of land in Perthshire. Apparently the original pension was of a most iniquitous character. James Hay, Earl of Carlisle, had upon the accession of Charles I. a grant of the Island of Barbadoes, as a sort of compensation for property expended about the court and in general extravagant and voluptuous living. On the death of James, Earl of Carlisle, in 1660, without issue, William, Earl of Kinnoul succeeded to the Barbadoes estate, which, in 1661 was ceded to Charles the II., who, in lieu thereof, granted the £1000 per annum for ever to the Earls of Kinnoul.

Amongst the continuing pensions specially worthy of notice there is one of £4,000 a-year payable for ever to the Duke of Marlborough. This pension, originally of £5,000 per annum, was granted by Letters Patent by Queen Anne, in 1706, to the Duke of Marlborough and his heirs in consideration of the "meritorious services" of the Duke. By an Act of Parliament, 5 & 6 Anne, c. 4, the annuity of £5,000 was granted out of the Post Office Revenues for ever to the Duke of Marlborough, the Duchess, and his heirs, and to go with the title. This pension was paid out of the Revenues of the Post Office until 1857, when by the 19 Vic., c. 59, it was transferred to the Consolidated Fund as a pension of £4,000 a-year, which is the sum now paid. The Duke of Marlborough owns 2,755 acres in Buckinghamshire, 1,534 acres in Wiltshire, and 21,944 acres in Oxfordshire. In the event of the failure of heirs male to the body of the Duke of Marlborough, the Honor and Manor of Woodstock, with Blenheim Palace, ought to revert to the nation. J. Winston Spencer Churchill, the present and sixth Duke of Marlborough, is a Tory and is Lord Lieutenant of Ireland, his official salary for which is £20,000 a-year.

His Grace is a patron of fourteen livings. His Grace also receives £91 5s. 3d. per year for his pay as officer in the army.

In the payments of 1876 there appeared an item of £2,160 payable to "the heirs of the Duke of Schomberg." In one Parliamentary return for 1869 this £2,160 figures as "three-fourths of an annuity granted by King George I. to Maynard, Duke of Schomberg, and his heirs;" and in a Treasury minute for 1853, the actual recipients of this Schomberg pension, nominally as the heirs of the Duke of Schomberg, were stated to be the following persons, in the several proportions given after their respective names, viz.; the Duke of Leeds, £1,080, C. Eyre, £720, P. Powys, £360, R. Gosling, £360, Colonel Macleod, £288, Henry Macleod, £72. The portion of the pension payable to C. Eyre was redeemed in 1855 by the payment to him of £19,399 18s., and last year the sum of £29,101 was paid to the Duke of Leeds to redeem the portion payable to him. The original grant of the pension to Frédéric Amand, the first Duke of Schomberg, was by Letters Patent of William and Mary, and was expressed to be out of the Post Office Revenues. In the estimate dated 10th August, 1699, although the Duke had been killed at the battle of the Boyne on the 11th July, 1690, the pension figures under the head "Pensions and Perpetuities" as "Duke Schonberg, on the Post Office, £4,000 per annum." George Godolphin Osborne, ninth and actual Duke of Leeds, owns 3,117 acres in Buckinghamshire, 5,911 acres in Cheshire, 5,911 acres in Cornwall, 3,234 acres in the North Riding, and 10,034 acres in the West Riding, of York.

Another curious pension is one of £4,000 per annum, also payable for ever, which figures in the national accounts as payable to trustees for the use of William Penn and his heirs and descendants for ever, in consideration of his meritorious services and family losses from the American war. The original William Penn died in 1718; we do not know who was the William Penn who, in 1790, was judged so worthy.

Under the 43 George III., c. 159, a pension of £3,000 per year is payable for ever to the representatives of Jeffery, Earl Amherst. The present recipient of this pension is William Pitt Amherst, second earl, who owns 741 acres of land in Essex, 4,269 acres in Kent, and 1,789 acres in Warwick. William Carpenter affirms that General Sir Jeffrey

Amherst, the first grantee of the pension, "was a creature of George III.," and obtained the pension "without merit of any description." In the Black Book, published by Effingham Wilson forty-eight years ago, the editor says:—

"This is one of the most objectionable of the hereditary pensions. It was transmitted by the uncle of the peer, Sir Jeffrey Amherst, a favourite of George III., and placed by him at the head of the army; when, as a commander-in-chief, he introduced and protected such barefaced jobbing and traffic in commissions as both disgraced and ruined our military power. The loyalty of that day was not to entertain even a suspicion of the misconduct of the individual who had the ear of Royalty, however flagrant, and thus the Court favourite died in the full enjoyment of the rewards of his baseness."

Horatio, third Earl Nelson, is the son of the nephew of a Norfolk Church of England clergyman, the Rev. William Nelson, who was created an earl with a pension of £5,000; having been born the brother of Horatio, Baron Nelson of the Nile. Admiral Lord Nelson received pay, pensions, and presents to a large amount. After his death, £20,000 was granted out of the people's money to Mrs. Bolton and Mrs. Matcham, two sisters of the well-rewarded admiral, and £90,000 was, in addition, voted for the purchase of an estate and mansion for the Rev. William Nelson, Prebendary of Canterbury, and Norfolk vicar. At present Earl Nelson receives from the pension list £3,500 and the balance of £1,500 is received by the Countess Frances Elizabeth Nelson. The estate bought for his lordship's father's uncle is, we believe, in Wiltshire, 5,735 acres.

The Duke of Wellington receives £4,000 per year, and in addition to this, the sum of £700,000 was granted to his father, the late Duke, in addition to his ordinary pay and extraordinary allowances, and in addition to a like annuity of £4,000 a-year for life. The present Duke owns 15,847 acres of land in Hants and 2,246 acres in Herts. The total annual income of the "Iron Duke" during the latter years of his life was about £43,178—a very fair yearly pay.

The non-existent Earl of Bath receives, or some persons as his heirs receive to-day, a pension of £1,200 per annum. This pension was originally £8,000 and was granted to the Earl of Bath—£3,000 out of the revenues of the Duchy of Cornwall, £2,500 out of the Post Office, and £2,500 out of the firstfruits and tenths. The Parliamentary return of

1869 states the £3,000 pension to have been originally granted by King William III., and also states it to have been granted by Charles II. On the 12th August, 1715, the pension of £3,000 was transferred by Royal Sign Manual Warrant of George I. from the charge of the Duchy of Cornwall to the Hereditary Excise, as from the previous 24th June, in effect increasing the income of the Prince of Wales by that amount. In 1826, Lord Melbourne, who had somehow become entitled to receive a moiety of this pension, obtained from the country the sum of £30,000 in discharge of his portion of the pension. If in America Cabinet Ministers used their influence to obtain heavy money compensation for pensions originally granted without reason, the English Press would soon expose the corruption of republican administrations. Here corruption is unknown, for this is a monarchy.

On the 9th of June, 1694, William III. granted two pensions, each of £2,000 per year, to Henry Lord d'Auverquerque, one pension to be paid out of the revenues of the principality of Wales, and the other pension to be paid out of the revenues of the Duchy of Cornwall. On the 24th December, 1698, Lord d'Auverquerque was created Earl of Grantham. In 1732, Earl Cowper married into Earl Grantham's family, and for this latter service the Earls Cowper received, and down to 1853 continued to receive, four-fifths of each of the above pensions. In 1853 Earl Cowper received two several sums—on the 5th April, £40,000, and on the 13th May, £43,000—as compensation for foregoing the annual allowance so gallantly deserved. The pension of £2,000 being payable out of the Duchy of Cornwall the actual result was to benefit the present Prince of Wales to the extent of £43,000. F. Thomas de Grey, seventh Earl Cowper, P.C., K.G., owns 2,787 acres in the county of Derby, 10,122 acres in Herts, 2,078 acres in Kent, 1,064 acres in Northampton, and 5,294 acres in Notts. Countess Cowper owns 3,227 acres in Essex, 2,536 in Wilts, and 5,720 acres in the West Riding of Yorkshire. The Dowager Countess Cowper owns 8,888 acres in Bedfordshire. The motto of the Cowpers is "Tuum est" and includes the pension.

Amongst the small curiosities of the pension list we find £209 per year to Samuel Hallyer for not being Deputy Chaffwax. James Gordon Seton gets £442 for the like absence of service (it is to be presumed that he is a superior kind of non-deputy Chaffwax), while John Holdship, as actual ex-Chaffwax, gets annually £1,145 11s. The Hon. J. H. Knox gets as ex-Weighmaster of Butter £1,076 15s., and for not holding this sinecure office this honourable gentleman has personally received £49,530 10s. There is a gentleman of the same name who owns 6,909 acres of land in county Mayo. Can any of our readers tell us if the two Dromios are one? and if yes—what sort of a landlord he makes? There is another pensioner, Caleb Tyndall, who is also not a Weighmaster of Butter, who only receives for his non-service the paltry annual stipend of £118 6s. As Mr. Tyndall and Mr. Knox each do the same work, it seems unjust that they should not have the same pay. Each of them has been ex-Weighmaster of Butter for forty-six years, and prior to that date neither of them weighed any butter. Mr. C. Panton has for fifty-five years received £850 each year as ex-Clerk of the Pipe.

A pension of £600 a year to Lady C. M. Gardiner, as one of the bedchamber women in the household of the late Princess Charlotte of Wales, is stated, in the estimates, to have commenced on the 11th December, 1865. Now, as Princess Charlotte of Wales died on the 6th November, 1817, my curiosity was excited as to the nominal origin of this pension 48 years after the death of the Princess; stated in the Government estimates as having commenced on the same day, is a pension of £100 a year to Charles Andrews, footman to the same Princess, and the age at the time of retirement from office of this footman is declared to have been 65. Now, as Charles Andrew may be fairly presumed not to have continued as footman to Princess Charlotte of Wales after her death, it is difficult to understand what is meant by the retirement from office of Charles Andrews. The Princess Charlotte received first £6,000, then £13,000, and then £60,000 a year, besides special grants amounting to £69,777; and the Prince Leopold of Saxe-Coburg received £50,000 a year for marrying the Princess. Prince Leopold is supposed to have ceased to receive this pension from the date of his acceptance of the throne of Belgium. We still continue to pay pensions to persons belonging to the household of the late king of the Belgians, Edward Robert, gamekeeper to the king, gets £75; Charles Moore, the late king's steward, £85 10s.; and William Pitcher, the groom, £75. Recipients of pensions are long lived. One view of the pension to Prince Leopold, which I had not sufficiently regarded, has been forced upon me in examining the statements as to the Russo-Dutch Loan. In 1876 there is an item of expenditure for interest and sinking fund on Russian Dutch loan of £63,384. This money represents an annual payment of decreasing amount, which commenced in 1817 at £122,480, and which will end with a payment of £21,354 in 1915. The liability seems to have been undertaken at the close of the great war in 1815, for the purpose of "establishing the King of the Netherlands in his new sovereignty." The 55 George III., cap. 115, provided that Great Britain should only continue to pay her proportion of this Russian-Dutch Loan so long as the Belgic provinces remained part of "the dominions of his Majesty the King of the Netherlands." In 1830 Belgium formed itself into an independent State, and its secession was decreed on the 25th August, 1830. Prince Leopold of Saxe-Coburg was made King of the Belgians, and in consequence of the severance of Belgium from Holland, Great Britain ought no longer to have continued to pay for interest and redemption of the Russo-Dutch loan. A new treaty was, however, entered into on the 16th November, 1831, between this country and Russia, and the engagement to continue the payments was renewed.

Mr. E. G. Johnstone was Clerk of Patents to the Attorney-General, and Solicitor-General for England. On the 1st October, 1853, his office was abolished by the 15th and 16th Vic. cap. 83, and he, as compensation for the abolition of this office, receives £850 per annum. Mr. Johnstone also receives £528 a year addition "as long as he holds the office" (*vide* Civil Service Estimates, 1874, p. 456), notwithstanding that, as the office has been abolished for nearly a quarter of a century, his holding is hardly an ordinary one.

Miscellaneous Expenditure.

Amongst miscellaneous expenditure to March 1st, 1878, £439 3s. 4d. is charged for fees paid on the installation of Prince Frederick William of Prussia as Knight Companion of the Garter, and £380 is paid for special packets for conveyance of certain "distinguished persons," whose names and destinations are not given. £7320 is charged as the cost of conferring the distinction of the Order of St. Michael and St. George upon several colonists, and of completing the insignia of the various classes of the Order.

The secret inquiry into the frauds on the London Stock Exchange cost £600. If it had been public it would not have been dear at £6000; but with closed doors and with millionaire culprits sitting on it, the whole procedure is a sham. There are several ancient fees, which have no merit except their antiquity, and which, although small, ought all to be struck out of our annual national expenditure—the City of London, £7; Duchy of Lancaster, £100; Duke of Rutland, £20; Duke of Norfolk, £60; The Bursar of Trinity College, Cambridge, £5; the Dean and Chapter of Norwich, £5.

If any evidence should be needed of the marvellous effect on health and life of the receipt of a government pension, it may be found in the item of £261, paid in 1878, "for relief of certain distressed Spanish subjects resident in this country, without the means of subsistence, who were employed with the British army, or under British authorities, in Spain, or who have otherwise rendered service to our military operations in that country during the war from 1808 to 1814." Suppose the persons who so assisted us in 1808 to have been only 25 years of age, they must now have attained the ripe age of 95. But these are only infants compared with the unnamed American loyalist who has figured for the last half-century on our national accounts, and who still continues to draw his £18 a year. What age had he attained to at the time of the Declaration of Independence? and what service had he done to be immortalised on the face of our estimates? Assume the loyalist to have been precocious, and to have exhibited his interest in Imperial politics at a very early age, as did Mr. Disraeli's famous school-girl—say ten years old—even then he would, to-day, be 112. I should like to know that American loyalist, and, in any case, I affirm that a pension is far more effective than Parr's life pills for the prolongation of human life.

We now come to the Civil List and the annuities paid to members of the Royal Family.

In 1856 the Liverpool Financial Reform Association reprinted a precise statement of the cost of the Royal Household, and about seven years ago Sir Charles Dilke caused a considerable stir in this country by his famous speeches at Newcastle and elsewhere on the expenditure of the Royal Household. Since then, Mr. J. C. Cox, of Derby, has published, in pamphlet form, an essay on the same subject. A parliamentary return, ordered to be printed by the House of Commons on the 26th July, 1869, contains the only accessible official information as to the origin of the Civil List.

On the 19th of March, 1872, Sir Charles Dilke in the House of Commons treated the subject at great length in a vain endeavour to obtain parliamentary investigation or more complete official returns. This speech he afterwards republished.

The Civil List, which is now understood to mean the annual sum granted by Parliament for the support and maintenance of the sovereign and royal household, formerly meant much more. The first Civil List Act passed by Parliament was the 9 and 10 William III., cap 23, by which £700,000 per annum was voted. This included—as the accounts for the year 1700 show—all the expenses of the nation except interest, management, and repayment of National Debt, army, navy, and ordnance. The following are the approximate items of the cost of the Royal Family per annum :—

Her Majesty the Queen, £385,000. Income of the Duchy of Lancaster, £42,000; including a compensation annuity from the Consolidated Fund, the total income of the Duchy is about £69,000. As Duchess of Lancaster Her Majesty receives £101 every year from the nation as an ancient fee. Cost of royal palaces inhabited, or partly inhabited, by Her Majesty, or inhabited without parliamentary authority by pensioned members of the royal family, £35,680. Cost of royal yachts paid by the country, amount not at present ascertainable. The *aides de camp* to the Queen are charged separately in the army estimates.

Her Majesty's enormous private property in foreign funds and landed estate is not included here, although the whole of this property must have been obtained by her from moneys economised out of the allowance made by the nation to herself and to Prince Albert, as the Duke of Kent, her father, died hopelessly insolvent, and the Prince Albert had practically no estate when he married.

There is a further sum of £1500 voted annually to Her Majesty to enable her to be charitable in Scotland, and a smaller sum of £300 to enable her to be charitable in Ireland, and there have also been yearly votes of about £1500 for racing plates to be given in Her Majesty's name. In Scotland the vote for Queen's plates comes to £218.

There is no pretence for the allegation that the Duchy of Lancaster is the private property of the Queen. In the reign of Anne, the revenues of the Duchy of Lancaster were not only part of the Civil List, but the Crown was restrained from making grants except under the provisions of 1 Anne, c. 7. So far as I am aware, although a recital was introduced into an Act of George III. that the king is possessed of himself, his heirs, and successors, of the possessions of the Duchy, it was not until 1830 that any claim of purely private property was set up. On December 1, 1830, William IV., in a letter written to Earl Grey, claimed the Duchy "as his separate, personal, and private estate, vested in His Majesty by descent from Henry VII. in his body natural, and *not in his body politic as king.*" This claim is monstrously absurd, as William IV. in his body natural was most certainly not the heir male of Henry VII., even if the Duchy had passed by natural succession.

The Princess Royal has an annuity of £8000. Her Royal Highness is Crown Princess of Prussia and received a grant of £40,000 on her marriage.

Prince of Wales and Princess of Wales, £50,000.

Net income of Duchy of Cornwall about £70,000. The total income of the Duchy in 1875 was £101,828.

The Duchy of Cornwall is the result of a charter of Edward III. stated to be confirmed by a statute of 11 Edward III., which statute is not in the revised statutes. The Duchy of Cornwall is not and cannot be the private property of the present Prince of Wales, who can only have a life estate in it, yet parts of the Duchy have been sold, but no return has, so far as I am aware, been made of the capital moneys received, or of their disposition, though in some years the receipts from such sales have been many thousands of pounds. There were formerly three pensions —one of £3000 a year to the Earl of Bath, another of £2000 a year to Lord D'Auverquerque, and a third of £300 to Sir Peter Killigrew, all payable out of the revenues of the Duchy of Cornwall. These pensions have all been transferred to the cost of the nation, thus increasing the net income of the Duchy of Cornwall. Interest on £602,720 Duchy of Cornwall accumulations in 1861, say £18,000 per annum. Sir Charles Dilke, in Parliament, stated these accumulations without contradiction at £743,000. Landed property rents, say, yearly, £8000. Military income as colonel of several regiments and field-marshal, not included.

There is no record here of the property inherited by the Prince of Wales from his father, nor can any information be given, as the will is illegally kept secret.

Occasional sums are voted for the repairs of His Royal Highness's residence. In one year £8000 was paid for this. In 1876, £550 was charged. This year £6450 is the figure of expenditure. Last year it was £4100.

There is an item each year in the national accounts of £16,216 paid to the Receiver-General of the Duchy of Cornwall for loss of duties on the coinage of tin. This item is, in fact, an annuity paid by the nation to the Prince of Wales. Although then enormously rich, His Royal Highness the Prince of Wales was content to receive from the people on the occasion of his coming of age, a parliamentary grant of £23,455.

The Duke of Edinburgh, £25,000. The naval income is not included in this annuity, nor is any account taken of the value of the hereditary rights to the Dukedom of Saxe-Coburg, and which are variously estimated. The Duke of Edinburgh has now a large additional income from his wife.

Prince Arthur, £15,000. No estimate is here made of the yearly value of the premises belonging to the nation occupied, without any parliamentary authority, by the Prince, and for which he pays no rent.

Prince Leopold, £15,000.

Princess Alice, £6000. On marrying Prince Louis of Hesse, Her Royal Highness received a grant of £30,000.

Princess Helena, £6000, and a grant of £30,000 on her marriage to Prince Christian of Schleswig-Holstein-Sonderburg-Augustenburg.

Princess Louise, £6000, and a grant on her marriage to the Marquis of Lorne.

Princess Augusta, Duchess of Cambridge, £6000 (the Financial Reform Almanack for 1878 gives this at £3000 only). In addition we spend a large sum of money to repair Her Royal Highness's apartments in St. James's Palace, and we pay the rent of her stables in Brick Street, Piccadilly.

Princess Mary of Cambridge, £5000 (married to the Duke of Teck). The White Lodge, Richmond Park, is occupied by the Duke and Duchess of Teck, and no sort of rent or compensation is paid by them to the nation, nor is there any parliamentary authority for the occupation.

Princess Augusta of Mecklenburgh-Strelitz, £3000.

Prince George, Duke of Cambridge, £12,000.

This does not include His Royal Highness's salary as Field Marshal Commanding-in-Chief, and Colonel of several regiments, nor does it include any benefits derived by the Duke of Cambridge from any rangerships or other posts held by him. As far as can be ascertained, the military salaries of the Duke of Cambridge are, as Field Marshal Commanding-in-Chief, £4432; as Colonel of the 17th Lancers, £1350; as Colonel of the Grenadier Guards, £2200; as Colonel of the Royal Regiment of Artillery, as Colonel of the 60th Rifles, as Colonel of the Corps of Royal Engineers, for these three it is not clear whether or not he takes salary. It is extremely difficult from the military estimates to say if these are given accurately. In the army list Honorary Officers are distinguished by the addition of the word Honorary, and none of the above are so marked.

Some persons pretend that the amounts paid to the royal family are justly due to them as part compensation for valuable properties surrendered by them to the nation. The only property belonging to the Brunswicks when they came to England was their Hanoverian property; this they not only kept, but actually added to out of English taxpayers' pockets. They surrendered nothing. When James II. was declared to have forfeited the Crown, and his heir male was disinherited, it is clear that the nation, or Parliament on its behalf, gave a distinct schedule of revenues for the royal maintenance, first to William of Orange, and then to Queen Anne and the children of the Electress Sophia, but there was no sort of private inheritance for the newcomers to surrender in return. They, at that time, were not even the heirs to the private estate of James II., if he had left any private estate in this country.

In the early stages of the Civil List the grants to members of the royal family were made by the Monarch for the life of the Monarch. In 1737 Frederick, Prince of Wales, applied to Parliament for a larger allowance than had been made to him by George II., and the King then objected that Parliament had nothing whatever to do with the maintenance of the royal family.

In order to find out the real cost of the royal family it is needful to examine the whole of the financial accounts with the most careful scrutiny. In the Naval expenditure for 1877, £1262 4s. was charged for conveyance of Her Majesty and the Royal Household. It was stated in the House of Commons that the amount voted for the journey of the Prince of Wales to India was more than sufficient, and that a small surplus had been left undisbursed. Despite this there is, on page 210 of the "Naval Estimates," the following item:—"Expenses incurred in connection with the visit of H.R.H. the Prince of Wales to India, £4,360 14s. 8d." Lumped in an item of £3386 8s. 7d., so that it is impossible to fix the exact amount, I find: "Pay of equerry to the Duke of Edinburgh" and "allowance to messes of Her Majesty's ship *Sultan*," while H.R.H. the Duke of Edinburgh was in command; and this year, £11,000 is to be devoted for "Conveyance by sea of the Royal Household, entertainment of royal personages, and other small or unforeseen expenses."

The True Principle of Taxation.

The true principle of taxation should be, that every member of the State who earns more than is necessary for the mere subsistence of himself and his family should contribute towards the national taxation in due proportion to his ability to pay, and to his stake and interest in the nation. It is submitted that at present the main source of revenue from taxes in the United Kingdom is the earnings of the labourer, and that even the burden of the income tax, assessed taxes, and other taxes, which seem to fall exclusively, or principally, on the richer classes, are really ultimately borne almost entirely by the producing classes.

All taxes direct and indirect, paid by the producers or importers of commodities; or paid by the dealers therein, and all taxes direct and indirect incurred on the productions of land, must in the end be paid by the consumers of house commodities and productions. Taxes originally paid to the tax collector by the producer or importer of any commodity, and by the traders and dealers therein, are all repaid by the ultimate consumer in the augmented price of the article he purchases.

TORYISM FROM 1770 TO 1879.

BY

CHARLES BRADLAUGH.

FROM 1688—when the Whig Revolution which dethroned James II., and took away the possible succession from James II.'s son, affirmed the principle that "the people of the land, fully and freely represented," have the right to take back from the wearer of the crown the authority entrusted by the nation to the monarch—down to the accession of George III., the Tories were rigidly excluded from office. During this period of nearly eighty years the Tories were consistent haters and revilers of the reigning members of the House of Hanover. No words we have ever uttered or written were half so bitter against the Brunswicks as those which came from Tory lips and Tory pens. As the Tories were not allowed to dip into the national purse they were eloquent in and out of Parliament in favour of national economy. Tories not being permitted, except in rare instances, to be commissioned officers, we have strong denunciations of the evils of standing armies from Tories, both in the House of Lords and in the Commons. With the coming to the throne of George III. there was a marked change in Tory utterances, if not in Tory principles. George III. was a natural Tory. Buckle says of him that he was despotic as well as superstitious, and he adds: "Every liberal sentiment, everything approaching to reform—nay, even the mention of inquiry—was an abomination in the eyes of that narrow and ignorant prince." The "great Commoner" who in the very Cabinet Council talked "of being responsible to the people," was no fitting minister for a true Tory King; so by the aid of Lord Bute we have in 1770 Lord North as a real Tory Prime Minister, his administration lasting until 1782. None can doubt the pure Toryism of Lord North. On the 2nd March, 1769, he declared that he could not remember that he had voted for a single popular measure. It is to George III. and his worthy minister Lord North that we owe the whole bitterness of the struggle with the North American colonies. Lord North vowed that he would never yield until "he had seen America at his feet;" but like a true Tory, he placed England at the feet of America and yielded. Lord Hillsborough, his Tory colleague, a sort of Marquis of Salisbury of a century ago, said: "We can grant nothing to the Americans except what they may ask with a halter round their necks." King George III. threatened that if the colonists succeeded he would go to Hanover; but he repented and stayed.

What was the effect of this Tory struggle with the American colonists on our National Debt and national taxation? In 1770 the National Debt was £129,197,633. The war with the American colonies cost £139,521,035, and at its conclusion the Debt had increased to £245,466,855. Just prior to the commencement of the revolution in America the annual expenditure of Great Britain and Ireland was £10,866,580. In 1785, when the war had ended in the defeat, disgrace, and impoverishment of England, the tax-bill had increased to £26,841,141. As every one knows now, this Tory war resulted in the Republic of the United States, and this result was achieved by Tory obstinacy and Tory folly, absolutely against the wish of the majority of the American colonists. George Washington was Monarchical, until the Tories made him a Republican *malgré lui*. Two petitions from the colonists to the "King's Most Excellent Majesty" were treated with scorn and contempt by the King, and by Lords North, Dartmouth, and Sandwich, his Tory advisers. The struggle began with imperial brag and ended in national shame. Those who, in South Africa, employ Basutos, Fingoes, and Swazies under Lord Beaconsfield in 1879, may well read Lord Chatham's grand denunciation of the employment of Indian savages as our allies in North America in 1777. "Who is the man," asked the great orator, "that—in addition to these disgraces and mischiefs of our army—has dared to authorise and associate to our arms the tomahawk and scalping-knife of the savage? To call into civilised alliance the wild and inhuman savage of the woods, to delegate to the merciless Indian the defence of disputed rights, and to wage the horrors of his barbarous war against our brethren—my Lords, these enormities call aloud for redress and punishment. Unless thoroughly done away with, it will be a stain on the national character." The Tory minister, the Earl of Suffolk, replied that "in a contest with rebels there were no means which God and nature might have placed at the disposal of the governing powers to which they would not be justified in having recourse." Lord Chatham's indignation knew no bounds, and in words of fire he denounced the employment of "these horrible hell-hounds of savage war." Now Tories sanction the employment of Basutos to help to steal Baphuti cattle, and assegai Baphuti wounded, while we, Christians and civilised, explode dynamite in the caverns where Baphuti women and children are hidden. As late as 1782, when the Whigs were moving resolutions in both Houses of Parliament in favor of peace with America, the Tories still encouraged the King to continue the mad and suicidal war.

From 1783 to 1801 we had the Tory Ministry of William Pitt, and in the compass of this Tory rule are crowded so many iniquities—injustice to India, cruelty and treachery to Ireland, the struggle against political progress in England and Scotland, and the war with France—that if there were no other Tory sins in the whole record of the past 100 years, these would be sore enough, and disastrous enough in their consequences, to make all honest working men guard an undying enmity to Tory Governments. Warren Hastings, the Indian Governor-General, had been impeached for fraud, corruption, for hiring out English soldiers to invade the land of the Rohillas as wholesale butchers, ravagers, and destroyers, and for murder, under the cover of the law, of an inconvenient witness against him. It was the Tory Ministry that protected the Tory Governor-General of India in his wanton course of bloodshed and dishonor. In those days there were English members of the House of Commons with the courage to impeach, but the Tories covered the crime with a party vote, and left, without redress, to the oppressed in Hindustan only the memory of their wrongs, to grow ultimately into mutiny when despair of all justice had made the bitterness of life unendurable. Then it was the Rohilla, now it is the Afghan, and to-morrow it will be some other scientific frontier, if for our shame we endure these Beaconsfields and Salisburys much longer. The Irish story has been told so often that men speak as though the repetition of the record of our shameful doings had in some degree remedied or absolved the wrong we had done. But it was not only the Tory cruelty in Ireland under Pitt, it was not only the breach of faith to the Catholics at the time of the Act of Union, it was the consistent and persistent hindrance by the Tories of all approach to religious liberty through more than a quarter of a century of embittered struggling. In the teeth of his own distinct pledge the Tory Pitt in 1805 directly voted against Lord Grenville's resolution in favor of the removal of Catholic disabilities. True to Tory instincts, in 1807 Lord Liverpool and the Duke of Portland secured the rejection of Lord Howick's proposal to enable persons of every religious persuasion to hold commissions in the army. The Tories might have made Ireland loyal by justice; they made disaffection chronic by keeping the pressure of injustice always acute. Even when, after the masterly agitation conducted by Daniel O'Connell, the Tories at last gave way to the claim for Catholic emancipation, they were only moved by fear. Eloquence found them deaf, entreaty found them stern, but the threat of civil war found them coward.

The Tory Duke of York, putting his hand to his left breast, near the region where the heart should have been, pledged himself in the House of Lords that the measure for the relief of the Roman Catholics should not be carried, "so help me God." The virtuous and Tory Duke of Cumberland menaced the nation that he would leave it for ever if it dared to pass the Bill. But Tory resistance was vain. On the 4th of April, 1829, the Duke of Wellington declared that his unconvinced Cabinet had been compelled to submit to the popular will, being at last thoroughly convinced that they had no choice between concession and civil war. It was not that they would have cared for the horrors of civil war if they had dared to believe they would have won, but they feared defeat. It is only men with the sustaining courage of principles who can again and again, and with foreknowing persistence, fight losing battles, and since the Tories have been faithless to the Stuarts they have had no principles. And, except that modern opinion limits their power for mischief, the Tories of to-day are to Ireland as were the Tories of Pitt, Portland, Liverpool, Castlereagh, and Wellington. It was on the 2nd of December, 1868, that Mr. Disraeli declared that he would continue to give an uncompromising resistance to the disestablishment of the Irish Church. The Tories made '98; they sowed the seed for '48; they planted the roots of Fenianism; they it is whom we must indict for the continuing discontent in our sister isle. We come back again to the Ministry of Pitt, to the war with France, which arose out of the bargain made by Lord Elgin in 1791 to support the Royal Family of France—that is, to encourage, with armed support, weak and vacillating Louis XVI. to betray the very Constitution he had solemnly sworn to maintain. Without English subsidies, furnished by the Tory ministers, the European princes could have given small aid to the tottering Monarchy of France. The Tories feared that the contagion of liberty would be too fierce, and they made a war which endured from 1793 to 1815; and again, lovers of an Imperial policy, look at the effect of this war on our National Debt and national taxation. The war cost, in hard cash, £989,636,449. Before the war began the annual taxation of Great Britain and Ireland was £18,349,344; in 1815, when the war finished, the tax-bill had swollen to £77,887,335. Before the war commenced the National Debt was £247,874,434; when the war had finished England's future industry was mortgaged to repay £861,039,049, besides the capital value of the terminable annuities.

The political liberty we use to-day, the right of meeting we enjoy to-day, the cheap Press we read to-day, have all been won in spite of bitterest Tory opposition. Under Pitt the most infamous repressive laws were passed against tongue and pen.

One statute of 1796 declared that if a man permitted lectures or debates on any subject whatever without licence of a magistrate he might be fined £100 a day, and that if a man without a similar licence lent books, newspapers, or pamphlets, he might be fined £20. Under Lords Liverpool, Sidmouth, and Castlereagh, acts were passed in 1819 which actually prohibited the publication of a cheap pamphlet or a cheap newspaper until the publisher had given two sureties to the extent of £800 not to publish anything seditious. These statutes were only repealed under Mr. Gladstone in 1869, and after many a journalist had been ruined. In the period between the accession of Pitt to power and the termination of the long administration of Lord Liverpool, how many poor men went over and over again to gaol to win us free speech and free Press! In Scotland, Gerald, Skirving, Palmer, Muir, Margarot, and a host of others paid the penalty for their advocacy of reform; some died in the plantations, others died at home from dungeon fever. In London, Erskine's grand defence of Hardy, Tooke, and Thelwall, and in Manchester his brilliant pleading for Walker and his fellow-prisoners, serve to show us a little how the struggle was conducted, and the later fights, as in 1820, when a whole regiment of poor men were on trial with Hunt and Balmforth at Lancaster —all these mark the fashion in which political liberty has been painfully battled for and slowly won, despite Tory rule. And the present Tory Ministry is true to its old Tory traditions; while it dare not gag the Press in England, it has issued a Press gag law in India, and has stifled the Press in Cyprus. It dare not now use yeomanry to disperse a political meeting in Lancashire, as it did sixty years ago, but it ventures on a similar outrage in South Africa.

In office or out of office the Tories tried to keep bread dear until they were beaten by Cobden and the men of the anti-corn-law movement. In office and out of office the Tories hindered reform, until in the struggle prior to 1832 they were affrighted by Bristol riotings, Nottingham burnings, and the threat of Attwood and his Birmingham men that they would march on London. As they were in 1830, so they were in 1866, when Lord Derby, on the 9th July, as Tory Prime Minister, declared that he would not introduce a Reform Bill, but modified his opinion fourteen days later, when the Hyde Park railings were on the ground in Park Lane. The measure of reform of 1867 grew into its ultimate shape under pressure of large meetings held throughout the land. And as Tories have been, in office and out of office, since 1770 to 1874, so have they been under the present Ministry, from 1874 to 1879. When they came into office in 1874, our national expenditure amounted to £73,270,000, not including the sum paid for the "Alabama" claims. In 1878 our admitted national expenditure was £85,407,000, but this does not include many items for the Afghan war, which India cannot pay if she would, and ought not to pay if she could. These eighty-five and a half millions do not include the whole of the items of the disbursements in South Africa, although it is hopeless to expect that the South African colonies can contribute much to this cost. The Tories have taken from the nation each year a larger sum in respect of the National Debt, and yet the national indebtedness is to-day actually larger than when they came into office. In March, 1874, the debt was nominally £779,283,245, but as the estimates of the outgoing Government showed a receivable surplus of income as against expenditure on the current year, of more than five and a half millions, the real balance should only be taken at seven hundred and seventy-three and three-quarter millions. In March, 1879, the National Debt was admittedly £778,078,840, but this left out many millions to be added of Indian and South African war debt, and who dares say to how much the butcher's bill has already swollen or will swell the debt before this year has finished?

Lord Sandon pleads that our Imperial interests need this enormous expenditure. I answer that our national interests do not need it. In England we want no Empress and will not have one. Lord Sandon says that the expenditure is required for the protection of our colonies. I reply that this wanton waste for powder and steel is only required in those colonies where we practise injustice, annexation, and oppression.

The bill of indictment against the present Tory Ministry is a most serious one. In November, 1875, they bought from the late Viceroy of Egypt—at a time when they ought to have known him to be utterly insolvent—a large quantity of practically worthless shares, for which £4,080,000 was paid. These shares not even giving a right to speak or vote in the Company, the Tory Ministry have since purchased other more valuable shares to qualify salaried directors to watch over the valuable property so acquired. As this purchase was actually most illegally completed, and the money treasonably paid before Parliament was consulted on the matter, an extravagant rate of interest was paid by the Government to the Messrs. Rothschild, by whom the scheme was temporarily financed. To cover this reckless waste of public money to Rothschilds the Prime Minister made two statements, both of which he either knew to be, or might have known to be, positively untrue—1. That Rothschilds had, at the request of the Government, bought the shares, and might have been compelled to keep them if Parliament had not endorsed the transaction. 2. That Rothschilds had found one million in gold on the 1st of December, 1875, and might have been called on to find the remaining three millions on the following day—the facts, on the contrary, being that Rothschilds refused to be, and were not, parties to the purchase, except as lenders of the purchase-money, and that they expressly stipulated against being called on to find the three millions except at dates convenient to themselves. Subsequently to this the whole conduct of the Ministry in Egypt has been characterised by deception so far as the Ministerial explanations to Parliament are concerned, and by gross fraud on the nation.

The six millions' vote prior to Berlin was obtained by a fraud on the country; the Government, afterwards pledging itself that the abstract of the secret agreement with Russia was wholly unauthentic, thus led infatuated Jingoes to believe that Lords Beaconsfield and Salisbury were really advocating a bold policy at Berlin. Lord Beaconsfield made a wantonly false boast of having secured at Berlin an enduring peace when in Europe Austria was invading Bosnia; when the plans for the invasion of Zululand were already submitted to and approved by the Duke of Cambridge; and when the schemes for forcing a quarrel on Shere Ali, in breach of our solemn treaty, and in defiance of our deliberately pledged word, were being eagerly hurried on. In South Africa, in absolute bad faith, the Tories have most illegally destroyed the Dutch South African Republic. They have quarrelled with the Gaikas, the Galekas, and the Pondos, burning their kraals, stealing their cattle, and shooting their women and children. The Tories have landed us in a quarrel with the Baphutis, who have three times beaten us back from Moirosi's mountain, despite that English Christians have thrown dynamite to explode in the caverns where Baphuti men, women, and children lay hidden. These Tories planned long beforehand the invasion of Zulu territory, and sent reinforcements to enable Lord Chelmsford to make the invasion, and yet Lord Salisbury calls our defeat at Isandalana "an unexpected attack made by savages on one of our colonies, which came on us like a thunderclap." They have decorated as a hero the Lord Chelmsford who, in coward terror, left our dead unburied for four long months.

With the warning of thirty-eight years since before their eyes, with a solemn treaty binding this country not to force European residents upon the Court of Cabul, the Tory Government have wantonly disregarded treaties, promises, and warnings, and they have, in breach of their own distinct statement to the English Parliament, tried to compel the late Shere Ali to receive a British resident at Cabul. These Tories have succeeded in deceiving the present English Parliament by false and fraudulent representations as to what was really happening in India and Afghanistan, and now, by excluding the representatives of the Press, except under most disgraceful conditions, they prevent the real truth from reaching the English people. Lords Beaconsfield, Salisbury, and Lytton are responsible for the death of Sir Louis Cavagnari, as Lord Beaconsfield and Sir Bartle Frere are responsible for those who died at Isandalana. They were warned over and over again that there was danger to any European resident at Cabul, but Sir Bartle Frere mocked the warning in 1875, and Lord Lytton not only mocked the warnings prior to and after the entry of Sir Louis Cavagnari amongst the Cabulese, but he actually permitted lying telegrams of safety and quiet to be published in England in lieu of the discomforting reports which continually reached the Government.

What has this Tory Government—now said to be about to dissolve Parliament—to show to the people as compensation for this waste of treasure and loss of life? Seven thousand troops brought from India and marched back again, just enough to teach the inhabitants of Hindustan—whom we govern in their own country at the point of the bayonet—that we were not strong enough to hold our own in Europe without the help of Hindu swords. Cyprus, "a place at arms," desolate and fever-stricken, leased from the Porte at a high rent, which we are to hold as vassals of the Sultan to practise there a little slavery, a little Press-gagging, and some priest-shaving. The Asia Minor Protectorate, a dissolving view in a political magic lantern with the slides twisted and blurred. We are repudiated by Turkey; Safvet Pasha himself told me that England had betrayed Turkey into war by promises of support which had never been kept. We have made Italy uneasy. Germany ridicules our pretence of boldness, and France regards us with mistrust. At home trade is bad, our people are hungry and unemployed. But their verdict is to be given at the polling-booth on the day of the general election.

Printed and Published by CHARLES BRADLAUGH and ANNIE BESANT,
at 28, Stonecutter Street, London, E.C.

THREE HUNDREDTH THOUSAND.

December, 1879.

CATALOGUE OF WORKS

SOLD BY THE

FREETHOUGHT PUBLISHING COMPANY,

28, STONECUTTER STREET, FARRINGDON STREET, E.C.

Orders should be sent to the Manager, Mr. W. J. RAMSEY, accompanied with Post Office Order, payable at Ludgate Circus, or Cheque crossed "London and South Western Bank."

The Freethinker's Text-Book.—Part I. By C. BRADLAUGH. Section I.—"The Story of the Origin of Man, as told by the Bible and by Science." Section II.—"What is Religion?" "How has it Grown?" "God and Soul." Each Section complete in itself, with copious index. Bound in cloth, price 2s. 6d.
    Part II., by ANNIE BESANT.—"On Christianity." Section I.—"Christianity: its Evidences Unreliable." Section II.—"Its Origin Pagan." Section III.—"Its Morality Fallible." Section IV.—"Condemned by its History." Bound in cloth, 3s. 6d.

History of the Great French Revolution.—By ANNIE BESANT. Cloth, 2s. 6d.

Impeachment of the House of Brunswick.—By CHARLES BRADLAUGH. Sixth edition. 1s.
    The boldest indictment of the present reigning family ever published, with an Appendix on the Civil List.

What does Christian Theism Teach?—A verbatim report of two nights' Public Debate between the Rev. A. J. HARRISON and C. BRADLAUGH. Second edition. 6d.

God, Man, and the Bible.—A verbatim report of a three nights' Discussion at Liverpool between the Rev. Dr. BAYLEE and C. BRADLAUGH.
    This is the only debate extant on the purely Socratic method. 6d.

Heresy; its Morality and Utility.—A Plea and a Justification. By CHARLES BRADLAUGH. 9d.

On the Being of a God as the Maker and Moral Governor of the Universe.—A verbatim report of a two nights' Discussion between THOMAS COOPER and C. BRADLAUGH. 6d.

When were our Gospels Written?—A Reply to Dr. Tischendorf and the Religious Tract Society. By CHARLES BRADLAUGH. 6d.

Has Man a Soul?—A verbatim report of two nights' debate at Burnley, between the Rev. W. M. WESTERBY and C. BRADLAUGH. 1s.

Christianity in relation to Freethought Scepticism and Faith.—Three Discourses by the BISHOP OF PETERBOROUGH, with Special Replies by CHARLES BRADLAUGH. New edition, reduced to 6d.

Is it Reasonable to Worship God?—A verbatim report of two nights' debate at Nottingham between the Rev. R. A. ARMSTRONG and C. BRADLAUGH. 1s.

National Secular Society's Tracts.—1. Address to Christians. 2. Who was Jesus? 3. Secular Morality. 4. The Bible and Woman. 5. Secular Teachings. 6. Secular Work. 7. What is Secularism? 8. Who are the Secularists? 9. Secular Responsibility. 7½d. per 100, post free. 10. Fruits of Christianity, by ANNIE BESANT. 2d.

My Path to Atheism.—Collected Essays of ANNIE BESANT.—The Deity of Jesus—Inspiration—Atonement—Eternal Punishment—Prayer—Revealed Religion—and the Existence of God, all examined and rejected; together with some Essays on the Book of Common Prayer. Cloth, lettered, 4s.

Marriage: as it was, as it is, and as it should be. By ANNIE BESANT. In limp cloth, 1s.

Verbatim Report of the Trial, The Queen against Bradlaugh and Besant.—Neatly bound in cloth, price 5s., post free. With Portraits and Autographs of the two Defendants.

Second Edition, with Appendix, containing the judgments of Lords Justices Bramwell, Brett, and Cotton.

PAMPHLETS BY ANNIE BESANT.

	s.	d.
The True Basis of Morality. A Plea for Utility as the Standard of Morality ...	0	2
Auguste Comte. Biography of the great French Thinker, with Sketches of his Philosophy, his Religion, and his Sociology. Being a short and convenient *resume* of Positivism for the general reader	0	6
Giordano Bruno, the Freethought Martyr of the Sixteenth Century. His Life and Works	0	1
The Political Status of Women. A Plea for Women's Rights ...	0	2
Civil and Religious Liberty, with some Hints taken from the French Revolution ...	0	3
The Gospel of Atheism ...	0	2
Is the Bible Indictable? ...	0	2
England, India, and Afghanistan ...	0	9

		s.	d.
The Story of Afghanistan		0	2
The Law of Population: Its consequences, and its Bearing upon Human Conduct and Morals. 35th thousand		0	6

An additional twenty thousand of this have also been printed in America, and a translation has been issued and widely sold in Holland.

	s.	d.
Liberty, Equality, and Fraternity	0	1
Landlords, Tenant Farmers, and Labourers	0	1
The God Idea in the Revolution	0	1
The Gospel of Christianity and the Gospel of Freethought	0	2
English Marseillaise, with Music	0	1
English Republicanism	0	1
Essays, bound in one volume, cloth	3	0
Christian Progress	0	2

Large Portrait of Mrs. Besant, fit for framing, 2s. 6d.

A splendidly executed Steel Engraving of Mrs. Besant, price 2d.

PAMPHLETS BY C. BRADLAUGH.

	s.	d.
Hints to Emigrants, containing important information on the United States, Canada, and New Zealand	1	0
Cromwell and Washington: a Contrast	0	6

A Lecture delivered to large audiences throughout the United States.

	s.	d.
Five Dead Men whom I Knew when Living. Sketches of Robert Owen, Joseph Mazzini, John Stuart Mill, Charles Sumner, and Ledru Rollin	0	4
Jesus, Shelley, and Malthus, an Essay on the Population Question	0	2
American Politics	0	2
Life of George, Prince of Wales, with Recent Contrasts and Coincidences	0	2
Real Representation of the People	0	2
Toryism from 1770 to 1879	0	1
Letter to Albert Edward Prince of Wales, on Freemasonry	0	1
Why do Men Starve?	0	1
Poverty and its effect upon the People	0	1
Labour's Prayer	0	1
The Land, the People, and the Coming Struggle	0	2

	s. d.
Plea for Atheism	0 3
Has Man a Soul? New Edition	0 2
Is there a God?	0 1
Who was Jesus?	0 1
What did Jesus Teach?	0 1
The Twelve Apostles	0 1
The Atonement	0 1
Life of David	0 2
Life of Jacob	0 1
Life of Abraham	0 1
Life of Moses	0 1
Life of Jonah	0 1
A Few Words about the Devil	0 1
Were Adam and Eve our First Parents?	0 1
Large Photograph of Mr. Bradlaugh for framing	2 6
Autobiography with Portrait	0 3
Taxation; how it originated, who bears it, and who ought to bear it	0 6
The Laws Relating to Blasphemy and Heresy	0 6

Or to be obtained in volumes.

Political Essays.—By C. BRADLAUGH. Bound in cloth, 2s. 6d.

Theological Essays.—By C. BRADLAUGH. Bound in cloth, 3s.

Five Debates between C. BRADLAUGH and Rev. Dr. BAYLEE, in Liverpool; the Rev. Dr. HARRISON, in London; WILLIAM BROWN, M.A., in Leeds; THOMAS COOPER, in London; and the Rev. R. A. ARMSTRONG, in Nottingham. Just published, bound in one volume, cloth. Price 3s.

The Value of this Earthly Life. A Reply to W. H. Mallock's "Is Life worth Living?" By EDWARD B. AVELING, D.Sc., F.L.S., Fellow of University College, London.

Wealthy and Wise. A lecture introductory to the Study of Political Economy. By J. HIAM LEVY. 6d.

Past and Present of the Heresy Laws.—By W. A. HUNTER, M.A., Barrister-at-Law, Professor of Jurisprudence, University College, London. (The Counsel who so ably defended Mr. EDWARD TRUELOVE before the Lord Chief Justice of England, and again before Mr. Baron Pollock). Price 3d.

Court Flunkeys; their Work and Wages. By G. STANDRING. Price 1d.

The Education of Girls.—By Henry R. S. Dalton, B.A., Oxon. Second Edition. Price 6d.

Ish's Charge to Women. By H. R. S. Dalton. 4d.

Religion and Priestcraft. By H. R. S. Dalton. 2d.

L'Impot sur le Capital. Par Menier, Député. 1s.

On the Connection of Christianity with Solar Worship. By T. E. Partridge. 1s. (Translated from Dupuis.)

Clericalism in France.—By Prince Napoleon Bonaparte (Jerome). Translated by Annie Besant. Price 6d.

Noah's Flood. By G. W. Foote. 1d.

Creation Story. By G. W. Foote. 1d.

Futility of Prayer. By G. W. Foote. 2d.

Secularism, the True Philosophy of Life. By G. W. Foote. 4d.

The Cause of Woman.—From the Italian of Louisa To-Sko. By Ben W. Elmy. Price 6d.

Studies in Materialism.—By Ben. W. Elmy. Price 4d.

Thoughts on Religion and Society.—By H. Glasse. Price 2d.

Lectures of Colonel Robert Ingersoll.—"Oration on the Gods." Price 6d.—"Oration on Thomas Paine." Price 4d.—"Heretics and Heresies." Price 4d.—"Oration on Humboldt." Price 2d.—"Arraignment of the Church." Price 2d. These can be supplied in one volume neatly bound in limp cloth. Price 1s. 6d.

City Missionaries and Pious Frauds.—By W. R. Crofts. 1d.

The Ten Commandments.—By W. P. Ball. Price 1d.

Religion in Board Schools.—By W. P. Ball. 2d.

The Devil's Pulpit, being Astronomico-Theological Discourses.—By the Rev. Robert Taylor, B.A., of St. John's College, Cambridge; author of the "Diegesis," "Syntagma," &c. (Reprinted verbatim from Richard Carlile's original edition). Published in fortnightly numbers. 2d. Vol. I. now ready, containing twenty-three numbers, in neat cloth, 4s.

Natural Reason versus Divine Revelation.—An appeal for Freethought. By Julian. Edited by Robert Lewins, M.D. 6d.

The Dyer's Hand.—By Alexander J. Ellis. 2d.

Cabinet Photographs of Mr. Bradlaugh and Mrs. Besant.—2s. each.

Cabinet Photograph of Mabel Emily Besant.—2s.

Cartes de Visite, taken from the above three, each 1s.

The Methodist Conference and Eternal Punishment: Do its Defenders Believe the Doctrine?—By Joseph Symes, formerly Wesleyan Minister. 3d.

Hospitals and Dispensaries, are they of Christian Growth? By J. Symes. 1d. New and revised edition.

Man's Place in Nature, or Man an Animal amongst Animals. By J. SYMES. 4d.

Philosophic Atheism. By J. SYMES. 2d.

Robert Cooper's Holy Scriptures Analysed, with Sketch of his Life. By C. BRADLAUGH. 6d.

Thomas Paine's Common Sense.—With New Introduction. By CHARLES BRADLAUGH. 6d.

New Theory of Poverty.—By H. AULA. 1d.

Liberty and Morality. By M. D. CONWAY. 3d.

Hovelacque's Science of Language. With Maps. Large Crown 8vo. 5s.

Molesworth's History of England from the Year 1830 to the Resignation of the Gladstone Ministry. Three vols. Crown 8vo. 15s.

Topinard's Anthropology. With a Preface by Professor BROCA. With numerous Illustrations. Large crown 8vo. 7s. 6d.

The Romantic Legend of Sakya Buddha. By the Rev. SAMUEL BEAL. Crown 8vo, pp. 408, cloth. 12s.

Lange's History of Materialism, translated by E. C. THOMAS. 10s. 6d.

Thomas Carlyle on the French Revolution. 3 vols. 6s.

Guyot's Earth and Man; or Physical Geography in its Relation to the History of Mankind. With additions by Professors AGASSIZ, PIERCE, and GRAY. 12 Maps and Engravings on Steel, some Coloured, and a Copious Index. Crown 8vo, cloth extra, gilt, with Illustrations. 4s. 6d.

The Meaning of History. Two Lectures delivered by FREDERIC HARRISON, M.A. 8vo, pp. 80, sewed. 1s.

History of Rationalism: embracing a Survey of the Present State of Protestant Theology. By the Rev. JOHN F. HURST, Revised and enlarged. Crown 8vo, pp. xvii. and 525, cloth. 10s. 6d.

Thomas Carlyle's Cromwell. 5 vols. 10s.

The Debatable Land between this World and the Next. With Illustrative Narrations. By ROBERT DALE OWEN. Second Edition. Crown 8vo, pp. 456, cloth. 7s. 6d.

Threading my Way: Twenty-seven years of Autobiography. By R. D. OWEN. Crown 8vo, pp. 344, cloth, 7s. 6d.

Faraday's Chemical History of a Candle. Edited by W. CROOKES, F.C.S. With numerous Illustrations. Crown 8vo, cloth extra 4s. 6d.

Faraday's Various Forces of Nature. Edited by W. CROOKES, F.C.S. With numerous Illustrations. Crown 8vo, cloth extra, 4s. 6d.

Shelley's Works, reprinted from the original MSS. In four handsome volumes, each complete in itself. Vol. 1, Early Poems. Volume 2, Later Poems. Vol. 3, Posthumous Poems. Vol. 4, Prose Writings. 2s. each.

The Population Question. By C. R. DRYSDALE, M.D. 1s.

Tobacco, and the Diseases it Produces. By C. R. DRYSDALE, M.D. 2d.

Alcohol. By C. R. DRYSDALE, M.D. 6d.

The History of Clerkenwell. By the late W. J. PINKS, with additions and Notes by the Editor, Edward J. Wood, complete in one vol., fully gilt, 800 pp., 15s.

Paine's Theological Works; including the "Age of Reason," and all his Miscellaneous Pieces and Poetical Works; his last Will and Testament, and a Steel Portrait. Cloth. 3s.

The Age of Reason. By THOMAS PAINE. Complete, including an Essay on his Life and Genius, with Portrait, 1s.

Paine's Rights of Man. A Reply to Burke on the French Revolution. 1s.

Essays on Miracles. By DAVID HUME. A new edition, complete, with all the notes. 2d.

The Immortality of the Soul Philosophically Considered. Seven Lectures by ROBERT COOPER. 1s.

Voltaire's Philosophical Dictionary. The edition in six, re-printed in two thick volumes. Two portraits and a memoir. 8s.

Life of David Hume. 3d.

Analysis of the Influence of Natural Religion on the temporal Happiness of Mankind. By PHILIP BEAUCHAMP (a pseudonym adopted by G. Grote, the historian of Greece). Pp. 123. 1s. 6d.

The Diegesis. By ROBERT TAYLOR (coadjutor of Richard Carlile, and imprisoned for blasphemy in Oakham Jail). 3s. 6d.

House of Life. Human Physiology in its Application to Health. By Mrs. FENWICK MILLER. Cloth, illustrated. 2s. 6d.

Shelley's Song to the Men of England. Set to Music for four voices. By HERR TROUSSELLE. 2d.

American Communities. By W. A. HIND. The only reliable history of American Communities. Splendidly printed on toned paper. 3s.

Error Book. The Queen v. Bradlaugh and Besant, containing the formal indictment and pleadings. 1s.

Three Years of the Eastern Question. By the Rev. M. Maccoll. 5s.

LIST B.

Special List of Second-hand Books and Remainders.—All the books in List B are at the lowest price, and no reduction can be made to the trade, the object being to supply readers of the *National Reformer* with literature at specially low rates.

Orders should be sent to the Manager, Mr. W. J. Ramsey, accompanied by Post Office Order, including the cost of Postage, which is inserted after the letter P. Where no postage is mentioned, to go by Sutton at cost of purchaser, and 2d. in addition to price must be sent for booking.

Howell's Capital and Labour.—Including Chapters on the history of Guilds, Trades' Unions, Apprentices, Technical Education, Intimidation and Picketing, Restraints on Trade; Strikes—their Objects, Aims, and Results; Trade Councils, Arbitration, Co-operation, Friendly Societies, the Labor Laws, &c. By GEORGE HOWELL. Published at 7s. 6d. Post free for 5s. 6d.

Volney's Ruins of Empires.—Crown 8vo. (Published at 8s. 6d.) 2s. P. 3d.

The Outcast.—By WINWOOD READE. New, cloth, handsomely bound, pp. 262. 1s. 6d. P. 3½d.

Bartholomew Fair, Memoirs of. By HENRY MORLEY, a verbatim reprint from the original edition, with eighty-one fac-simile drawings engraved on wood, post 8vo, cloth, new uncut (pub. at 5s.), 2s. 6d. P. 5½d.

The Religion of the Heart: A Manual of Faith and Duty. By LEIGH HUNT. Pp. 259. Neatly bound. 2s. 6d. P. 3d.

Ancient Mysteries described, by WILLIAM HONE. With Engravings on Copper and Wood. New, cloth, uncut. 2s. 6d. P. 6d.

The Apochryphal New Testament, being all the Gospels, Epistles, &c., attributed to Christ, his Apostles, and their companions in the first four centuries of the Christian Era. By W. HONE. 2s. 6d. P. 6d.

Morley (Henry, author of "English Literature,") &c., &c.), Clement Marot, and other studies, 2 vols. in 1, thick post 8vo, cloth, new (pub. at 21s.), 4s. P. 8d.

Taine (D.C.L., Oxon.), On Intelligence, translated from the French By J. D. HAYE and revised with additions by the Author, pp. 542, 8vo, cloth new, uncut (pub. at 18s.), 6s. P. 10d.

The Life and Times of the Hon. Algernon Sydney, English Republican. By A. C. EWALD, in two large volumes, new, cloth, uncut, 4s. (pub. at 25s.)

Correspondence of Charles Lamb, with an Essay on his Life and Genius. By THOMAS PURCELL. New, uncut, pp. 537, cloth, gilt lettered, 2s. 6d. P. 8d.

Rousseau.—By JOHN MORLEY. 2 vols. 7s. 6d. Published at 24s.

The Upas: a Vision of the Past, Present, and Future.—By Capt. R. H. DYAS. This book, which, translated into Italian, is having a wide circulation in Italy, traces the rise, reign, and decay of Superstition. Cloth, published at 10s., reduced to 2s. 6d. P. 7d.

The Works of Flavius Josephus. By WILLIAM WHISTON. With numerous illustrations. 2 vols. Very handsomely bound. Vol. I., pp. 693. Vol. II., pp. 661. Quite new, 8s. 6d.; published at 14s.

History of English Literature.—By H. A. TAINE, D.C.L., Translated by H. VAN LAUN. 2 vols., handsomely bound. Vol. I., pp. 531; Vol. II., pp. 550, 12s.; published at 15s.

Household Words.—Conducted by CHARLES DICKENS. Strongly bound. New, uncut, each volume, 2s.; published at 5s. 6d.

Vol. 8 contains "A Dead Secret" and other tales. Various papers on Constantinople, the Dardanelles, and Greece. A round of Christmas stories.

Vol. 9 contains the whole of the essays on Turkey and Greece, by a Roving Englishman, written at the close of the Crimean War.

Vol. 14 contains the story of "The Wreck of the Golden Mary," also the famous papers "A Journey due North," and "A Journey to Russia."

Divine Revelation or Pseudo-Science.—By R. G. S. BROWNE, B.D. Written against Evolutionists. Pp. 120. 6d. P. 2½d.

Ireland under British Rule.—By Lieut.-Colonel H. J. W. JERVIS, R.A., M.P. Neatly bound. Pp. 321. 2s. P. 7½d.

Histoire de la Commune.—Par P. VESINIER. The original French edition. Handsomely bound in cloth. Price 1s. 6d. P. 6d.

Views of the Deity, Traditional and Scientific.—A Contribution to the Study of Theological Science (written against the Materialist Position). By JAMES SAMUELSON. Pp. 171. New and uncut, 1s. 6d. P. 3½d.

Diversions of the Echo Club.—By OLIVER WENDELL HOLMES, the great American writer. Reduced to 1s., post free.

Thomas Wentworth, Earl of Strafford, and Lord Lieutenant of Ireland, The Life of. By ELIZABETH COOPER. 2 vols. 8vo, cloth, uncut, new (published at 30s.), 5s.

Hans Breitman's Christmas, with other Ballads, reduced to 6d., post free.

Hans Breitman as a Politician, with other Ballads, reduced to 6d. Post free.

The Story of the Commune.—By a COMMUNALIST. Reduced to 6d. Post free.

The Last Days of a Condemned.—By VICTOR HUGO. With Obervations on Capital Punishment, by Sir P. Hesketh Fleetwood, Bart, M.P. Cloth, 1s. P. 3½d.

Castelar's (Emilio) Life of Lord Byron, and other Sketches. Translated by Mrs. ARTHUR ARNOLD. 8vo, cloth, new, uncut (published at 12s.), 3s. 6d. P. 7d.

The other Sketches are—Victor Hugo, Alexander Dumas, Emilo Girardin, Daniel Manin, Adolphe Thiers.

David Fredrick Strauss, in his Life and Writings.—By EDWARD ZELLER. Cloth, new and uncut (published at 5s.) Pp. 160. 1s. P. 4d.

Zoological Mythology; or, the Legends of Animals. By ANGELO GUBERNATIS. 2 vols., pp. 874, new, uncut, £1 (published at 28s.).

The Essence of Christianity.—By LUDWIG FEUERBACH. Translated by MARIAN EVANS. Pp. 340, neatly bound, new, uncut, 2s. 6d. P. 6d. Published at 6s. The translator is celebrated under the *nom de plume* of George Eliot.

Letters on Bibliolatry. Translated from the German of G. E. Lessing, by H. H. BERNARD, Ph. Dr. Pp. 144. 2s. P. 4d. Published at 5s.

The Sphere and Duties of Government.—By WILHELM VON HUMBOLDT. Pp. 203. 2s. 6d. P. 3d. Published at 5s.

The Ancient World.—By J. A. G. BARTON. Pp. 339. Bound in cloth. 1s. 6d. P. 4d.. Published at 6s.

Fresh Revision of the English Old Testament. By S. DAVIDSON, LL.D. 1s. P. 3d. Published at 5s.

The Book of Job. By J. A. FROUDE, M.A. Pp. 38. Neatly bound. 1s. Post free.

The Philosophy of Kant. Lectures by VICTOR COUSIN. Translated from the French. With a Sketch of Kant's Life and Writings. By A. G. HENDERSON. Pp. 194. Neatly bound. 2s. 6d. P. 5d. Published at 6s.

The Book of Genesis and its Relation to the Hebrew Chronology. The Flood, the Exodus of the Israelites, the Site of Eden, &c., &c. From the Danish of the late Professor RASK. With a Map of Paradise and the Circumjacent Lands. Pp. 126. 2s. P. 2½d. Published at 2s. 6d.

The True History of Joshua Davidson, Christian and Communist.—By Mrs. LYNN LYNTON. Sixth Edition. New, handsomely bound in cloth, printed on thick paper, pp. 279. Price 1s. 6d. P. 4d.

Life and Pontificate of Leo. X.—By WILLIAM ROSCOE. Neatly bound, quite new, pp. 425. 1s. P. 2½d. A standard Historical authority.

Rossel's Posthumous Papers. Translated from the French. Pp. 294. New, bound in cloth, 1s. 6d. P. 4d.

Empire in India. By MAJOR EVANS BELL. Pp. 412. Bound in cloth. 2s. 6d. P. 6d. Published at 8s. 6d.

Reduced to 3d., if sent by post 1d. extra. Any 8 of the undermentioned
Half Hours with the Freethinkers:—
Lord Bolingbroke, Lord Shaftesbury, Shelley, Anthony Collins, Spinoza, Charles Southwell, Charles Darwin, Descartes, Heinrich, Heine, Thomas Carlyle, George Combe, Lord Herbert of Cherbury, Theodore Parker, W. J. Fox, Thomas Paine, Mrs. E. Martin, G. H. Lewes, Voltaire, Volney.

Letter to the Queen on her Retirement from Public Life. (Published at 1s.) 3d. P. 1d.

Revolt of the Field. By ARTHUR CLAYDEN. 1s. P. 3½d.

Republican Superstitions. By MONCURE D. CONWAY. 2s. (Published at 7s. 6d.) P. 3d.

The Gooroo Simple. A Satire on Hindu Religion. Gilt edges Gaily bound in cloth and freely illustrated. 2s. 6d. P. 3½d.

The Survival, with an Apology for Scepticism. Pp. 471. 1s. P. 7d

Australian Views of England. By HENRY PARKES. Pp. 11. 1s. P. 3½d.

Elementary Chemistry. By Rev. H. MARTYN HART, B.A. New, neatly bound in cloth, 1s. 6d. P. 3½d.

Santo Domingo, Past and Present, with a glance at Hayti, with Maps and numerous Engravings. By S. HAZARD. Cloth, richly gilt, crown 8vo, pp. vvi. and 511. 5s.

Arminius (James, D.D., of Leyden), The Works of, with Brandt's Life of the Author, with numerous extracts from his private Letters, a copious and authentic account of the Synod of Dort and its proceedings. By JAMES NICHOLS. With Portrait of Arminius from a scarce Dutch print. Three large vols. 8vo, new, in cloth (published at £2 8s.), 10s. 6d.

Order and Progress.—By FREDERIC HARRISON.
        Part 1.—Thoughts on Government.
        Part 2.—Studies of Political Crises.
Published by Messrs. Longmans & Co., at 14s., reduced to 3s. 6d. P. 9d. 395 pages neatly bound in cloth.

Isis and Osiris, or the Origin of Christianity. By JOHN STUART GLENNIE, M.A. (New edition) 3s. 6d. P. 8½d. Published by Messrs. Longmans at 15s. 432 pages.

Parallel Lives of Ancient and Modern Heroes. By CHARLES DUKE YONGE. Pp. 270. Neatly bound. Published at 4s. 6d. 1s. 6d. P. 3½d.

Travels in the Philippines. By F. JAGOR. With numerous Illustrations and Maps. Pp. 370. Cloth, handsomely bound Published at 16s. 3s. P. 8d.

The Papal Conclaves, as they were and as they are. By T. ADOLPHUS TROLLOPE. Pp. 434. Cloth, handsomely bound. Published at 16s. 4s. P. 8½d.

The Trades Unions of England. By M. LE COMTE DE PARIS. Translated by NASSAU J. SENIOR. Edited by THOMAS HUGHES, M.P. Cloth, new, uncut, 2s. Published at 7s. 6d. P. 4d.

    This book, together with **Capital and Labour,** by GEORGE HOWELL, present views of Trade Unionism from entirely different standpoints.

Plutarch's Lives. Langhorne's Translation, Text and Notes complete and revised (Grecian section). Cloth, new and uncut, 2s. P. 6d.

National Christianity; or, Cæsarism and Clericalism. By the Rev. J. B. HEAD. Cloth, new and uncut, 2s. (Published by Messrs. Longmans at 10s. 6d. P. 7d.

A Visit to the Seat of War in the North (the Crimean War). By LASCELLES WRAXALL. Pp. 106. 6d. P. 1½d.

Sketches of the Hungarian Emigration into Turkey. By A. HONVED. 6d. P. 1½d.

Pictures from the East. By JOHN CAPPER. Describing especially Ceylon. Pp. 162. 6d. P. 2d.

A Visit to Belgrade, describing Semlin, the Danube, and Servia generally. Pp. 105. 6d. P. 1½d.

Montenegro and the Slavonians of Turkey. By COUNT VALERIAN KRASINSKI. This most interesting book ought, at the present time, to be most eagerly read. Pp. 152. 8d. P. 2d.

Florian and Crescenz : a Village Tale from the Black Forest. By BERTHOLD AUERBACH. Translated by META TAYLOR. 6d. P. 1½d.

Alfieri : his Life, Adventures, and Works. By C. MITCHELL CHARLES. 6d. P. 1½d.

Oriental Zigzag : Wanderings in Syria, Moab, Abyssinia, and Egypt. By CHARLES HAMILTON. Handsomely illustrated, cloth, new and uncut. Pp. 304. 2s. 6d. P. 6d.

History of Rome, its Structures and Monuments, from its Foundation to the end of the Middle Ages. By DYER (THOMAS H., LL.D.), 8vo, cloth, new, uncut, with coloured Map. Pp. 420, (Published at 15s., by Messrs. Longmans) 5s. P. 9d.

Causality ; or, the Philosophy of Law Investigated. By JAMIESON (Rev. GEORGE). Second Edition, greatly enlarged, 8vo, cloth, new, uncut. (Published at 10s. by Messrs. Longmans) 3s. P. 7d. Contents : The Factors and Principles of Causality ; the Philosophy of the Conditioned ; the Conditioned and the Unconditioned ; the Grounds of Causality ; the Philosophy of Matter ; the Philosophy of Mind ; the Philosophy of the Abstract Sciences ; the Philosophy of Theology ; the Absolute (impersonal and personal) ; the Infinite ; the External Relative with the Infinite ; Reason in the Absolute, &c.

Man with the Iron Mask. By MARIUS TOPIN. Translated and edited by HENRY VIZETELLY, with fac-simile. Crown 8vo, cloth, new, uncut. (Published at 9s.) 2s. 6d. P. 5d.

Bryant (William Cullen), Orations and Addresses. Portrait, thick post 8vo, cloth, new, uncut. (Published at 7s. 6d.) 2s. 6d. P. 6d.

The Age and the Gospel : Essays on Christianity, its Friends and Opponents. By the Rev. B. FRANKLAND, B.A. This is a controversial book on the Christian side. New, cloth. 303 pp. 2s. P. 5d.

Tales from the Fjeld. A Second Series of Popular Tales, from the Norse of P. CHR. ASBJORNSEN. By G. W. DASENT, D.C.L. Pp. 375. Handsomely bound in cloth. Published at 10s. 6d. 2s. 6d. P. 5½d.

Life and Conversations of Dr. Samuel Johnson. (Founded chiefly upon Boswell.) By ALEXANDER MAIN. With a preface by GEORGE HENRY LEWIS. Pp. 441. Handsomely bound in cloth. Published at 10s. 6d. 3s. 6d. P. 5d.

Wanderings in the Interior of New Guinea. By CAPTAIN J. A. LAWSON. With Frontispiece and Map. Pp. 282. Handsomely bound. Published at 10s. 6d. 2s. 6d. P. 5d.

A Compendium of English History. From the Earliest Times to A.D. 1872. With copious quotations on the leading events and the Constitutional History, together with Appendices. By HERBERT R. CLINTON. Pp. 358. Neatly bound. Published at 7s. 6d. 2s. 6d. P. 5d.

Geography Classified. A systematic manual of Mathematical, Physical and Political Geography. With Geographical, Etymological and Historical Notes. By EDWIN ADAMS, F.R.G.S. Pp. 357. Published at 7s. 6d. 1s. 6d. P. 4d.

Grammaire Française. Par L. DIREY. Pp. 171. Neatly bound. (Published at 3s.) P. 2d.

Latin Grammar. By L. DIREY. P. 179. Neatly bound. (Published at 4s.) 6d. P. 2d.

English Grammar. By L. DIREY and A. FOGGO. Pp. 136. Neatly bound. (Published at 3s.) 6d. P. 2½d.

Longinus on the Sublime. A new translation, chiefly according to the improved edition of Weiske. By a Master of Arts of the University of Oxford. Pp. 92. 1s. P. 1½d.

Hallam's Europe during the Middle Ages. Pp. 720. Cloth, quite new. 2s. 8d. P. 6d.

Hallam's Constitutional History of England. Pp. 970. Cloth, quite new. 3s. 9d. P. 8d.

English Life of Jesus. By THOMAS SCOTT. Cloth, new and uncut, 2s. 6d. P. 5d.

Catechisme du Libre Penseur. Par EDGAR MONTEIL. Published at 3s. 6d. Reduced to 1s. P. 3d.

An Essay on Classification. By LOUIS AGASSIZ. 8vo. Pp. vii. and 381. Cloth. Published at 12s. Reduced to 5s. P. 6d.

Myths and Myth-Makers; Old Tales and Superstitions, Interpreted by Comparative Mythology. By JOHN FISKE, M.A., LL.B., Lecturer on Philosophy at Harvard University. Crown 8vo. Pp. 260. Cloth. Published at 10s. 6d. Reduced to 5s. P. 5.

Light, and its influence on Life and Health. By Dr. FORBES WINSLOW. Cloth, new and uncut. Pp. 301. 1s. P. 4d.

Obscure Diseases of the Brain and Mind. By Dr. FORBES WINSLOW, M.D., D.C.L., Oxon., &c. &c. &c. Fourth edition, revised. Pp. 618. Neatly bound in cloth, new and uncut, 3s. 6d. P. 9d. A great Bargain. This work is a most important one to psychologists, and is offered at a very low price.

Unorthodox London; or, Phases of Religious Life in the Metropolis. By the Rev. Dr. MAURICE DAVIES. Two volumes bound in one. Contains: South Place Chapel, Finsbury—MONCURE D. CONWAY on Mazzini—Colonel WENTWORTH HIGGINSON on Buddha—Unitarianism, a Sunday Lecture, by Professor HUXLEY—Tabernacle Ranters—The Walworth Jumpers—Bible Christians—Plymouth Brethren—A Quakers' Meeting—Dr. CUMMING—Seventh Day Baptists—Christadelphians—Moravians—Father IGNATIUS at Home, &c. 465 pages. 2s. 6d. P. 6½d. Published originally in Two Volumes at 28s.

Orthodox London. By the same Author. Two volumes bound in one. Contains: The Rev. H. R. HAWEIS—Father STANTON—Mr. FORREST—Rev. T. TEIGNMOUTH SHORE—Mr. LLEWELLYN DAVIES—Mr. MAGUIRE—Dean STANLEY—Canon LIDDON—Canon MILLER—Mr. STOPFORD BROOKE—Midnight Mass—Archbishop of York—Bishop of London—Bishop of Manchester—Bishop of Lincoln, &c., &c. 458 pages. 2s. 6d. P. 6½d. Published originally in Two Volumes at 28s.

Chapters on Man, with the Outlines of a Science of Comparative Psychology. By C. STANILAND WAKE. Pp. 343. 2s. 6d. P. 4½d. Published at 7s. 6d.

The Principles of Surgery—Clinical, Medical, and Operative. An original analysis of Pathology, systematically conducted, and a critical exposition of its guidance at the bedside and in operations. Representing the principles of the earliest and most exact Diagnoses, Etiology, Prognosis, and Therapeutics, Medical and Operative. By Frederick James Gant, F.R.C.S., Surgeon and Pathological Anatomist to the Royal Free Hospital, &c., &c. 860 pp. Neatly bound in cloth, quite new, and uncut. 3s. 6d. P. 1s. A rare opportunity.

Origines Biblicæ; or, Researches in Primeval History. By C. T. BEKE. 2s. P. 5d.

Prophet of Nazareth. By E. P. MEREDITH. 7s. 6d. P. 8d.

Quite New, and a rare bargain.

Charles Knight's Pictorial Shakespeare. Containing a Biography in one vol. by CHARLES KNIGHT; the historical plays in two vols.; comedies in two vols.; tragedies in two vols.; and doubtful plays in one vol.—in all, eight vols. Royal 8vo, splendidly bound in cloth, gilt. Illustrated with hundreds of fine engravings. These are published at £3 12s., but will be supplied by the Freethought Publishing Company at £2 2s.

The Life and Labours of Albany Fonblanque. Neatly bound, cloth, 546 pp., quite new and uncut. Published at 16s. 4s. P. 9½d.

Foundation of Christianity: a Critical Analysis of the Pentateuch and the Theology of the Old Testament. By GEORGE B JACKSON, A.B. "A searching and uncompromising inquiry into the origin and credibility of the religion of the patriarchs." Published at 2s., paper in perfect condition, 6d. P. 2d.

Life and Character of Richard Carlile. By GEORGE JACOB HOLYOAKE. Post-free, 6d.

Volney's Lectures on History. Post-free, 6d.

Confessions of Rousseau: with a preface by GEORGE JACOB HOLYOAKE. 170 pp., cloth, new, neatly bound, 1s. P. 2d. This is the edition published by Messrs. Holyoake at the Fleet Street House.

Half-hours with the Freethinkers. First and second series. By C. BRADLAUGH and JOHN WATTS. Cloth, new, and uncut, containing forty-eight lives, 2s. 6d. P. 3d.

Trial of Theism. By GEORGE JACOB HOLYOAKE. Cloth, new, and uncut, 1s. 6d. P. 2d.

Clarke's Critical Review. Published at 5s. 6d. 446 pp., cloth, new and uncut, 2s. 6d. P. 3½d.

THE
GOLDEN LIBRARY SERIES.

All New, Handsomely Bound, and Uncut.

Reduced to 1s. 3d. each. If sent by Post 3d. each extra.

Bayard Taylor's Diversions of the Echo Club.

The Book of Clerical Anecdotes.

Byron's Don Juan.

Emerson's Letters and Social Aims.

Godwin's (William) Lives of the Necromancers.

Holmes's Professor at the Breakfast Table.

Hood's Whims and Oddities. Complete. With all the Original Illustrations.

Irving's (Washington) Tales of a Traveller.

Irving's (Washington) Tales of the Alhambra.

Jesse's (Edward) Scenes and Occupations of Country Life.

Leigh Hunt's Essays: A Tale for a Chimney Corner, and other Pieces. With Portrait, and Introduction by EDMUND OLLIER.

Mallory's Sir Thos. Mort d'Arthur: The Stories of King Arthur and of the Knights of the Round Table. Edited by B. MONTGOMERIE RANKING.

Pascal's Provincial Letters. A New Translation, with Historical Introduction and Notes by T. M'CRIE, D.D., LL.D.

Pope's Complete Poetical Works.

Rochefoucald's Maxims and Moral Reflections. With Notes, and an Introductory Essay by SAINTE-BEUVE.

St. Pierre's Paul and Virginia, and the Indian Cottage. Edited, with Life, by the Rev. E. CLARKE.

Lamb's Essays of Elia. Both Series Complete in one Volume.

"A series of excellently printed and carefully annotated volumes, handy in size, and altogether attractive."—*Bookseller.*

THE NATIONAL REFORMER. Journal of Radicalism and Freethought. Edited by C. BRADLAUGH.

WEEKLY—PRICE TWOPENCE.

Post free to any part of Great Britain, 2s. 8½d. per quarter. To Europe or America, 3s. 3d. per quarter.

With its large and constantly-increasing circulation, THE NATIONAL REFORMER—which is constantly reviewing works on Theology, Philosophy, Politics, and Sociology—is an admirable Advertising Medium, especially for Publishers.

SCALE OF CHARGES FOR ADVERTISEMENTS.

	£ s. d.
First Thirty Words	£0 1 6
Every additional Ten, or part of Ten Words	0 0 6
Quarter Column	0 12 6
Half a Column	1 0 0
Column	1 14 0
Page	3 0 0

Special Arrangements may be made for repeated insertions.

www.ingramcontent.com/pod-product-compliance
Lightning Source LLC
Chambersburg PA
CBHW031816230426
43669CB00009B/1159